W9-AHS-142

On
Writers
and
Writing

Books by John Gardner

NOVELS
The Resurrection
The Wreckage of Agathon
Grendel
The Sunlight Dialogues
Nickel Mountain
October Light
In the Suicide Mountains
Freddy's Book
Mickelsson's Ghosts
Stillness and Shadows

NONFICTION
The Life and Times of Chaucer
The Poetry of Chaucer
On Moral Fiction
On Becoming a Novelist
The Art of Fiction

STORIES
The King's Indian
The Art of Living and Other Stories

POETRY
Jason and Medeia

TRANSLATION
Gilgamesh (*with John Maier*)

FOR CHILDREN
Dragon, Dragon
Gudgekin the Thistle Girl and Other Tales
The King of the Hummingbirds and Other Tales

On Writers and Writing

JOHN GARDNER

Introduction by Charles Johnson
Edited by Stewart O'Nan

Addison-Wesley Publishing Company
Reading, Massachusetts   Menlo Park, California   New York
Don Mills, Ontario   Wokingham, England   Amsterdam   Bonn
Sydney   Singapore   Tokyo   Madrid   San Juan
Paris   Seoul   Milan   Mexico City   Taipei

For acknowledgments regarding previously published material, see page 297.

Many of the designations used by manufacturers and sellers to distinguish their products are claimed as trademarks. Where those designations appear in this book and Addison-Wesley was aware of a trademark claim, the designations have been printed in initial capital letters (e.g., Band-Aids).

Library of Congress Cataloging-in-Publication Data

Gardner, John, 1933–
    On writers and writing / by John Gardner ; introduction by Charles Johnson ; edited by Stewart O'Nan.
      p. cm.
    Includes index.
    ISBN 0-201-62672-1
    ISBN 0-201-48338-6 (pbk.)
    1. Books—Reviews. I. O'Nan, Stewart, 1961– . II. Title.
PS3557.A71205 1994
809.3'04—dc20   93-50798
                                                        CIP

Copyright © 1994 by the Estate of John Gardner
Introduction copyright © 1994 by Charles Johnson

All rights reserved. No part of this publication may be reproduced, stored in a retrieval system, or transmitted, in any form or by any means, electronic, mechanical, photocopying, recording, or otherwise, without the prior written permission of the publisher. Printed in the United States of America.

Cover design by Jean Seal
Text design by Ruth Kolbert
Set in 11-point Janson by CopyRight, Inc.

1 2 3 4 5 6 7 8 9-DOH-9998979695
First printing, February 1994
First paperback printing, March 1995

CONTENTS

INTRODUCTION BY CHARLES JOHNSON *vii*

"Bartleby": Art and Social Commitment *1*

An Invective Against Mere Fiction *13*

More Smog from the Dark Satanic Mills *35*

Witchcraft in *Bullet Park*, by John Cheever *55*

Alice in Wonderland, by Lewis Carroll *60*

The Breast, by Philip Roth *65*

The Way We Write Now *70*

Saint Walt *78*

The Adventurer, by Paul Zweig *86*

Beyond the Bedroom Wall, by Larry Woiwode *90*

Amber (Get) Waves (Your) of (Plastic) Grain (Uncle Sam) *95*

JR, by William Gaddis *101*

The Acts of King Arthur and His Noble Knights,
   by John Steinbeck *112*

Lancelot, by Walker Percy *119*

Falconer, by John Cheever *124*

The Castle of Crossed Destinies, by Italo Calvino   *130*

Daniel Martin, by John Fowles   *134*

The Silmarillion, by J. R. R. Tolkien   *140*

The Stories of John Cheever   *145*

Dubin's Lives, by Bernard Malamud   *149*

Sophie's Choice, by William Styron   *154*

A Writer's View of Contemporary American Fiction   *163*

Bellefleur, by Joyce Carol Oates   *199*

Italian Folktales, edited by Italo Calvino   *205*

Fiction in *MSS*   *212*

What Writers Do   *216*

Cartoons   *228*

Julius Caesar and the Werewolf   *237*

General Plan for *The Sunlight Dialogues*   *258*

INDEX   *289*

INTRODUCTION

ON THE DAY OF HIS FATAL MOTORCYCLE ACCI-
dent on September 14, 1982, on a lonely though not particularly
dangerous curving stretch of road in Susquehanna County, Pennsyl-
vania, John Gardner, the embattled advocate for higher artistic and
moral standards in our fiction, was snatched at age forty-nine from
the stage of contemporary American literature before we could properly measure either his contribution to literary culture or the man himself. In the wake of his staggeringly prolific, driven, and very public
life as a popular novelist, critic, teacher, and classics scholar, he left
behind a workroom loaded with intriguing projects: some recently
completed, like his widely used handbook on craft *The Art of Fiction*;
some unfinished, like his proposed opus *Shadows*; and some works,
such as the novel *Stillness*, written for the purpose of "self-therapy"
during his stormy first marriage, that he might not have published in
the form given to us posthumously. There were, of course, rumors
flying that his death was suicide, that he willingly rode the machine
that became one of his symbols, a '79 Harley-Davidson *hog*, into obliv-
ion. But as always the truth is otherwise, more banal than rumor, and
far more illustrative of the mission that made him one of the most
inventive novelists and outstanding writing teachers of our time: he
died en route to yet another meeting with one of his students at the

State University of New York (SUNY)–Binghamton, with yet another stack of manuscripts strapped to the back of his black, monstrous bike.

As one foot soldier in that coast-to-coast army of young artists he inspired and influenced forever, perhaps his only black former apprentice now publishing (for reasons I don't know, he also claimed Toni Morrison), my filing cabinet, indeed my entire home, groans with material by and about Gardner, for it was his peculiar trait, like D. H. Lawrence, to externalize on the page everything he felt, thought, and experienced as a way of taking control of his life. One library wall in my house holds a still life he painted in 1980, a present to me and my wife when we bought our first home in Seattle (a city he disliked, though he never told me why); it is balanced on either side by his lovely Lord John Press broadside "On Books" (a paean to their physical beauty) and his eulogistic poem to his dearest friend, sculptor Nicholas Vergette, who died of cancer in 1974. Thirty of his books, criticism, translations, poetry, and adult and children's fiction stretching from *The Forms of Fiction* (1962) to *Stillness and Shadows* (1986) fill one bookshelf in my study, along with copies of his literary journal *MSS* (in its earliest incarnation he published early works by Joyce Carol Oates and William Gass), and no less than ten critical volumes on his work that range from studies of his major novels to his short fiction to collected interviews (he gave more than 140). On the shelf below sits his photograph: he peers out from the frame, tired, shorthaired in 1982, wearing his black fisherman's sweater, Dunhill tobacco smoke streaming from the pipe in his mouth. Somewhere in one of my desk drawers is one of his big churchwarden pipes he gave me two decades ago in an effort to wean me off cigarettes.

In disorganized envelopes I have stacks of his letters (some of our correspondence is in a special collection devoted to him at the University of Delaware, and has been edited by a black graduate student); the copy for produced radio and theater plays ("The Temptation Game," "Helen at Home") and unproduced ones ("Death and the Maiden") for opera librettos and musical comedies; videotapes of the low-budget film based on his best-selling novel *Nickel Mountain* and the animated version of *Grendel* (which I know disappointed him, being the Walt Disney fan he was), plus a tape of his freewheeling public-television "Writer's Workshop" interview with James Dickey and William Price Fox before an audience of baffled yet enchanted University of South

Carolina students (to whom he—relaxed, longhaired, and handsome in his black leather jacket and maybe a little drunk—said, "What happens when you have a really fine character is that you get not only a sense of that kind of person in that kind of town but yourself and everybody around you. Finally you get a kind of control over the universe, a kind of fearlessness from having understood other people"); handwritten essays on the nature of moral art he gave me when he guided me through the composition of my novel *Faith and the Good Thing*; his lecture notes (faded dittos now) from classes on the epic and black literature he taught at Southern Illinois University in the early 1970s; yellowed book reviews (happily, most are now collected in this extremely valuable addition to Gardner scholarship), prefaces, introductions, letters to the editor, and statements he wrote for popular magazines, obscure journals, now-defunct publications, and to endorse novels long forgotten; and his early interviews, one of which he granted as a favor to me on January 21, 1973, when I was a young reporter and philosophy master's-degree student at Southern Illinois University. There he confessed his affection for the works of R. G. Collingwood and Alfred North Whitehead, his belief in the "connectedness" of all life, his disdain for most famous writers at the time, then, in a way both grim and optimistic, concluded:

> I think a certain kind of America is doomed, though something greater may be coming. The novelist and only the novelist thrives on breakdown, because that's the moment when he can analyze the beauty of the values that are falling and rising. . . . The end of a great civilization is always a great moment for fiction. When the old England at the end of the nineteenth century fell, along came Dickens; when Russia fell apart, along came Tolstoy. . . . One looks forward to the fall of great civilizations because it gives us great art.

Over two decades I've returned again and again to this profusion of archival documents, remembering minutiae about the man, his work, and always I come to the same conclusion, that no American fiction writer in our generation will be able to match the incredible ambition, the unusual aesthetic project—two parts Dickensean and one part Sartrean—that this farm boy from upstate New York brought to Yankee literature in the postwar years.

I was twenty-four years old when I drifted into his orbit, and perhaps he saw me as an oddity among his other Carbondale students, not simply because I was black but in terms of the creative baggage I brought along behind me: two published books of comic art; more than a thousand individual political drawings, some of which he'd encountered on the editorial pages of the town newspaper, the *Southern Illinoisan*; and an early how-to-draw PBS series I'd hosted, which most likely he'd seen when flipping channels (he wouldn't have missed the first season of "Kung Fu"). I say oddity because, as the only professional cartoonist among his Southern Illinois writers, my imagination and creative skills at the time were directed toward a stylized, broad-stroke form of expression—caricature, boiling things down to their essential visual traits—that Gardner himself favored in his favorite writers (for such influence on his work see his lively essay "Cartoons," in this volume). Included in my baggage were six novels I'd written in the two years before I met Gardner, all heavily influenced by the Black Arts movement and authors I then admired (Richard Wright, James Baldwin, John A. Williams). Naturally, I knew of him before we met in the fall of 1972 in his workshop "Professional Writing," which convened in the evening at his farmhouse on Boskeydell Road. Like R. Buckminster Fuller, he was a local celebrity, particularly after he published *Grendel*, which cemented his reputation among critics. Friends of mine took his English classes, and spoke with excitement about him; they also said he was the bitterest man they'd ever known—this because for fifteen years he wrote in virtual obscurity as an underpublished author whose closet spilled open with brilliant, original fiction. Enrolling in his course, I wasn't sure what to expect.

What I *did* know after pounding out six novels, and reading as widely as I could in literature and philosophy as well as every handbook on craft and theory I could find, was that after writing a million words of fiction I needed a good teacher, a genuine mentor, a senior craftsman with greater experience than mine whom I could apprentice myself to, adding what he'd learned to what I'd already discovered. That circumstances should have brought me, six book-length manuscripts under my arm, to the Gardners' home on a rainy September night is one of those formative, fork-in-the-road events in my life that I have never fully been able to unkey. A few editors who'd rejected my fiction remarked that I could stand improvement on such matters as "voice" and "prose rhythm." Gardner's reply was, "Oh, I can help you with *that*." And it was true: he prided himself, as a trailblazer of the New Fiction that arose in the early 1970s, on his prodigious understanding of technique, his gift for voice and narrative ventriloquism, his magisterial, musical prose, which, for example, in the opening paragraph of his story "John Napper Sailing Through the Universe," achieved nearly perfect pitch in fully cadenced, poetic lines that seamlessly fused image and idea. He was, I learned soon enough, so immersed in modern, medieval, and classical philosophies that on any occasion in his office, in his car, as we walked across campus, or at a party, he could answer my graduate-student questions about the history of ideas and offer, always to my shock, his own thought-provoking opinion on the strengths and weaknesses of any Western metaphysical system—as well as opinions, always fresh, about any aspect of theater, painting, sculpture, music, or popular culture.

True enough, there were in the early 1970s a few good authors teaching creative writing (which, incidentally, Gardner once told me was "a joke" in terms of how it was then approached, a touchy-feely affair with little foundation in skill acquisition), and any one of them could have added to my repertoire of technique. John Barth, say, with whom Gardner felt a certain competitiveness, most likely because our national magazines heralded him as *the* high priest of literary invention. Or his friend William Gass, whose symphonically orchestrated books he often praised. But for *this* Illinois colored boy raised happily in the African Methodist Episcopal church in a Chicago suburb by a conservative, hardworking father and a mother with the soul of an actress, it was Gardner's personality, not just his knowledge of *techne*, that made him both an artist and a human being I could deeply respect. Unlike his equally skillful postmodern contemporaries, experimentalists and polytechnical innovators who rolled their eyes or looked confounded when the touchy subject of religion or spirituality came up, Gardner—the son of a sermonizer—was as frank and forthcoming as Flannery O'Connor about the significance of morality and the life of the spirit in literature. He praised my characters in *Faith* for their "dignity," a characteristic he complained was missing in so many stories, all by acclaimed authors, who (he felt) wallowed in fashionable despair, entropy, defeatism, cheap fireworks, and a cynical vision of humankind. (By the way, for the ancient Greeks, the word *cynic* meant "doglike.")

Gardner, and perhaps *only* Gardner, had the courage to say, as he does in "A Writer's View of Contemporary American Fiction," that "at a conservative estimate, 90 percent of the so-called new fiction is soporific." Read: boring, despite its dazzling originality.

Added to that, and most important of all, I saw in Gardner's boundless self-confidence and passion for writing in the early '70s exactly the same do-or-die love I had since my teens for drawing. For Gardner, writing was not a "career." It was not so pedestrian an enterprise as to be ranked among the various professions from which we might freely choose—doctor, lawyer, soldier, or stockbroker. On the contrary, it was more like a calling. ("Fiction is the only religion I have," he told a *New York Times Sunday Magazine* reviewer.) It was one way for men and women to make their stab at immortality, heal the conflicted human heart, transcend the idiocies of daily life (yet help us at the same time see how heroism can reside in ordinary living), and celebrate the Good. Sometimes it seemed as if Gardner was interested in nothing short of fiction worthy of winning a writer lasting fame (glory) based on—and here is the trick—hard-won achievement. When pushed to the wall about his preferences, it seemed he *approved* of nothing less, and in our conferences and conversations he pushed me gently, then sometimes roughly, to imagine harder and with greater precision of detail, write with fairness for every character in my book, and hold in contempt any sentence I composed that fell below the level of the best sentence I'd ever written. He was a teacher who could fill you to overflowing with confidence. He was also capable of wounding you in the most painful way by pulling the covers off your conceits and holding them up—like a puppy by its ears (his image)—before you.

In "A Writer's View of Contemporary American Fiction," which nicely categorizes fictional visions in terms of their relationship to religion, Gardner identifies himself as a "troubled Christian orthodox writer." Can anyone who knew him doubt that he saw something akin to salvation in art? Late one spring afternoon I drove to his farmhouse to pick up one of my chapters. He sat alone in the house that day at the long, mead hall–size table in his dining room, drinking whiskey from a Mason jar and editing a home movie, a western, his family and friends had written and performed. On the table nearby were recent reviews of *Jason and Medeia*. Many of them were negative. One reviewer had called Gardner a "clever student." I knew these notices angered and disappointed him. Timidly, I nodded toward the reviews, asked him what he thought, and he replied quietly, hardly looking up from his editing machine, "They just try to keep you from getting to heaven."

All this was heady stuff for me; it was precisely the kick-in-the-fanny, challenging wake-up call that I'd been hungering for a teacher to give me. Unbeknownst to him, I took notes on even his casual remarks about fiction. I read his three-decker, architectonic novel *The Sunlight Dialogues* with a pencil in my fist, flagging every linguistic device, strategy, and technique I did not know. I ordered all his earlier works of criticism. And since the melodic substructure of his best prose fascinated me, I copied out in longhand the first chapter of *The Wreckage of Agathon*, a work he felt disappointed with, but by transcribing each of his sentences onto a notepad I discovered that, as I turned from one page to another, I could *feel* how his next sentence had to flow, what metrical beats it needed to have, even if I had no idea what its content might be. Slowly, I began to see. Gradually, a picture of man and method began to emerge. By degrees, the musical *logos* of his fiction became something I was able to intuit and feel from within, as well as the greater artistic game plan behind his challenging himself from book to book, story to story, by selecting different classical or contemporary literary forms (or several combined) to serve as the ground, the general shape or mold for his stories—a mold he could reconfigure as he wrote, and at the same time use to stay in touch with other writers, living and dead, who'd also used that form.

At dinner one evening I heard his wife, Joan, joke about the archaic language Gardner displayed in *Jason and Medeia*; she said it was there because she'd chided him about not having any "big words" in his novels. So Gardner took his magnifying glass and walked through every word in *The Compact Edition of the Oxford English Dictionary* before revising his update of the classic story. We laughed, but her anecdote haunted me for days. I thought if Gardner had gone to such trouble (a task I now believe every writer needs to perform), then perhaps I should do the same with a Christmas present my parents had given me, the 2,129-page *Webster's New Twentieth-Century Dictionary*. It took me five months to plough through it, night after night, during my first year in the philosophy Ph.D. program at SUNY–Stony Brook, and the exercise proved invaluable.

So yes, I painstakingly studied Gardner, testing my regimen and secular, post-Christian "religious" faith in the discipline of fiction against his own (and always I fell short). If he recommended a book, I bought then pored over it, regardless of the century or culture that produced it. I'm convinced no one else could have gotten me—a philosophy student then oriented toward Marxism and, in fiction, toward protest literature—interested in *Morte d'Arthur*, Geoffrey Chaucer, Longinus, the Wakefield pageant cycle, Fulgentius, *Beowulf*, or Caedmonic poetry. But he did, because he, like his fellow post-sixties "experimental" writers, had found a way to make the practice of fiction interesting again after decades of naturalism. Not that they couldn't write in the great tradition of American naturalism—they did, now and then, just to show they could, to show that naturalism was but *one* of the innumerable ways a story could be told and the universe imagined and interpreted. "I believe that the art of the thirties, forties, and fifties was fundamentally a mistake," Gardner told Joe David Bellamy in a 1973 interview, "that it made assumptions that were untrue about art, basically wrong assumptions that went wrong in the Middle Ages, too. . . . It seems to me that we are a play out of the seventeenth century. Seventeenth-century civilization is us. . . . In the fifteenth and sixteenth centuries all the genres break down. It becomes impossible to write a straight romance, or a straight anything. And everybody who is anybody starts form-jumping."

He credited himself and other New Fictionists rightly for developing fresh strategies for solving the problem of viewpoint, opening our fiction to exciting new (and sometimes old) ontologies, and for unsealing a door to "fabulation" closed since the mid-nineteenth century. Inside that room of fictional possibilities was a tale- and yarn-telling tradition still close to the roots of oral storytelling, where one could find philosophical insight in fairy tales, folktales, and myths: stories about fantastic creatures—golems and grendels—we are not likely to bump into at the corner supermarket, but in the New Fiction we could. For in the universe of the mind (and the college-based experimentalists were interested in nothing if not mind, perception, epistemology), Frankenstein's monster and J.F.K., quarks and Pegasus, Rip Van Winkle and Chairman Mao all existed side by side as phenomenal objects for consciousness, none more "real" than another in our dreams or between the covers of a book. In what Gardner called "the vivid and continuous dream" that is art, each could be a meaning dramatized, allowed to live, and lead us to laughter and tears and learning as powerfully as did the ghost and flesh in the Middle English poem "The Debate of Body and Soul."

Here, in short, was a post-1960s "school" of writers who found a way of freeing the imagination, but in Gardner's case it involved a return to ancestral traditions and forms. Perhaps now we take for granted this "turn" in American storytelling from sod-busting "realism," what with television offering us a series about a family of dinosaurs, Hollywood dishing up films about coneheads and characters based on video games, and literary writers like Valerie Martin retelling the Jekyll and Hyde story from the viewpoint of Jekyll's housekeeper in her superb psychological thriller *Mary Reilly*. But thirty years ago, at the moment Gardner was fusing realism and fantasy in his midwestern farmhouse, Joanna Russ in the East was just then looking at medieval literature in terms of its lessons for the "New Wave" of speculative fiction that emerged in the early '70s, and replacing sci-fi's earlier reliance on the "hard" sciences of physics and chemistry with an interest in the latest research from such fields as biology and anthropology (her friend Samuel R. Delany was looking at theories of language games and much, much more); and in the West, Ishmael Reed was studying Egyptian myths and taking Saturday-morning cartoons as a model for editing his novels. As in the politics of the '60s, the *moment* called for innovation, throwing out nets in every direction—pop culture, high culture, Third World culture, science—in the hope that as writers they could haul to the surface something to propel fiction's evolution.

However, Gardner differs in many important respects from these other innovators. "Newness" for its own sake did not appeal to him. And in contrast, for example, to Russ (whose essays include a defense of man-hating) and Reed (who once called Western cultural forms "diseased"), he was dissatisfied with pyrotechnics and novelty if their purpose turned out to be nothing more than political or religious propaganda; if character—which is at the core of his aesthetics—suffered; if cartoon strategies, for all their fun, completely abandoned fidelity to mimesis, and lost the authorial generosity that comes only from minutely rendered details of setting and social gesture; if, in the end, he felt the novelty of the New Fiction replaced convincing models of moral behavior with events and emotions that slyly and subversively promoted something unhealthy for humankind. "A healthy life is a life of faith," he told Bellamy, "an unhealthy, sick, and dangerous life is a life of unfaith." Nevertheless, a writer could not preach his faith in a story. It had to be concretized, the idea incarnated—made flesh—in specific people, places, and things delivered with *haeceittias* (*thisness*). Real art was not, he said, in the sermon we hear in church on Sunday morning, but instead in "the arches and the light."

Looking back over the collected pieces in *On Writers and Writing*, we see that during his spectacular career much of Gardner's energy was invested in defining, evaluating, and trying to correct—in his criticism and stories—the products of the New Fiction school, of which he was a leading figure. At times he was guilty (as he admits) of its self-conscious excesses that distract us from the "fictional dream," but he was always struggling to use the positive contributions of this period to create a lasting work worthy of the best in Dickens, Melville, and Tolstoy. It is also true that as he scrapped with his brothers and sisters in the movement for the New, he was revising and refining his theory that the process of fiction itself is moral and life-affirmative. But just a moment. Is this really a "theory"? And is it really "morality" that Gardner means? It's clear from his criticism that he was firmly opposed to "moralizing." Apparently, he was not intractably Christian, insofar as he said a finely done work could make him believe in the value of a Buddhist vision. I think, just maybe, we are better off seeing his interconnecting essays in this book as presenting a credible *description* of what happens when writers write well. And rather than using the inflammatory word "moral," we might be more accurate if we say that what Gardner wanted was a *responsible* fiction, one that did not insult the intelligence of readers as thoughtful and educated as himself.

"All my life," he wrote his fiancée Susan Thornton, whom he was to marry on September 18, four days after his fatal accident, "I've lived flat-out. As a motorcycle racer, chemist, writer . . . I was never cautious." This was hardly something Gardner needed to tell us. We could see it in everything he did. While he helped those of us fortunate enough to study with him believe we could distinguish ourselves as artists, provided we were willing to sweat enough, be unsatisfied enough, rewrite enough, none of us believed we could match *his* breakneck schedule. I cannot speak for his New Fiction contemporaries, but I know for a fact that Gardner could write for seventy-two-hour stretches without sleep; compose an introduction to one of his collections of poetry and portions of *The Art of Fiction* while recuperating in a hospital bed from an operation for colon cancer. Some critics believe Gardner's incredible drive, his "fire in the belly," dated back to his teens and the accidental death of his younger brother, a tragedy he blamed himself for and dramatized in his story "Redemption." As to the truth of this childhood "wound," I cannot say. But I do know he was a writer who boasted he could read in twenty-seven ancient and medieval languages by the time he earned his Ph.D. at age twenty-five, and that in his late forties he polished up his Greek in order to provide his students at the Breadloaf Writers Conference with his own translations of Homer. He traveled to Japan in the '70s to lecture and returned with sixteen stories by Kikuo Itaya—an eighty-five-year-old writer hardly known in his homeland, which Gardner translated with Nobuko Tsukui, introduced with a memorable essay called "Meditational Fiction," and published under the title *Tengu Child* with Southern Illinois University Press.

Week after week on the pages of the Sunday *New York Times Book Review*, and in other national forums for literary discourse, he attempted to separate novelistic wheat from the chaff, genuine fiction from fakery. However, Gardner was not given to writing puff pieces, reviews I would call no better than extensions of the blurbs and promotional copy in press releases. Always his intention was to understand, to imagine the various alternatives an author had at his or her disposal for solving problems on the level of the sentence or for a book's overall structural design, to *analyze* what constructions in the stories of writers he admired—Saul Bellow, Vladimir Nabokov, Marguerite Young, John Cheever, Larry Woiwode—worked, and which ones did not. Only in his reviews do we find a consummate teacher and technician examining the works of his peers as he would an assignment turned in by one of his students in a college writing class. Often the effect is shocking—he said *that* about John Updike?—but it is a testament to Gardner's professionalism that publicity and public acclaim never blinded him to the basic question every reviewer and critic must ask: What exactly *do* we have here? (As an analogue, consider the equally courageous reviews of black fiction by MacArthur fellow Stanley Crouch.) In principle, it seems, very little contemporary fiction worked perfectly for Gardner; like an elder craftsman disappointed by his finest achievements, he regarded even the most lauded literature by others as being in need of some repair.

He lectured, read, and taught across America and abroad for twenty years. His students included the famous (Raymond Carver took his first class at Chico State) and scores of aspiring writers who mailed him manuscripts—perfect strangers whose work he corrected with the same meticulous, line-by-line editing he brought to his own fiction. What could prompt a busy man to behave this way? An incident he enjoyed relating reveals something about the demons that drove him. After one of his readings, a woman approached him and said, "You know, I think I like your stories, but I'm not sure I like *you*." He did not hesitate before he replied, "That's all right, I'm a better person when I write," meaning that no matter how pigheaded, stupid, or imperfect a writer might be in his personal life (and certainly the stories of how badly many outstanding writers have lived are legion), what he did on the page offered an opportunity—perhaps the *only* chance for some—to speak with clarity and precision, work in a spirit of love and compassion, and revise his thoughts and feelings to the point where they could be most helpful and do no harm. In an unpublished 1976 preface to the writing exercises that now appear in *The Art of Fiction*, he wrote that a sane, moral writer

> never forgets that his audience is, at least ideally, as noble and generous and tolerant as himself, so that to turn characters into cartoons, to treat his characters as innately inferior to himself, to forget their reasons for being as they are, to treat them as brutes, is disgraceful. . . . If you write, even through the mouth of a sympathetically observed character, something Tolstoy, Socrates, or Jesus would not write—think twice. You live in a world in which it's possible to buy flavored, edible panties (strawberry, lemon-lime—), a world where the word "asshole" passes for elevated diction. Think about it.

Seventeen years later we are demanding that record companies place rating labels on "gangsta" rap music filled with obscenities, the abuse of women, and calls for killing police officers; and television and motion pictures must now contend with a groundswell of public backlash against the gratuitous, make-believe violence that some feel is related to the streets of urban America turning into combat zones. If Gardner had lived, the current hand-wringing over depictions of violence and cruelty, and the sense that moral demands apply even to make-believe, might have prompted him to say, "I told you so," and repeat his oft-stated belief that "even bad art is powerful."

To put this simply, Gardner's energy, his self-punishing schedules, his devotion to all good fiction wherever he found it, *shamed* those of us who watched him work, and still had the audacity to call ourselves writers. Just the same, he labored with self-doubts. In a 1977 *Atlantic* interview, he said, "I'm one of the really great writers; I haven't proved that yet, but I feel that it's coming." Did it come? More specifically, did any of the New Fiction novelists create works that have become part of the language, the culture? As I grow older and find myself less ensorcelled by pyrotechnics and more appreciative of spirited storytelling and old-fashioned page-turners, I wonder how various characters and tales have down through the centuries become common coin in our culture. Melville, of course, languished for years before being redis-covered, as did Zora Neale Hurston; and surely there is often more than a little media hype, literary and academic fashion, politics, and the impact of Hollywood involved when an author's efforts become a household word.

Be that as it may, the rare event does occur when a serious writer creates something that becomes emblematic for some sector of our experience. In "More Smog from the Dark Satanic Mills," Gardner praises Pär Lagerkvist's *The Holy Land* for compressing the complexity and difficulty of modern life "into a few stark and massive symbols in which all our experience and all human history are locked." To my eye, this event arises when a writer—traditional or experimental, literary or pulp—stumbles consciously or unconsciously, by genius or dumb luck, upon an archetypal character (Raskolnikov, Lolita, Candide, Huck Finn) or an imaginative situation (as in Fowles's *The Collector*, Dickey's *Deliverance*) or a flexible concept that organizes a welter of complex feelings and ideas (Ellison's *Invisible Man*, Heller's *Catch-22*, Haley's *Roots*). In some cases this naming, this dramatizing, crystallizes an expe-rience we all know but until the creation occurs have not found a way to utter. Or it may be a fictional situation or premise so fertile (Malory's *Morte d'Arthur*, Goethe's *Faust*, Defoe's *Robinson Crusoe*) and intriguing that other writers feel compelled to keep retelling it, updating it for their age, going it one better, as Gardner himself did with the

Beowulf legend. Did the New Fiction of the early '70s body forth its "King Lear," its *Oliver Twist*, its great white whale? Eleven years after Gardner's death the jury is still out, as perhaps it must be, though I think it safe to say that the intense interest in Gardner's work in the decade after his death, the effort finally to take measure of the man, suggests happily that his devotion to good writing will result in longevity for his books on writing craft, for *Grendel* as an example of the New Fiction's principles at their best, and, one hopes, for his short and long fiction as well.

Gardner would have been sixty this year. Readers born too late to remember the post-1960s debates and battles over fiction's purpose might find it difficult to feel the passion or the reason for fierce position-taking that crackles along the surface of Gardner's book reviews. These are *more* than reviews. They are brief position papers, extensions of his ongoing thoughts about art's meaning; but a few readers might ask, why all the fuss? After all, by the mid-1980s—when the concept of "moral" fiction was no longer tied so tightly to Gardner himself— few, if any, major American novelists questioned in their interviews and public statements the significance of a moral vision for fiction, even if they had distanced themselves from Gardner when he was alive, which many did after he published *On Moral Fiction*. For most authors today moral responsibility in their products is a *given*, though as always the definition of what defines "moral" varies from writer to writer, as it should. But it was Gardner who served as our point man, our "trip wire" in the task of clearing away land mines planted by less faithful novelists and critics along the path where traditional ethical concerns and artistic creation meet.

Furthermore, if three decades ago during the heyday of the New Fiction, writers were arguing about technique, today the battlefield of aesthetic debate has shifted to "multiculturalism," to denunciations of English departments for marginalizing women and writers of color, and to a dismissal of the very canon of "dead white male writers" Gardner's scholarship was based upon. Oh yes, he died too soon by ten years, long before we had finished with him. We needed his intimate knowledge of the classics, his great love of fine storytelling regardless of the culture or race that produced it, and his compelling arguments against easy art and proselytizing in these years that have seen English departments politicized and torn apart from within at so many major American universities.

Moreover, we needed the author of "Amber (Get) Waves (Your) of (Plastic) Grain (Uncle Sam)," who was one of Jimmy Carter's favorite writers, when the Grand Old Party of his parents caved in to the religious right and Pat Buchanan during the 1992 presidential campaign, retreating from politics proper to cultural warfare in the form of appeals to "family values" and the priority of "character." Aren't these matters— values and cultural vision—that reside at the heart of what one might call "Gardner country"? We wonder: Where might he have positioned himself in respect to Allan Bloom, Roger Kimball, Dinesh D'Souza, and Rush Limbaugh (who could easily be a Gardner concoction, one of his "earnest babbling . . . short-legged, overweight, twitching cartoon creations")? How might he have responded to our present controversy over abortion (there is one answer in *Mickelsson's Ghosts*), homosexuality (he tries to understand how one man can love another in *Freddy's Book*), or Hillary Clinton's "politics of meaning" speech (our First Lady might do well to read *October Light*)? Because Gardner was that species of poet-philosopher on whom nothing in the social world was lost, we can find hints in his huge *oeuvre* for these questions and use them to construct responses to present dangers, guesses that are consistent with his position at the time of his death—but, sadly, that is the very best we will be able to do.

As his former student and friend, I thankfully add *On Writers and Writing* to my burgeoning shelf of books by and about John Gardner. I have no idea what words appear on his headstone in upstate New York, no idea if the man's fierce spirit lives on, but for years I've entertained the thought that these lines by Italian poet Jacopone da Todi might be fitting for how most of us would like to remember his furious and illuminating passage among us.

> *La guerra e terminata:*
> *de la virtu battaglia,*
> *de la mente travaglia*
> *cosa nulla contende.*

> *The war is over.*
> *In the battle of virtue,*
> *the struggle of spirit,*
> *all is peace.*

CHARLES JOHNSON
Seattle, 1993

"Bartleby":
Art and Social
Commitment

I N "BARTLEBY," MAN LOOKS AT MAN, ARTIST
looks at artist, and God looks at God. To understand that the narrator is at least as right as Bartleby, both on the surface and on symbolic levels, is to understand the remarkable interpenetration of form
and content in the story. Most Melville readers have noticed that on
one level, Bartleby can represent the honest artist: he is a "scrivener"
who refuses to "copy," as Melville himself refused to copy—that is,
as he refused to knock out more saleable South Seas romances. But
if Bartleby is the artist, he is the artist manqué: his is a vision not
of life but of death; "the man of silence," he creates nothing. A better
kind of artist is the lawyer, who, having seen reality through Bartleby's
eyes, has turned to literature. Nor is he the slick writer: "If I pleased,"
he says, "[I] could relate divers histories, at which good-natured gentlemen might smile, and sentimental souls might weep." That is, popular
fiction. The phrase "If I pleased" is significant: "please" is the narrator's substitution, later, for Bartleby's infectious "prefer." Like Bartleby,
the narrator does what he prefers to do—but within certain reasonable
limits. The reader may weep or smile at Bartleby's story, but the narrator's chief reason for choosing it is that he is seriously concerned
with "literature." Close reading reveals that the story he tells is indeed
a highly organized literary work, a story that is as much the narrator's

as it is Bartleby's, ending with the narrator's achievement of that depth of understanding necessary to the telling of the story.

An important part of what the narrator at last understands is the conflict between the individual and society. The individual feels certain preferences which, taken together, establish his personal identity; society makes simultaneously necessary and unreasonable demands which modify individual identity. Thus the individual's view of himself and the view others have of him can become two quite different things separated by a substantial wall (communication is difficult); thus, too, the socialized man's identity and his view of his identity can be walled apart (self-knowledge is difficult). And man's dilemma cannot be resolved, for if one insists on one's own preferences and thereby affirms one's identity, one finds oneself, like Bartleby, walled off from society and communion with other men; and on the other hand, if one gives in to the necessary laws of social action, one finds oneself, like Bartleby's employer, walled off from active obedience to the higher laws of self and, in a sense, reality. Wall Street is the prison in which all men live.

The conflict between the rule of individual preference and the necessary laws of social action takes various forms in "Bartleby." Conflicts arise between individual and social impulses within each of the first three scriveners, Turkey, Nippers, and Ginger Nut, and also between individual traits in the scriveners and the necessary requirements of their employer, whose commitment is perforce social, for he must do his job well to survive. But for the action of the story, the most important conflicts are those rooted in the relationship of the lawyer and Bartleby, that is, the conflicts between employer and employee, between the lawyer's kindly nature and his recognition of the reasonableness of society's harsh demands, and between Bartleby and the world.

In many ways the lawyer and Bartleby differ. The lawyer is a successful, essentially practical man with highly developed feelings for social position (he mentions coyly that he was "not unemployed" by John Jacob Astor), the value of his money (the office of Master in Chancery is "pleasantly remunerative"), "common usage and common sense," and above all, as he tells us John Jacob Astor has observed, "prudence" and "method." Bartleby, on the other hand, is merely a clerk with an obscure past, a man little concerned with practicality in the ordinary sense, and apparently quite uninterested in social position, money, or usage and sense. He is totally lacking in prudence—

he courts dismissal at every turn—and for method he relies on "prefer-ence," often preference "at present." The narrator at first cannot under-stand Bartleby, for good reason, and Bartleby prefers not to understand the narrator or the society the narrator represents. At the same time, the two characters are in some respects similar. Early in the story, the narrator tells us, "I am a man who, from his youth upwards, has been filled with a profound conviction that the easiest way of life is the best"; and Bartleby shares the narrator's profound conviction: what he cannot share is the narrator's opinion that the easiest way must be socially acceptable, or even "reasonable." The narrator is also like Bartleby in that he does not seek "public applause"; but Bartleby goes further, he does not avoid public censure. Finally, the narrator is decor-ous and "eminently *safe*"; so is Bartleby: the narrator is positive that Bartleby would not copy in shirtsleeves or on Sunday, and the narrator has "singular confidence in his honesty."

Perhaps partly because the narrator and Bartleby are both different and similar, the conflict between them triggers a conflict within the narrator's mind. He knows that as employer he has the authority to make demands of a scrivener, whatever the scrivener's preference, for if employers cannot function as employers, society cannot work; but despite his knowledge, the narrator cannot bring himself to force Bartleby to obey or get out. When Bartleby first refuses to comply with a request, the narrator merely thinks, "This is very strange . . . What had one best do?" and, being pressed by business, goes on with his work. When Bartleby refuses to comply with another request, the narrator is shaken and for a moment doubts the assumption behind employer–employee relations. When Bartleby uses it as a *modus ope-randi*, the narrator's opinion that "the easiest way of life is the best" conflicts with his equally firm opinion that the laws of social action are of necessity right; and in his momentary uncertainty the narrator turns to his office, a miniature society, for a ruling. Even their ruling is not much help, however, for to act on it would be to become involved in unpleasantness, and this the narrator would prefer to avoid in favor of some easier way—if any is to be found. Once again he avoids the issue, in the socially approved way, by turning his mind to his work.

Bartelby's unconventional insistence on his preferences, and his in-difference to the demands of his social setting, the office, leads the narrator to wonder about him, that is, to want to understand him.

He watches Bartleby narrowly and finds him more enigmatic than before. Bartleby never seems to leave, he exists on ginger nuts, and in the miniature society of the office his corner remains a "hermitage." Judgment cannot account for the man, and though imagination provides "delicious self-approval," it too fails to provide understanding. The conflict in the narrator's mind between acceptance of Bartleby as enigmatic eccentric, on one hand, and insistence on Bartleby's position as employee, on the other, leads to no action while the narrator is in a charitable mood; but when he is not, he feels a need to force Bartleby into revealing himself actively, not just passively—that is, to make himself vulnerable by showing "some angry spark answerable to my own." The narrator's goading excites the other scriveners, but it cannot reach Bartleby. At last, for the sake of keeping peace in the office, and also because some of Bartleby's preferences coincide with the preferences of society ("his steadiness, his freedom from all dissipation, his incessant industry"), the narrator comes to accept Bartleby, and the narrator's internal conflict is temporarily resolved.

When the narrator learns that Bartleby lives at the office, the internal conflict reawakens. As he looks through Bartleby's things, the narrator's judgment hurls him onto the truth: Bartleby is "the victim of innate and incurable disorder," in a word, he is mad. Common sense demands that he be gotten rid of, for, as the narrator sees, the practical fact is that "pity is not seldom pain," and one cannot work well (as one must in this world) when one is suffering. The narrator gives his scrinever one last chance: he asks Bartleby to tell him about his past; if Bartleby will answer like a sensible man, the narrator will keep him on. As he asks it, the narrator insists, sincerely enough, "I feel friendly towards you." And the effect is interesting: Bartleby hesitates a "considerable time" before answering, and for the first time his composure breaks—his lips tremble. "*At present*," he says (and he is using the phrase "at present" for the first time), "I prefer to give no answer." It seems that the narrator has cracked the wall between them; but if so, he does not know it at the time. The narrator's common sense goes deep and now, when he is on the threshold of his scrivener's secret self, self-delusion saves the narrator from what, as he rightly sees, cannot help Bartleby and can only hurt himself. Misinterpreting what has happened, he feels "nettled" and says, "Not only did there seem to lurk in [Bartleby's manner] a certain calm disdain, but his perverseness

seemed ungrateful, considering the undeniable good usage and indul-
gence he had received from me." Even so, common sense is not quite
triumphant: "I strangely felt something superstitious knocking at my
heart, and forbidding me to carry out my purpose [of firing Bartleby],
and denouncing me for a villain if I dared to breathe one bitter word
against this forlornest of mankind." Instead of sensibly dismissing the
mad scrivener, the narrator chooses mercy, not justice, and humbly begs
Bartleby to promise to be a little reasonable "in a day or two." Bartleby's
answer, of course, is as delightfully mad as the request: "At present
I would prefer not to be a little reasonable." And Bartleby, or the will
of the individual, wins. Indeed, individualism is doing very well: Everyone in the office is saying "prefer" these days. Social dicta become
polite suggestions waiting upon the individual's taste ("If [Bartleby]
would but prefer to take a quart of good ale every day. . ."); legal eti-
quette becomes a matter of individual choice (the narrator is asked
what color paper he prefers for a certain document). Bartleby's success
is complete when, preferring to do no more copying, and preferring to
remain in the office, he gets the narrator to prefer to put up with him.

In voluntarily choosing to accept Bartleby as "the predestined purpose of my life," the narrator makes a choice which, unfortunately, he
is not free to make. From the point of view of society, the choice is
odd, unacceptable (like Colt's choice to murder Adams—a choice Colt
would not have made, the narrator says, if the two of them had not
been alone). Bartleby is such an oddity in the office that at last the
narrator must choose between Bartleby and his own professional reputation. As the sane man must, the narrator chooses society and denies
Bartleby: he moves out of the office. When moving out proves insuffi-
cient—for society holds him accountable—the narrator reluctantly goes
the whole route: he would not have acted with the cruel common
sense of the landlord, but preferring to choose the inevitable, he gives
the testimony requested in the landlord's note. The betrayed Bartleby
pronounces the judgment: "I know you." Even now the narrator feels
friendly toward Bartleby, and certainly he cannot be blamed for his
action; nevertheless, betrayal is betrayal, and both of them know it.

The sequel provides us with an insight into the background of
Bartleby's derangement and provides the narrator with belated understanding of his scrivener. As the narrator understands the matter, and
we have no reason to doubt his interpretation, Bartleby's former

occupation as dead-letter clerk heightened the natural pallid hopeless-
ness of Bartleby's character by giving him a queer and terrible vision
of life. The narrator thinks, as Bartleby must have thought before him,
"Dead letters! does it not sound like dead men?" Letters sent on mis-
sions of pardon, hope, good tidings—errands of life—end in pointless
flames; and the dead-letter clerk sees no other kind of mail (if, in fact,
there is any other kind). What he knows about letters he comes to
know of man. The bustle of activity, scrivening, clerking, bar-tending,
bill-collecting, traveling—all tumble at last against the solid wall, death.
Bartleby prefers not to share the delusions of society. For him, the
easiest way of life is the best because whether one spends one's time
"not unemployed" by John Jacob Astor or spends it "sitting upon
a banister," one dies. He is not "luny," as Ginger Nut thinks, but mad.
Estranged from the ordinary view of life (he does not even read the
papers), Bartleby perceives reality; thus whereas the narrator, when
he looks out his windows, sees at one end a wall "deficient in what
landscape painters call 'life'" and at the other end "a huge, square
cistern," Bartleby sees, respectively, death and the grave.

Except at that moment when he is tempted to feel affection for
the man who feels friendly toward him, there is within Bartleby no
conflict at all. He is dead already, as the narrator's recurring adjective,
"cadaverous," suggests. Whatever the exigencies of the moment, he
cannot be made to forget the walls enclosing life. He has walked for
some time in the yard "not accessible to common prisoners," for the
yard in the Tombs is life itself: "The surrounding walls, of amazing
thickness, kept off all sounds behind them. The Egyptian character
of the masonry weighed upon me with its gloom. But a soft imprisoned
turf grew under foot. The heart of the eternal pyramids, it seemed,
wherein, by some strange magic, through the clefts, grass-seed, dropped
by birds, had sprung." But though Bartleby suffers no conflict within,
he is engaged in a conflict more basic than that in which the narrator
is involved. The narrator wishes to avoid unpleasantness—and if possible,
to do so without loss of self-respect. Bartleby wishes to shape his own
destiny, at least within the little space between the walls of birth and
death. The narrator, when he has "looked a little into 'Edwards on the
Will,' and 'Priestley on Necessity,'" slides into the persuasion that his
troubles have been predestined from eternity, and he chooses to accept
them, voluntarily relinquishing his will to "an all-wise Providence."

But Bartleby insists on freedom. When the narrator suggests that he take a clerkship in a dry-goods store, he answers, "There is too much confinement about that." The narrator's reaction: "why, you keep yourself confined all the time!" misses the point, for confinement, if one chooses confinement, is free agency, and circling the world, if required of one, is not. Melville makes the point dramatically. When Bartleby will neither tour Europe with some young man nor live in the narrator's home, the narrator flees from Bartleby, the landlord and the tenants who may again besiege the law office. He runs from the building, up Wall Street toward Broadway, catches a bus, surrenders his business to Nippers, and turns to still wilder flight, driving about in his rockaway for days. In his restless flight he is less free than the man on the banister.

But in the end, no individual, not even Bartleby, can be free. The freedom of each individual curtails the freedom of some other, as poor Colt's freedom curtails the freedom of Adams (murdered men have no preferences), and as Bartleby's freedom curtails that of the narrator. Thus the limits imposed upon freedom by the laws of Nature are narrowed by the laws of society: Bartleby must be jailed. Inside the prison, "individuals"; outside, "functionaries." Betrayed by the narrator and the society he represents, confined in a smaller prison and, as he says, knowing where he is, Bartleby has only one freedom left: he may prefer not to live. And he does.

Melville suggests in various ways that the conflict between Bartleby and the world (and the conflict within the narrator's mind) is one between imagination and judgment, or reason. Judgment supports society: ethical law is the law of reason; imagination, on the other hand, supports higher values, those central to poetry and religion: moral law is the law of imagination. Ethical law, always prohibitive, guarantees equal rights to all members of the group, but moral law, always affirmative, points to the absolute, without respect to the needs of the group. Thus ethical law demands that scriveners proofread their copy; but the narrator says, "I cannot credit that the mettlesome poet, Byron, would have contentedly sat down with Bartleby to examine a law document of, say five hundred pages. . ." And when the narrator sees that Bartleby is mad and must be dismissed, that is, when common sense bids the narrator's soul be rid of the man, the narrator cannot bring himself to go to Trinity Church. Reason and imagination also divide the narrator's mind: each time Bartleby's stubborn preferences force the narrator into thought, the narrator thinks in two ways, by imagination (when he sees in poetic or religious terms) and by reason (when he works out logical deductions after studying facts); and the results of the two ways of thinking differ sharply. Reason tells the narrator that Bartleby exists on ginger nuts but somehow does not become hot and spicy; "imagination," explaining "what proves to be impossible to be solved by his judgment," tells the narrator that Bartleby is a "poor fellow" who "means no mischief" and "intends no insolence." When the narrator examines Bartleby's belongings, imagination leads him close to an understanding of Bartleby the individual: as he detects, through empathy, the loneliness of Bartleby, he sees that he and Bartleby are "both sons of Adam," and he begins to suffer "sad fancyings—the chimeras, doubtless, of a sick and silly brain." He adds, "Presentiments of strange discoveries hovered round me. The scrivener's pale form appeared to me laid out, among uncaring strangers, in its shivering winding sheet." Reason, however, leads the narrator in a different direction. He sees that the man is mad (a social judgment) and that, after giving Bartleby a fair chance to prove himself sane, he must fire him. Throughout the story, the narrator's generous impulses, as well as his attempt at self-justification when common sense fails to drive out the sense of guilt, take religious form: by leaps of faith, or imagination, he understands Bartleby, and when he is considering doing harm to Bartleby for the sake of his own reputation, he consoles himself with words like "charity" and "love," allowing himself to believe that what he plans is after all for Bartleby's good, not his own. (The narrator is self-deluded, not hypocritical, for as he tells the story now he understands and, usually, acknowledges the mistakes he made at the time of his Bartleby troubles. Mistakes he does not acknowledge openly he treats in comic terms, as he treats his ethical perversion of the moral injunction "that ye love one another.")

If the narrator's interpretation of Bartleby's madness is correct, imagination, presenting a metaphor which relates dead letters and men, is the basis of Bartleby's plight. In other words, he is a man who has seen a vision and, holding true to his vision, can no longer operate in the ordinary world. In a sense, he is a queer sort of fanatic, operating on the basis of a religion of his own.

Obviously the conflicts in "Bartleby," together with the germs of symbolic extension of meaning, are rooted in character; and the legitimacy of the conflicts, whether they are seen as conflicts between the individual and society or between will and necessity, is equally clear. Thus the story is not a melodrama (between, say, the stupid reviewer of *Pierre* and the pure, heroic author) but an honest fictional representation of a dilemma which, in ordinary life, cannot be resolved. In the end the narrator understands. Learning that Bartleby was a dead-letter clerk, he achieves Bartleby's vision: he sees by a leap of imagination exactly what Bartleby must have seen—dead letters, dead men, limited human freedom. This vision is the terrible outcome foreshadowed earlier: "And I trembled to think that my contact with the scrivener had already and seriously affected me in a mental way. And what further and deeper aberration might it not yet produce?" From the beginning the narrator has been imaginative—in fact, like Bartleby, has been given to "fancyings" and "chimeras"; but unlike Bartleby, he also possesses judgment. When he needs to, he can control his fancies. Unlike Bartleby, he creates: he originally created his practice, he has created "recondite documents," and he is now creating a work of art. Reason must impose order upon the chaos of imagination.

Symbolism in "Bartleby" supports this view of scrivener as visionary and narrator as creator. The religion of ordinary scriveners is the routine of the law office or the will of the lawyer: the narrator speaks of Turkey as the "most reverential of men," values his "morning services," and cannot get him to give up his afternoon "devotions"; and the narrator tells us that Turkey eats ginger nuts as though they were "wafers." Bartleby is another matter: his arrival is an "advent," there is nothing "ordinarily human about him," he is full of "quiet mysteries," and when the narrator leaves Bartleby alone in the office Bartleby stands "like the last pillar of a ruined temple." He dies at last among "murderers and thieves." And whereas Bartleby is Christ-like, the narrator is Jehovah-like: the voice behind the story, like the voice behind *The Confidence-Man*, is mythical, for the speaker here is God, the story of his reluctant change from the legalistic, tribal deity of the Old Testament to the God of Love and Justice in the New Testament. As Melville treats the material, Christ is not a son of God but (as the Old Testament Jehovah sees him) an "incubus," thus not a revelation sent by God to man but rather a nightmare creature who drives God into self-knowledge (as, on the literal level, Bartleby drives the lawyer to self-knowledge).

The narrator and Jehovah are linked in numerous ways. The narrator is officially "Master" in Chancery. Like Jehovah, he keeps out of the public eye and works "in the cool tranquillity of a snug retreat." The narrator's first scrivener, Turkey, is the militant archangel Michael. His nickname is possibly meant to suggest not only the red-necked, irascible fowl emblematic of thanksgiving but also the terrible Turk. He has a face which "beams," "blazes," and "flames" like the sun, and he considers himself, rather insolently, the narrator's "right-hand man." He uses his ruler as a sword and is in charge of the narrator's forces, marshalling and deploying "columns" (the narrator speaks later of his "column of clerks"), and charging "the foe." His "inflamed" ways are always "worse on Saturdays" (the Sabbath). The second scrivener, Nippers (pincers),[1] is symbolically linked with Lucifer. He is a "whiskered, sallow, and, upon the whole, piratical-looking young man" who suffers from "ambition" as well as indigestion. He is impatient with the duties of a mere copyist, and his ambition is evinced by "an unwarrantable usurpation of strictly professional affairs, such as the original drawing up of legal documents." (The Devil is famous for making pacts: consider poor Faust.) His indigestion (spleen) is "betokened in an occasional nervous testiness and grinning irritability, causing the teeth to audibly grind together. . ., unnecessary maledictions, hissed, rather than spoken, in the heat [inferno] of business. . ." He has his own kingdom, for the narrator says, "Among the manifestations of his diseased ambition was a fondness he had for receiving visits from certain ambiguous-looking fellows in seedy coats, whom he called his clients." He is "considerable of a ward-politician," occasionally does "a little business at the Justices' courts," and is "not unknown on the steps of the Tombs." As gods and would-be gods control willful men, so Nippers jerks his desk about as if it were "a perverse voluntary agent and vexing him." The third scrivener, Ginger Nut (Raphael, perhaps— for Milton the messenger and sociable angel), is official cake (or "wafer") and apple (forbidden fruit?) purveyor for the establishment.

Much of the humor in "Bartleby" depends upon the reader's perceiving the symbolic level, for comic effect arises out the tendency of surface and symbolic levels to infect one another: the narrator, an ordinary man, is comic when he behaves like God, and God is comic when he behaves like man; and other tensions between surface and symbol (Turkey—Michael, Nippers—Lucifer) work in the same way.

Ground-glass folding doors (through which, presumably, we see darkly) divide the narrator's premises into two parts. "According to my humor," the narrator says, rather pleased with himself, "I threw open these doors, or closed them." He also takes pleasure in his clever disposition of Bartleby: Bartleby sits inside the doors (all others are outside) but sits behind a screen "which might entirely isolate Bartleby from my sight, though not remove him from my voice." Puns frequently contribute to this humor. The words "original" and "genius" work as they do in *The Confidence-Man*. And when the narrator becomes resigned to Bartleby he says, "One prime thing was this—*he was always there*. . ." (Melville's italics). When the scrivener's being "always there" proves a not unmixed blessing, the narrator says:

> And as the idea came upon me of his possibly turning out a long-lived man, and keep occupying my chambers, and denying my authority; and perplexing my visitors; and scandalizing my professional reputation; and casting a general gloom over the premises; keeping soul and body together to the last upon his savings (for doubtless he spent but half a dime a day), and in the end perhaps outlive me, and claim possession of my office by right of his perpetual occupancy. . . I resolved to gather all my faculties together, and forever rid me of this intolerable incubus.
>
> Ere revolving any complicated project, however, adapted to this end, I first simply suggested to Bartleby the propriety of his permanent departure. . . But, having taken three days to meditate upon it, he apprised me, that his original determination remained the same; in short, that he still preferred to abide with me.

(The funniest barrage of puns in the story is *keeping soul and body together to the last upon his savings*.) But the effect of the symbolic level is not always—and is never entirely—comic. When the narrator abandons his office to Nippers at the time of Bartleby's arrest, one is more distressed than amused. One is moved, too, by the rich final line of the story: "Ah, Bartleby! Ah, humanity!" A man who behaves like God may be queerly admirable. The narrator puffs up his chest like God, but he is also capable of infinite compassion, he is dedicated to the spirit of the law (he will not get rid of Bartleby by laying an essentially false charge on him), and he can survive.

The lawyer-turned-artist is creative, like God, because he has judgment. He has imagination like "the mettlesome poet, Byron," but unlike Byron (Melville seems to suggest) the lawyer has the judgment to see that the commitment of art is to man. One reason for the social commitment of art, as we have seen, is that society cannot operate without voluntary or involuntary diminution of the individual will. But Melville offers, in "Bartleby," another reason as well. The final line of the story is both an equation and an opposition: "Ah, Bartleby! Ah, humanity!" Man lives on a walled-up street where the practice of law flourishes and justice is operative only in the mind. If justice is to be introduced into the ordinary world, if man is to receive recompense for being stopped in mid-action by dry lightning (like the narrator's man from Virginia), justice must come either as a Christian afterlife or as a transmutation of purely conceptual experience—that is, as art. The first seems no longer certain: the office of Master in Chancery is now defunct, "a [damned] premature act." We must find some other pleasant remuneration. The betrayed Bartleby gets justice and mercy at last, though; for Bartleby, whose freedom was limited in life by the inescapability of death, is now transmogrified to eternal life in art. Before Bartleby, the office was governed by law; but the recondite document at hand is a New Testament of sorts, at once ethical and moral. It insists upon law in this world, but it also provides justice. Though life must of necessity be characterized by limited freedom, voluntary self-diminution, there will be, after life, art. The artist rolls the stone away—that is the narrator's creative act—and man escapes from the Tombs.

NOTE

1. For suggestions concerning the names "Nippers" and "Ginger Nut" I am indebted to E. M. Glenn of Chico State College.

An Invective
Against
Mere Fiction

AS EVERYONE KNOWS, THE WHOLE TEN-
dency of modern life and thought is against the absolute. Metaphysics
is out, "alternative conceptual systems" are in. Kings are out, pluralism
is in. Relativity is all. But however useful relativism may be as a way
of running daily life—keeping fascists out of power, keeping tea parties
civilized—it has nothing to do with art. Relativism denies those finalities toward which man's spirit has always groped. To admit that there
are no finalities is to put the spirit out of business; to say that finalities
are a matter of personal assertion is to make the spirit's business
insignificant.

Despite the vogue of relativism, good painters and composers continue to make absolute affirmations, but they do so in spite of their
critics, their happy, horn-swoggled audiences, and the richly rewarded
hacks who call themselves painters or composers. As for literature,
the two most important of the established novelists in America are
that great gossip Saul Bellow, with his "personal vision," and that master
of illusion, prankster, puzzler, Vladimir Nabokov. Both are solid writers,
but neither is so vulgar or obsolete as to admit his fiction (as Chekhov
said) "tells the truth." The fact is that, despite their protestations, Bellow
and Nabokov do tell the truth, insofar as they are significant writers—
Bellow clumsily, Nabokov with careful craftsmanship.

To put it another way, writers work out in words their intuitions—their private certainties—of how things are. Good writers have right and significant intuitions, and they present their intuitions intact by means of masterful technique. To deny the possibility of absolute intuition is either to scrap the art of fiction or to look patronizingly on the fool who works at it. Ultimately, the critic or publisher's abnegation of the absolute turns weak but serious writers into hacks and promotes the publication of books by natural-born bus drivers.

I am not really saying that only one book should have been published this season—*Omensetter's Luck.* I approve of books on chess, stories about boys and dogs, and one or two other things. What I mean I must say by examples. Before I do that, though, I must add one truism more. In the absolute world of fictional truth, the novelist speaks of what might be, *In Cold Blood* notwithstanding—speaks of people and events about whom the reader is not likely to feel any violent urge to disagree, though sometimes he ought to. The critic, on the other hand, declaims the truth about an actuality, a book, waving the old flag of Absolute Taste in the face of all common sense. To the relativist's rhetorical question "Who is to judge?" the critic leaps up, red beard flying, banging his crutches, screaming, "Me!" Laughter. Tentative applause. If the man has any brains, any dignity, he soon learns to speak of demonstrables like Form, as if construction in a novel were far more important than what the novel is constructed to do. Or he learns to speak of Personal Vision, becoming sideshow barker for freaks. Since novelists are people too, the critic learns to make careful distinctions between the work and the man who worked it out, as if a man who thinks and feels like Capote *could* have written like Graham Greene this time, unfortunately, he didn't. What is important to notice here is that the capitulating critic is right. Art is not all that important, or anyway most art. Nevertheless, it may be observed of clowns, especially red-bearded, bespectacled clowns who bang their crutches—they persist.

Now to the examples and what I mean about Fiction and Information and Escape and Truth. My object, I should explain at once, is to comment on everything in this enomous hodge-podge stack of books I've been sent by the editors of *The Southern Review* and make of the hodge-podge a clean demonstration of what distinguishes fictional truth from mere fiction.

AN INVECTIVE AGAINST MERE FICTION / 15

When Peter Faecke published *The Firebugs* in his native Germany—
he was then twenty-three—he was "hailed by leading literary critics,"
according to the jacket, "as a writer of startling originality and proven
artistic achievement." The tale, told backwards and inside-out, concerns
(1) town guilt, (2) a man in search of lineage, (3) racial conflict and
guilt (Jews and Germans, not whites and Negroes), (4) an idiot, (5) an
all-knowing detective-lawyer-uncle, (6) sawmills, (7) arson. Faulkner
reheated, a thick and bitter brew. From an absolutist's point of view,
Faecke is a hack.

Usually the pandering of writers and publishers does not come to
outright fraud, however. One finds, for instance, young writers who
are devoutly sincere, like Marilyn Hoff (*Dink's Blues*) and Gene Horowitz (*Home Is Where You Start From*). Miss Hoff has written a college
novel that sounds like a college girl's letter home, full of ellipses and
girlish opinions about civil rights and free will and imagination, in the
obscene popular magazine style: "The next day was Friday, November
22. When *it* happened [my italics] I was grabbing lunch in the snack
bar." Shock of recognition? Book also has symbols. Horowitz's book—
much better written—is about the generations, how the younger can't
learn from the older, how no two people can communicate, and so
on. Horowitz is good at rendering scenes from New York Jewish life,
and as a sociological study his novel is interesting. The trouble is that
sociology is not, itself, interesting. It deals with the moment, as
Kierkegaard would say. It provides mere information. Horowitz wallows
in trivial detail, having neither the barbaric wisdom of Melville, who
scorned such stuff, nor the philosophical insight of Tolstoy (or, in a
smaller way, Peter Taylor), who can make gossip significant. Perhaps
because his experience is limited, perhaps because he has been taken
in by fashionable nonsense, Horowitz's attempts at universalizing come
to nothing: however popular it may be to assert that each generation
must learn on its own, the assertion is false. If a second generation
can't learn from a first, the reason is that the second generation has
a basic and uninteresting fault: it lacks the ability to empathize or think
and thus understand. Great writers deal with problems which confront
a healthy, intelligent man, however grotesque the fictional representative; small writers deal with social or physiological traps. (Captain
Ahab may be mad, but he's a piece of Melville, by no means a fool,
a weakling, or merely a victim of social conditions.) Marilyn Hoff

got published because the racial question sells. Mr. Horowitz got published because alienation is in. Neither writer has clarified the human situation, though both make a youthful, feeble attempt. Both have been encouraged to market simpleminded opinions and undisciplined talent.

The pandering of grown-up writers is more troublesome. Take, for instance, Margaret Lane (*A Night at Sea*). A love triangle—husband, wife, mistress. Husband and wife go to the old symbolic sea and ruminate among the usual poetic-sounding nautical fittings for two hundred pages. Wife decides she should kill herself, the Christian thing to do. Takes pills while piloting the boat, despite the arguments of common sense and a ghostly voice. Boat is wrecked, husband dies, and wife finds that life is, for mysterious reasons, worth living after all. The writing is professional, and the analysis of characters is subtle, so that the immortality of the argument has effect. Infidelity is justified because we ought to be "free," ought to "fulfill outselves," according to Miss Lane. And as everyone knows, nothing in this world is really satisfying but sex. Or take Willard Motley (*Let Noon Be Fair*): a sad story— annoyingly well told, in its slick way—of American exploitation. It used to be that in beautiful, natural Mexico girls fornicated for free on the beach, but then came the gringos, paying the girls, on one hand, preaching to them, on the other. Now Mexico is dirty and rotten and guilt-ridden and capitalist, like America. Motley, like Miss Lane, makes money on fashionable lies, in this case the lie that Americans are basically hypocrites and fools and every other country in the world is nicer. Motley is wrong, as wrong as any Bircher, and his publisher (Putnam) should be trounced. One might say the same of the Trident Press, publishers of Don Tracy's maudlin and would-be sensational *Bazzaris*, except that a book so extremely clumsy can have no effect whatever. The probably unwitting social and moral thesis is absurd, the technique embarrassing.

I am of course not saying that every book must be significant, but only that a man who thinks he is significant—thinks himself an artist— had better be right. Helen MacInnes's *The Double Image*, a tale of intrigue and espionage, is good entertainment, though not art and never meant to be. Alexander Fullerton's *Lionheart* is now and then moderately entertaining, though hardly as exciting as Fullerton thinks, unless the style is pure desperation. Even the writers of entertainments have to be trivially honest, that is to say, convincing. MacInnes usually is,

Fullerton isn't, but the imperfection of his craft is not bothersome. One does not judge a lemon drop by the same standards one uses in judging a lifeboat.

On the other hand, the mere intent to be amusing and insignificant is no guarantee of success for the entertainer. Consider Jean Stafford's *A Mother in History* (not a work of fiction but a handy example). It is tasteless to write unimportantly of important matters—the assassination of a President, the background of an assassin. Miss Stafford's original object was serious enough, however unpretentious: to seek an intuitive, feminine understanding of Oswald's mother. But Miss Stafford has sold out to the snobbish, complacent, chattering ladies' magazines. For instance: "Accustomed as she was to public speaking, Mrs. Oswald did not seem to be addressing me specifically but, rather, a large congregation... Taking advantage of my anonymity in this quiet crowd and of the fact that her back was turned, I looked around the room in the snoopy way women do when they are in other women's houses..." A moment later Miss Stafford speaks of "a writing desk where orderly piles of papers were laid out to which my Paul Pry eye would be bound to stray." Throughout her narrative, Miss Stafford superciliously calls attention to Mrs. Oswald's grammar, her pronunciation, her vulgarity. Mrs. Oswald is straight out of Flannery O'Connor, but at least her demonic stupidity is honest. Miss Stafford, who used to write serious fiction, has taught herself to be what Longinus calls "frigid"—emotionally trivial.

I have an ulterior motive for dragging in Jean Stafford. I want to make a distinction between art and entertainment, one in which "fiction" in the old sense has no place. I have said that great writers avoid mere social or physiological traps and that entertainers—that is, writers of spy stories, animal stories, amusing interviews, and other books to escape with—are successful if they amuse without offending our sense of what is fitting. These were convenient simplifications. Good writers do deal with trivial problems and trivial people. When they do, however, they recognize the triviality of their material and force the reader— perhaps for the first time—to recognize it too. Mere entertainment, then, provides escape from the way things are; entertaining *art* clarifies. Entertainment fails when considerations inside or outside the work force the reader to muse soberly on Truth—not the truth of fact, but the truth of human values. Entertaining art, on the other hand, fails whenever it turns into pure entertainment (shooting in the wrong direction) or whenever it falls into error (a shot in the right direction, but a miss). From a technical point of view, both entertainment and art require craftsmanship, but since style is one of the chief devices for liberating truth, it should be obvious that the richer the language, the worse the entertainment. Or to put the thing neutrally, entertainment requires cleverness, art richness. Needless to say, neither art nor entertainment very often get what they require. It is also hardly necessary to mention that most books are neither art nor entertainment but a mixture of the two—Bellow's *Herzog*, for instance: part vision, part prattle. Nevertheless, the distinction is right and useful, and books which violate the distinction are unsatisfying, like music from a French horn that leaks air on certain notes.

Entertaining art does get its due in Anthony Burgess, even in his relatively slight first novel, *A Vision of Battlements*, belatedly published last winter. The comedy is lighter than that in Burgess's later books, but the artistic focus is the same. Characters who are not trivial, or wouldn't be if the world were put together right, find themselves entangled in the triviality of the world—in this case, the world of military system. The central character is a serious composer whose noble but inept attempts to manage where a Truth-man does not fit throw comic light on both the impossible ideal (which we all the more earnestly affirm) and the social realities which keep the ideal out of reach. Not that the tale is a melodrama. The army is all too eager to be a friend of art, education, and all that: it joyfully makes lists, sends out directives, studies the appropriate and inappropriate regulations; but it is as hard for military system to adapt to art as for art to adapt to military system. The hero's name is Ennis, his story a burlesque of Virgil's epic. No empire has been founded yet when the book ends, but Ennis is still at it, laboring like the insects in Burgess's splendid final paragraph. The language in *A Vision of Battlements* is not as ingenious as in the later Burgess novels, but it is sufficient, often very funny, rich in images which are at once clever and grimly appropriate.

And pure entertainment, of a sort less formulaic than the usual spy story or animal story, gets its due and then some in *Soft Soap*, the first of William Elsschot's *Three Novels*, superbly translated by A. Brotherton. *Soft Soap* is the story of a wise swindler named Boorman, managing director of *The World Review of Finance, Trade and Commerce, Industry,*

Art and Science, a publication with no subscribers. Most of the story consists of Boorman's half-Dostoyevskean, half-Dickensean talk about the world. His *Review* is a device for extorting money from other swindlers (the whole world), and the novelistic excuse for the talk is that Boorman is breaking in a new managing director. What makes the book delightful is that, though Boorman believes all the world to be crooked, Boorman is no whining cynic. He has enormous admiration for crooks:

> "Look, you do it like this," and he flicked open a thick directory and read out:
> *Washington Hotel—1100 rooms—electricity—bathrooms—lifts. Telephone 16305, 16306, 16307, 16308, 16309, 16310.*
> "You can see at once that the Washington Hotel is something for the *World Review* . . . They word the advertisements so that the innocent reader has visions of some immense labyrinth where he'd get lost without a guide. Then those phone numbers. They could just as well as have put one-six-three-o-five, a hyphen, and ten, but with each number printed separately you can hear a chorus of phones jangling as you read the advertisement. They know a trick or two!"

Soft Soap "exposes" everything under the sun—from politicians to funeral directors to unions to fat, sick ladies, and the inventiveness of the thing is amazing. *The Leg*, the second of the *Three Novels*, is shorter and almost as funny. Boorman grows remorseful and struggles to atone for his earlier swindling of a fat lady who now has a wooden leg. To no avail, of course. The swindled shall inherit the earth. The third novel is sadly disappointing—a moral tale, full of heavy-handed symbolism and all the virtuous emotion Elsschot poked fun at so cleverly in his earlier pieces. What has gone wrong here is interesting, or at any rate supports my thesis on art vs. entertainment. The longing and disillusionment which characterize all of Elsschot's work can make excellent entertainment, for there Elsschot mock-soberly takes patent illusion as his clown-hero's premise of reality and does not claim to say how things really are. But when, in an attempt at art, Elsschot describes the human situation as a sad case of longing and disillusionment, he mistakes a half-truth for truth, and the result is one more whimpering modern novel. At the same time, the very cleverness which makes the earlier short novels delightful is hollow and out of place here, while the attempt at richness introduced by symbols (mainly the sea) fails because the symbols are easy and awkwardly introduced.

I object on these same stylistic grounds to Heather Ross Miller's *Tenants of the House* and, more strenuously, John Nathan's translation of Yukio Mishima's *The Sailor Who Fell from Grace with the Sea*, which is probably no better in Japanese. Miss Miller's widely acclaimed style consists of "poetic" diction (houses are "dwellings"), high-falutin' sentences designed to intensify everyday situations, and trite bits of irony. By high-falutin' I mean: "But it didn't turn out that way. The vision that burned under the carbide lamps of the Carolina farmers as John Murdoch stood in their kitchens and talked of his church, his Mission, burned in the lamp of Destiny with a different blaze struck by another match." As for trite irony, take the chapter-opener, to be found in a hundred ladies' novels, "Summer came to Johnsboro in spite of the war." One might point to numerous instances of such sentimental writing in Miss Miller's novel, and I am tempted to do it if only from distress at the high praise her style has generally been given. But I won't. Three things should be said in her favor. Though she writes with a gilded shovel, she does not trade in patently moronic ideas or gossip for its own sake. Second, her symbols are more or less original and sometimes interesting. And third, the novel is infinitely better than its dust jacket—a picture of Poe's Miss Usher, with a green face and stormy blue hair.

As for Mishima's novel, the dust jacket is excellent. The prose, if one can isolate it from what it carries, is lean and spare, classical, like all Mishima's writing. The trouble is, there are brutally obvious stock symbols, intended ironically, in part, but nevertheless purveyors of untruth. The novel is about the sea and the land, youthful ambition and middle-aged disillusionment and compromise. The plot is as spare and classical as the prose: and the danger in a strictly classical plot which ends unhappily is that the doom must be inevitable as the plot and must be, at the same time, significant enough to justify the torture the reader must endure. Mishima tells of a sailor who once believed— and secretly believes yet—that he is set apart from the rest of mankind and will someday achieve some sort of glory. He becomes the idol of a group of schoolboys who have the same vague yearning for the extraordinary and the same conviction of personal superiority. The boys for unconvincing reasons train themselves in the heartlessness of a Nietzschean superman. For instance, in one powerfully upsetting scene, they murder and cut up a kitten. When the schoolboys discover that their hero is an ordinary man, compassionate, befuddled, gentle, like any common landsman, they resolve to destroy him exactly as they destroyed the kitten. The novel ends with the sailor drinking drugged tea, mumbling of his dream of glory, about to be liquidated: "Still immersed in his dream, he drank down the tepid tea. It tasted bitter. Glory, as anyone knows, is bitter stuff." We have heard before that glory is bitter—heard it so often we need to question the opinion. Mishima's division of humanity into landsmen and seamen, compromisers or wrongheaded glory seekers, is melodramatic, and the pious melodrama is completely unrelieved. Every character who figures in the story stands on one side or the other of the neat dichotomy: an actress who pitifully misses the Oscars year after year; a lady unwillingly compromising in her double role as land-rooted mother and mistress to a sailor; and on the other side, the sentimental sailor, the murderous boys. But there *are* in this world some who succeed, some who, as W. H. Gass says, "know how to be." As a psychological thriller Mishima's tale might be successful (though psychology for its own sake is no more interesting than sociology); but when accidental psychological limitations are elevated to cosmic verities by an awesome rumbling of symbolism, the result is falsehood and thus unsatisfying drama. In Mishima too, one may as well add, sex has much to answer for. The murderous son, Noboru, gets his great vision of the mysterious glory which is his supposed Destiny from peeping while his mother and the sailor make love. And as for the sailor:

> To a man locked up in a steel ship all the time, the sea is too much like a woman. Things like her lulls and storms, or her caprice, or the beauty of her breast reflecting the setting sun, are all obvious. More than that, you're in a ship that mounts the sea and rides her and yet is constantly denied her. It's the old saw about miles and miles of lovely water and you can't quench your thirst. Nature surrounds a sailor with all these elements so like a woman and yet he is kept as far as a man can be from her warm, living body. That's where the problem begins, right there—I'm sure of it.

Captain Ahab, I think, would spit.

If entertainment provides a moral holiday, whereas art tells the truth about human values, one must make up a third category for works which, fictional or not, deal frankly with mere fact. Both Frans Coenen's *The House on the Canal*, translated by James Brockway, and J. Van Oudshoorn's *Alienation*, translated by N. C. Clegg, published together in the Classics of Dutch and Flemish Literature series, one essentially non-fictional, the other a work of fiction, are successful accounts of non-universal fact. *The House on the Canal* is the chronicle of a real house and the family which actually lived there. The book is a sociological-historical piece, interesting because it is Dutch, well-researched, and gossipy; it is legitimate, as Gene Horowitz's book is not, because Coenen abstains from moral comment where there is none to be made. *Alienation* is a grueling psychological analysis, a painstaking clinical record of mental breakdown as seen from inside. The book has an effect much like one common effect of what I have called art: the reader is torn to bits. But the murder of the reader has no broad philosophical implications. If the madness of the central character has its basis in puritanism, the case is not presented as anything more than a special case. One reads in the way one reads about the emotional problems of Siamese twins. An excellent book, for its kind; neither art nor entertainment but an illustration of what the *Scientific American* could be if scientists let loose. A book of information.

Finally, as I said at the start, great literary artists give right answers to the right questions and do so with masterful craftsmanship. Such writers are rare, and a glance at the writers who have come closest shows why.

Take May Sarton first—*Mrs. Stevens Hears the Mermaids Singing*. Miss Sarton is a careful craftsman with considerable intelligence, but she is shallow. Her novel concerns an old lady poetess passionately dedicated to "getting down" the truth, to understanding, and so forth. Unfortunately, the lady we are supposed to admire is a posturing, self-pitying phony. She talks to herself in the stagy manner of an elderly lesbian (which she is): "Old thing, it's high time you pulled yourself together!" Or again, " 'Trapped by life,' Hilary muttered." And Miss Sarton, for understandable reasons, can't see through her. Two interviewers (lovers, to make a plot) are on their way to ask Mrs. Stevens about her life and work, and half the time while she waits for them Mrs. Stevens worries about the Meaning of Life, half the time dallies in (we are supposed to believe) characteristic feminine distress: "This room, too, gathered together a huge complex of living and harmonized it, all focused on the small intimate glimpse of the sea cut through scrub and brush, framed in French windows at the end. But would they disdain the flowered chintz on the sofa as old-fashioned? Would they register the two Impressionist paintings as not quite first class?" Besides a room which is really a poem she has the fond memory of a dead husband named Adrian, his mother, named Margaret (who used to bring one perfect rose in a glass), and a precious young homosexual friend named Mar (fussy names all). To Mar Mrs. Stevens shows her poems, with the following tiresome result:

> It was salutary to pit the new poems against someone so young and intransigent—so ignorant too—who would have none of her hardwon virtuosity, who forced her back and back to the essence who brought out the crude, original person. They fought bitterly, sometimes over a single word. Often she was in a rage when he left but the rage shot adrenalin through her, gave her the strength to begin a poem again, tear it apart, make it harder and stronger so she could hurl it at Mar the next day in triumph. She had not imagined that she would be so fertilized by a human being again.

And there are others, a brilliant cast of fops, mostly gay. Mrs. Stevens teaches people that "We have to dare to be ourselves." One wonders if such people *ought* to be themselves. Great writing requires a great person to do the writing. Miss Sarton leaves us with fine craftsmanship and a trivial view of man and—the real subject of the novel—poetry.

John Updike's *Of the Farm* is not much better. Again, the craftsmanship is impressive, but the people, like Updike in his present stage, are hypersensitive whiners. Every expert line tremulously whispers that the world is very sad: "Now in cool air I kissed her and her face felt feverish. Fall, which comes earlier inland, was present not so much as the scent of fallen fruit in the orchard as a lavender tinge in the dusk, a sense of expiration. The meadow wore a strip of mist where a little rivulet, hardly a creek, choked by weeds and watercress, trickled and breathed. A bat like a speck of pain jerked this way and that in the membranous violet between the treetops." The characters—an ad man, his mother, his wife and step-son—spend three days telling grim stories, quarrelling, feebly patching up, and, above all, watching each other, scrutinizing emotions. Everybody is jealous of everybody, and listening to their conversation is like listening to cross young lovers who'd be better off home in bed. The book is not mere sociology or psychology, however. It has a clear and driving moral, a kind of affirmation by default: vicious and self-centered people have to be moral to keep from killing each other. In short, the limitation of the novel is that its morality is grounded—as the Sartrean epigraph warns us—on a squinting and cynical vision, that is, a mistake. This streak in Updike has not always been quite so obvious, and one hopes he will get past it, whatever the cause.

Stylistically, Elizabeth Jane Howard's *After Julius* rings truer than May Sarton's book, and the analysis of characters is for the most part nearly as convincing as Updike's. Miss Howard's advantage is that she is wiser, emotionally healthier than the other two writers. She too enjoys scrutinizing motives, nuances of meaning in common speech, psychological interplay; but Miss Howard and her characters are not all inconvenienced at having been born. Take the character Daniel, for instance, at this point a stranger listening to a lady's sudden outpouring of grief and indignation:

> He listened, and nodded—more to show that he was listening than to indicate agreement or even understanding. He understood that she was not happy, all right, and of course, if people felt like that, they spent nearly all their time trying to find the reasons for it, and he knew that he wasn't there to find the reasons *for* her, just to provide comfort—a little ignorant warmth in this awful life of hers, jam-crammed with ideas and disaster and with no man to account for it or take her mind off herself.
>
> When she had no more to say she asked him what he thought. He thought.

The story is a kind of allegory in which three dissimilar women achieve their moral identity by means of what for them amounts to a private myth—Julius, killed at Dunkirk. The prose is smooth and serviceable, more clever than rich, not painfully self-conscious; and the controlling idea is worth the writer's trouble. What limits this pleasing novel is that, allegory or no, the book is merely a ladies' book, Miss Howard merely a ladies' novelist. If we read for escape, the serious theme distracts us from the pleasant chatter, the pretty scenes, the touching sentiments; once we are caught by the emerging idea, the gossipy detail stirs a tingle of impatience and we wish to get on to what counts.

The distinction I have made between art and entertainment is borrowed from Graham Greene, and it would be ungrateful to use it against him. Put it this way, then. Relatively speaking, *The Comedians* is a fine novel, especially for reading on a train. Greene himself has provided the standard. Near the start of the book the narrator says in passing, "I tried to read a novel, but the heavy foreseeable progress of its characters down the uninteresting corridors of power made me drowsy, and when the book fell upon the deck, I did not bother to retrieve it." The novel Brown is reading has some things in common with *The Comedians*, but Greene's book has nothing heavily foreseeable, no uninteresting corridors. *The Comedians* is partly informational (Totalitarianism in Haiti), partly entertainment (a well-plotted thriller). It also makes a casual pass at art, that is, Truth-telling, but here as almost always in Greene, Truth rides easy and manages not to be distracting—for two reasons. First, for all that has been made of it, Greene's Truth is—and has always been—comfortable and familiar, a piece of the plot. It has far less to do with the Catholic's problem (as Greene himself has insisted) than with the ordinary human problem, that of maintaining faith in and commitment to those absolute values—justice, freedom, loyalty—which for Greene seem increasingly remote from actuality. Greene's thesis is one that warms the heart, like sad, pretty girls and well-described exotic landscapes and amusing minor characters—a pair of devout vegetarians, for instance (as in this book). Second, Greene's form and manner are insistently popular. When serious art borrows a popular formula, the very manner forces one to recognize that the formula is for once being taken seriously. Consider Faulkner. An odd or striking technique, one which forces the reader again and again away from the formula to its inner meaning, is worthless if that meaning is trifling or thoroughly familiar, and Greene is right to adopt the form he does. But if the artist's vision is significant and exceptional it demands unique expression.

On the other hand, Crawford Power's *The Encounter*, which after fifteen years has now appeared as an Avon paperback, is a serious and original work of art held back from the first rank by Power's choice of conventional technique. Even so trifling a thing as the writer's way of beginning and separating chapters can limit the effect of a novel. The book opens *in medias res*, with a piece of conversation—a beginning which requires incredible skill to bring off. It is one of the two stock openings of spy stories, ladies' novels, and who-done-its, the other being *in medias res* description. Power's handling of chapter and episode, sometimes the individual sentence as well, call up the same unlucky associations. The whole effect of the conventional and popular technique—broken only in Father Cawder's meditations—runs counter to the main force of the novel, an impressive exploration of the idea of goodness. Power's central character, Father Cawder, is a Christian in the old-fashioned sense, a humiliator of the flesh, an uncompromising servant of God. He is an embodiment of goodness of a certain kind—as is almost every character in the novel. And his goodness, like that of the people around him, is both admirable and deadly. The central encounter is between Father Cawder and an acrobat named Diamond, who at first seems Cawder's opposite in every way: a sensualist, apparently uncommitted, finally a murderer. But in fact Diamond is Cawder and Cawder Diamond. No one in the novel is normative. The norm emerges as an impossible ideal at the imaginary center of the circle of characters—an ideal of human love as wise as God's. Father Cawder is no more capable of such love than is any other man. His tragedy is that he will not be satisfied with mere forgiveness, confession. He ends brooding on the image given him by his alter ego, the plunge into death and the divine radiance; but that death he cannot choose. Breaking off from his prayer of forgiveness, he becomes, in Power's brilliant close, a grim parody of the saintly martyrs of his faith, still mortifying the flesh but also turning—as imagery has suggested throughout—to stone.

Before I can turn to what seem to me the two most important novels published in the last few months—the last two novels in my stack—I must add to what I have said already one further observation about what makes art. Excellent craftsmanship is the limit of an intelligent and wise man—Graham Greene among entertainers, Anthony Burgess among what I am calling artists. The great artist, the "genius," to use an old-fashioned word, is the man who sees more connections between things than an ordinary man can see and has, moreover, a peculiar and *absolutely unerring* feeling for his medium. "Style" is as inadequate to describe this feeling for the writer's medium as "church" would be to describe a cathedral. (Part of the difference between a church and a cathedral is that the man who lives in a cathedral is a bishop.) Some men, beyond all doubt, have words bubbling in the holy wells where the rest of us have mere blood. In desperation one snatches at ludicrous phrases like "magical language." Fraudulent writers like Herr Faecke steal their magic from somebody good. Bad writers, only dimly aware of the mystery, trump up a style. (Strange to say, all bad writers come up with the same style, though its elements may be differently distributed from writer to writer.) Intelligent writers like Burgess in his later works (and Nabokov, too) painstakingly construct a style and pump into it artificial flavoring in the form of puns, anagrams, and other material not organically related to the thing being said. (Joyce engaged in this, but with a propriety his imitators miss: up to *Finnegans Wake* Joyce's books are tales of the artist told by the artist; the linguistic tricks are the traces or signs of the speaker, comparable to—and directly suggested by—the linguistic manner of the Holy Ghost as patristic exegetes understood him.)

Only two novels in this group are extraordinary for breadth of mind and verbal genius. One is Marguerite Young's *Miss MacIntosh, My Darling*; the other is William Gass's first novel, *Omensetter's Luck*.

Miss Young establishes at once (p. 4) the central question of her enormous epic of mind:

> What was the organization of illusion, of memory? Who knew even his own divided heart? Who knew all hearts as his own? Among beings strange to each other, those divided by the long roarings of time, of space, those who have never met or, when they meet, have not recognized as their own the other heart and that heart's weaknesses, have turned stonily away, would there not be, in the vision of some omniscient eye, a web of spidery logic establishing the most secret relationships, deep calling to deep, illuminations of the eternal darkness, recognitions in the night world of voyager dreams, all barriers dissolving, all souls as one and united? Every heart is the other heart. Every soul is the other soul. Every face is the other face. The individual is the one illusion.

The book is too big and too leisurely to read or judge in the usual way—a vast city of associations, classical and modern, in which floating spirits interpenetrate and external realities of time and place break down to become a startling myth of the archetypal human life. One recalls, for many reasons, the Joycean archetypes, Father, Mother, Son, Daughter, Poet. It is directly to Joyce, I think, that Miss Young is speaking, and she is saying No. No to the Aristotelean view of life as a conflict of generation, corruption, and re-creation; no to the Joycean theory of history, and, above all, no to the theory of love as constraint. Like Joyce, Miss Young knows what tales are worth telling—she has carloads of them, as does Joyce—and like Joyce she tells her tales with highly conscious, highly artificial style. The great difference, from which all further differences sprout, is that Miss Young is a thoroughgoing Platonist—a startling thing to encounter in our time. Thus while both boldly seize as their theme "Everything," the word means more (quantitatively) to Joyce than to Miss Young. Joyce offers a metaphysical explanation of the alphabet; Miss Young is not interested in the alphabet as such but only in the fact that spellings, right or wrong, reflect some remove from the Idea. Joyce is interested in particular responsibilities of specific kings and statesmen as well as the generic idea Kingship (the crown and scepter, hat and cane), and he relates these to the responsibilities of the father, son, and poet. Miss Young leaps at once to Kingship as love, with hats and cane-like objects (also cloaks, capes, robes) functioning as Freudian symbols. Her allusive style alludes always to the same eternal forms in their infinite disguises; her symbols all center in the same idea. And so, whereas the length of *Finnegans Wake* is justified by the density of the book, its analyses of particulars—places, occupations, institutions, rituals—the bloated length of *Miss MacIntosh* is an effect, simply, of system. The manifestations of recurrent embodiments of the Idea might, in one sense, be broken off at any point: they dramatize a vision which is just as clear and possibly even as convincing in the abstract. The book lacks the emotive power of compression, in short; but I am not sure the idea admits of compression. If so, Platonism pushed to its limit is not artistically viable. And if this is true, I must nervously report, Platonism is false.

The trouble with Platonism as a basis for art is that the realm of forms is a museum, and the world where forms find their expression is a junk shop. It is impossible for a thoroughgoing Platonist to love or respect the gew-gaws of actuality: he sees the actual as curious garments from an old trunk, and since people and places are all dim representations, emblems, signs—and signs, moreover, which he understands beforehand—he very naturally slides into finding greatest interest in the signs which are most grotesque.

> We had passed, on this journey, many curious pieces of rural architecture, an enormous coffee urn with its lid opened against the sky, a wigwam nightclub where, under a denuded oak, a melancholy buffalo was tethered, incongruous as the faded washing on the line. We had passed a windmill, a leaning tower, Noah's Ark, the old woman who lived in a shoe, but these were miles back, and there were now no buildings but those of the amorphous distance, little, low-roofed houses, small as ruined birds' nests, a child's face at some near window, the individuality blotted out by the watery greyness of the Middle West, the train as small as a toy train crossing a toy bridge.

At the same time, Platonism has its advantages, not the least of which is the freedom it gives to poetic fancy:

> There had been these seas of silk spun by martyred cocoons, silks so delicate that they might be drawn for miles through a wedding ring like clouds through the gold hoop of the absent moon, gossamers which might have been enclosed inside that casket which was a nut's shell, laces which seemed to melt, to dissolve at a touch, ribbons crumbling into fog and bands of silk disintegrating into dust and silks flowing into water as if water were their counterpart and moon-stained satins with torn skirts and white rosettes which might have been lying for years under the dust or in the waters of a grave—many bridal gowns and no bride's slippers—for this bride had lost her slippers long ago—many flounces, ruffles, skirts, underskirts—bridal gowns of all vintages and perhaps of that vintage which never was on earth, porous silks so thin that the least touch might cause them to fall into nothingness as snow might fall into a crucible of burning gold where a long-haired angel walked with folded wings and eyes which stared at Mr. Spitzer.

Miss MacIntosh, My Darling presents the world as a glittering moon-lit ruin, a dream; as death ("for were we not already dead, we who breathed and walked about, our breath like frozen plumes upon the winter air, our eyeballs cracking in the cold?"). Miss Young has put the best years of her creative lifetime into this book, and her craftsmanship, even genius, is impressive. But the book is fiction.

Omensetter's Luck, on the other hand, is true. It is an imperfect book, finally unsatisfying, but the work of an extraordinary mind. Whereas Miss Young's poetry is necessarily incantatory, all voices becoming one voice, and whereas her imagery is necessarily antique-shop imagery, Gass's language and imagery come from particular, real people and places closely observed—observed with intense love but also with that comic detachment which comes from the knowledge that all men are, like oneself, slightly ridiculous. It is a poetry made up of real people's turns of speech:

> Now folks today we're going to auction off Missus Pimber's things. I think you all knew Missus Pimber and you know she had some pretty nice things. This is going to be a real fine sale and we have a real fine day for it. It may get hot, though, later on, so we want to keep things moving right along. And now I'm going to begin the sale with the things back here by the barn. You've all had a chance to look at everything so let's bid right out for these fine things and keep things moving right along. . .

And poetry made up of the real world's images:

> The fire and the lamp made pairs of crossing shadows, one steady and firm, one leaping and vague. Her shadow spotted the wall and disappeared, drawn magically back beneath her chair as she rocked, then darting forth to climb the wall rapidly again. He found himself marking the height. Incredibly swift, it bent itself up from the floor, passing the picture, the long head reaching a mar in the paper and covering a cluster of leaves while the lengthening finial that followed behind struck a rose. . .

Gass's handling of language is unerring. And as a fictional strategist he is one of the best since Faulkner. Stripped to its thematic bones, *Omensetter's Luck* is a book about mind. The apparent hero, Brackett Omensetter, is a man who seems to have escaped that bane of our human existence, consciousness. He knows river currents, can whistle like the birds, makes love with joy and no sign of "desire in the ordinary sense." The apparent villain, Reverend Jethro Furber, a grotesque, tiny, spiderlike man, is pure consciousness and both hates and envies Omensetter. The battle between them is the ancient battle of intellectual vs. "natural man," reason vs. faith, intellectual control vs. "luck," but in Gass's novel the battle has a wide field: within the individual heart, within a town, within a nation, within all civilization.

The truth is that man must be conscious, at those times when it matters; must make moral choices, when it matters; must sometimes rise out of his material nature into mind: Jethro Furber is right and Brackett Omensetter self-deluded. But it is also true that to know "how to be" one must love and must have some measure of faith (in Gass's universe of Chance, a willingness to trust one's luck); and in this arena the intellectual is always a ridiculous creature. He is a "liar" in the sense that reason can support nearly anything, if it lacks what the natural man possesses, the certainty of the heart; and the intellectual is, as Jethro Furber rightly calls himself, "a dirty old man," for his very distance from his material nature makes him lust after it. On the other hand, the appealing natural man is wrong about himself, for he does possess consciousness, and his pretense to himself and others that he does not makes him dangerous.

For dramatic development of this idea, Gass takes two great American archetypes—the hearty frontiersman (Omensetter) and the hell-fire puritan preacher (Furber). In the first section of his novel, "The Triumph of Israbestis Tott," he shrewdly loads the dice—as they have always been loaded—for Omensetter: Israbestis Tott is a thoroughly likeable old man who admires Omensetter, hates Furber (as the section ends, Tott is squashing spiders). As local historian, Tott is the consciousness of the town of Gilean ("And how would [the boy] learn his history now? Imagine growing up in a world where only generals and geniuses, empires and companies, had histories, not your own town or grandfather, house of Samantha—none of the things you'd loved"). But though he understands town consciousness—his own town's history and geography—he does not understand either individual human consciousness or the history (or geography either) of the World. "Cats know how to live . . . Cats beat us at it bad. Now Brackett Omensetter, though—" In his role as individual, Tott is himself a natural man. The novel's second section, "The Love and Sorrow of Henry Pimber," on the surface supports but on a deeper level undermines the initially favorable view of Omensetter. Henry Pimber, who has affinities both with nature and with mind—lockjaw once made him outwardly a stone, inwardly a jangle of consciousness—loves Omensetter and looks upon him "almost as a personal savior." (Omensetter is a real name but also ironically suggests "the one who sets the omens," a god. Omensetter is a New Testament figure of faith and love; he contrasts with the Old Testament figure of reason and justice, Jethro.) In the end, because Pimber cannot qualify as a natural man (he lacks faith in Pimber's luck and Omensetter's love)—and because the loving but partly unconscious Omensetter fails to realize Pimber needs him—Pimber sinks toward despair and suicide. Still we view Omensetter favorably; the fault seems Pimber's. The third section, the bulk of the novel, concerns Gass's comitragic hero-and-villain, Furber: a lying, scheming preacher who lusts after women and writes outlandish dirty verses but also preaches—and thinks—brilliantly. He is consciousness fully developed, fully educated, but uncommitted: a mocker and despiser of the world and of himself, an at once comic and dead serious representative of the archetype poet-priest. Gass's theme becomes fully explicit the morning Furber preaches on the Creation story, making it a parable for our everlasting human desire for simplicity, a return to an animal-like state:

> God created always by division, taking the lesser part, transforming it into its opposite, and raising it above the rest. So should we change our worst into our best.
>
> Furber snapped his fingers. There was a good one. That was the kind of thing they liked. Should he say it again? But he was losing the thread.
>
> There is everywhere in nature a partiality for the earlier condition, and an instinctive urge to return to it. To succumb to this urge is to succumb to the wish of the Prince of Darkness, whose aim is to defeat, if possible, the purpose of God's creation.

But Furber himself cannot believe it, the words are mere words, a clever descant on his text. "Like a waterstrider, Furber rode a thin film of sense." Yet Furber is right, as he understands at last. Omensetter allows his own child to die of pneumonia—trusting to nature, Omensetter says; but Orcutt, the M.D. who should have been called, sees through him: "You and your damn fool theories." Recognizing his mistake, Omensetter becomes remorseful; and Furber becomes more like what is best in Omensetter. In his final gesture, Furber shows himself the one man in the novel who fully understands "the secret—how to be."

Gass is always dead right in his choice of which characters to use, how to treat each character, which scene to put first; he's dead right too in his handling of minor structural devices for the larger poetic rhythm of the novel. For instance, Omensetter's visit to Furber, late in the novel, is verbally (and convincingly) parallel to Furber's earlier visit to Omensetter's best friend—to whom Furber hissed monstrous and ridiculous lies about Omensetter. The recognition inherent in the device gives poetic force to a more important recognition, for it is in Omensetter's visit to Furber that we come to see what could only be suspected before, that Omensetter too is doomed to consciousness and lying. He reads books sometimes, he tells Furber, but not in the winter, "bad for the eyes."

Or praise the novel this way. *Omensetter's Luck* avoids every mistake I've had a chance to mention while discussing other novels in this review. Gass's novel is "informational"; life in rural Ohio a while ago, the progress of madness, the hatred of the world inherent in puritanism (from Plotinus forward); but here every line functions, and the meaning found in the material is there. The novel is funny in places, moving in places, but nowhere merely entertaining. And Gass steals from no one. The suggestion of one reviewer that Gass is a "jejune Joyce" is mere impudence. When Gass uses comic nonsense language it is strictly that; it has nothing to do with *Finnegans Wake*. And when Furber alludes to Empedocles he makes his allusion by fundamentally different principles from those in, say, *Ulysses*. One might point to Samuel Beckett, for equally striking and original comitragic vision as well as for similar delight in the absurdity of reason unchecked by commitment; but in *Omensetter's Luck* one finds only a few heelprints to signal Beckett's having passed through. Beckett may have given Gass his ideas of the world as circus or music hall, but Gass has his own experiences of circuses and music halls and his own ideas, different from Beckett's, on what makes those places real. Sooner say Gass is "influenced" by the comic strip and animated cartoon. Furber, Omensetter, Tott, and the rest are straight out of Al Capp except that they are convincingly human and not involved in paltry satire. And Gass's settings—a chair rocking in a firelit room, two men pacing before a forge, a snow-covered mountain in a shadow of birds—are the settings of a Disney movie come to *life*, as Disney settings never do. Gass's symbols (weather, a man skipping stones, a hanging man pecked by birds) are also strikingly original and are at the same time so firmly imbedded in the action that their force comes in the reader's blood, not merely into his head. Needless to say, given Gass's control of style and structure, nothing in the plotting and nothing in the treatment inadvertently call up association with a kind of writing the book is not.

The novel's faults are not failures of truth but failures of discipline. Gass dwells too long on Furber's thought. The first two sections, absolutely flawless, set up a dramatic action which jerks to a stop with the introduction of Furber in meditation; and when the action gets moving again it lacks its old power because Furber's thought has made the theme and symbols too explicit. In a great novel, action reveals its inner meaning like a stray, maybe dangerous mongrel taken in off the street. In *Omensetter's Luck* the action becomes too obviously the vehicle of ideas. Gass is right when he establishes connections poetically, without comment—for instance, the dissimilar reactions of Omensetter and Furber to weather—but wrong when, for instance, he again and again comments authorially on Furber's idea-spinning as "lying," forcing into the reader's head the relationship between the intellectual and the vicious gossip. Not that Furber should not think. The reader must see Furber's mind at work—partly for the sheer pleasure of it, partly so that he can draw conclusions about the action—but the conclusions must be the reader's if drama is not to be reduced to syllogism. The mistake in the Furber section is merely technical, however. It limits the power of the book, not the intelligence or truth. Gass has written perfect short stories and one of the best short novels ever produced by an American. He has everything it takes to produce a great novel.

Finally this. All of the popular lies I have shook my finger at throughout this essay—about Americans, about inevitable alienation, about sex and fulfillment, about longing and disillusionment, even the lie about art as opinion, Truth as that which sounds good—are revealed in *Omensetter's Luck* (as Israbestis Tott says) "as plain as a cow in a field."

More Smog
from the
Dark Satanic Mills

O<small>NE OF THE INCONVENIENCES OF LIVING</small>
in one's own time is that the filtering has not yet been done: you have
to hunt down the occasional first-rate contemporary book through
great gray heaps of trash. Not that trash is a bad thing. The money
a publisher makes on fashionable bad writers makes possible the publication of serious writers who eventually prove great. What is troublesome is not so much the trash as the imitation serious fiction which
obscures the real thing, the sickly stuff editors bloat to life-size in their
helpful letters to reviewers, who frequently echo (perhaps in good faith)
the grandiose phrases of the hint-sheets. I assume it's not really a
capitalist plot. Even to a city man I wouldn't sell a dead hog and pretend it was only asleep for a minute, but perhaps editors don't read
the novels they print. It's an attractive theory. They buy the novel
from an agent who has never read it either, he just "represents" it,
the way a number can represent two sick fish or two chickenhouses,
and to get them to buy it the agent throws in some other novel, cheaper
than it would have been otherwise, by someone like John Hersey, who's
safe. The editor gives the manuscript to a girl from Radcliffe, who
fixes the spelling and changes the parts that aren't clear to her, and
then somebody else who's read twenty-five pages writes the jacket blurb

which vaguely alludes to "outrageous humor" or "delicate insight" and the "deeper symbolic intent."

How pleasant it would be to be able to believe such theories! But the world, as we know, is no romance. Editors, even agents and jacket blurb writers, are as honest as they know how to be. The reason trivial contemporary fiction so frequently gets mixed up with better work is that nearly everyone involved with it, from the writer to the lady who forgot to send back the rejection slip from her reading club, is serious-minded and righteously committed to what are called the exciting new ideas of our time—in other words, to nonsense. Good writing may not be dead but merely in hiding, as usual, blocked out by smog from the dark satanic mills.

People have always known about themes and symbols and tensions, and people have always recognized that fiction has something to do with truth; but once, having strong churches where intransigeance and system were the main part of the entertainment, most people let fiction go about its business. Now fiction must be studied; it must support both ingenious theories of how fiction works and popular theories of reality. Since what fiction does is absurdly obvious and regular, not fit to support more than five full professors, it is made to do something else. Or, at best, what it does incidentally, with the side of its foot, is turned into a marvel and broken down to its constituent parts and analyzed and yodeled over as though it were something of unspeakable importance, like taxes. (How else can one explain the rage for empty pyrotechnics, for instance *The Sot-Weed Factor?*)

What true fiction does is celebrate, not preach. Which is why it tells the truth. For example, it takes two sensible ideas—the idea that a man should be responsible and the idea that a man should be himself, free, not, as we say, uptight—and it embodies these awkwardly conflicting ideas in, say, two people whom it fully respects (or else finds equally absurd, like us) and it puts these two people in a place and watches them act. Not for the purpose of proving one of the people a fool or a devil out of hell but because it is the nature and moreover the joy of the novelist simply to watch important, familiar things from inside. Art clears the head of small opinions, not because everything is relative, in view of art, but because some things are beautiful and need to be affirmed. Art celebrates, compassionately suspending its moral outrage for the moment.

This is a fairly simpleminded thing for art to do, and one can hardly blame college professors, who are serious people with promotions and families to think about, for objecting. No wonder Chaucer's Wife of Bath becomes a lesson against concupiscence, and Othello a lesson against romantic pride. Righteousness, like obscenity, is fun. The fact remains, fiction is moral as the universe is moral: in books as in life, killing people indiscriminately will probably bring you to a bad end; but unlike the universe as fondly as we conceive it, fiction is moral by accident.

Writers have been denying this for centuries. Nevertheless, the only boring characters in Dickens are the pillars of decency. The only stick figure in *Anna Karenina* is Levin, whom Tolstoy admires for his noble wooden head. In lesser writers, such as Faulkner at his worst—because panting after unreality is better than scorning the clowns who can't see it—the people who cast no shadows are the stark embodiments of evil. What the greatest writers have understood, and not just fitfully, is that people are understandably what they are, better or worse, imperfect when measured against the ideal and therefore comic or tragic or both. They leave the righteous moralizing to critics. To put this another way, what the best fiction does is make powerful affirmations of familiar truths. The trivial fiction which time filters out is that which either makes wrong affirmations or else makes affirmations in a squeaky little voice. Powerful affirmation comes from strong intellect and strong emotion supported by adequate technique. Affirmation and righteousness are as far apart as love and hate or art and criticism. Now to criticism.

Of the three great university doctrines at work in modern fiction, the least offensive is that a book is good or bad insofar as it is "well made"; the next in order is that fiction ought properly to teach right behavior, chastising sin; and the most offensive is that human beings are all mere clowns and tramps. Trivial books may sometimes be overrated because they "work," that is, because the symbols all click together neatly (as symbols in Melville and Shakespeare do not); but the truth is, great art does work, up to a point. It has to do with the structure of the human mind. What makes most modern fiction a howling bore is the vast heart-warming goodness discovered in vipers and toads, and the mechanical whine of self-pity.

For an excellent case of mechanical neatness and righteousness, consider John Knowles's little sermon *Indian Summer*. Like everything

Knowles has written, despite his protestations, the book is a carefully constructed little machine. It concerns a part-Indian young American hero by the name of, symbolically enough, Kin-solving (hyphenation mine), first name "Cleet," representing what he clings by. Where he lives, a town in Connecticut, there used to be great sailing ships—men of war and brigantines—but now the town has become puritanical, well-off, and dreary, and Kinsolving longs for freedom. The escape he wants is the modern equivalent of seventeenth-century New World sailing: an Alaskan freight airline. Every detail in the book is as neat as this equation. There is a theater symbol, elaborately tinkered (one of a hundred entrapment symbols), and the title of the novel works, like Anacin, three ways. The last section of the book, called "The Heir," treats how Kinsolving, true heir of the American spirit, in Knowles's opinion, rapes the wife of his antagonist, aborting her child and thus killing the false pretender to our heritage. (The medical details are a trifle obscure. "And they finished together," Knowles says of the rape—a piece of sexual sentimentality worthy of Norman Mailer himself—but somehow, much as the lady enjoyed it, she is shocked into abortion by the rape.)

One need not strenuously object to this symbolic patness, though it's obvious and therefore dull. What is objectionable is the simple-minded morality of the thing. It is the "new morality," of course, but just as foolish as the old one.

The concern of the book is man's conflicting urges toward freedom, on one hand, and security, on the other. All Knowles's details fall around these two values. The town is made up of puritanical Protestants and puritanical Irish Catholics (security by superstition); Kinsolving believes in living by his feelings and expects to go to a Happy Hunting Ground where throughout eternity you experience all the lives of all the people who have ever lived. Free Kinsolving loves Nature, dangerous or not; secure Wetherford, Connecticut, fears it, even when it's harmless. Free Kinsolving is like a lion; the people of Wetherford are like mice. The people of Wetherford take care of each other; Kinsolving does not bother to write to his adoring younger brother, who somehow hides from Mr. Knowles his grief. Kinsolving (we are told) believes in love; the Wetherford people incline to believe in rivalry and hate. Free people have deep and resonant voices (somehow this includes Kansas people and Eskimos); the prevailing tone of Wetherford voices is flat. One more opposition of this sort and I will quit. One night Mr. Kinsolving goes out naked to roll in the grass and, because he freely feels like it, does something in the grass which I think I will not spell out. A window opens and he hides in some bushes. The poor limited Wetherford soul looking out believes that what she caught a glimpse of was—a nun.

It's true that an excessive concern with security can be debilitating, can even, as Knowles says, turn into insanity. And it is true that the outmoded American dream of security through wealth and power is wrongheaded: no security comes. But in the passion of his preaching Knowles has not bothered to look closely at his people or even at his hoked-up symbols. It may be true that there are rich men whose sole motivation is hatred of others and of their natural selves, but one needs some kind of fictional proof, not mere assertion. And it may be true that the green-eyed natural stare of a one-quarter Indian boy can shatter the nerves of a Roosevelt "brain-truster"—but if so, Knowles misses the reason. People who stare, whoever they are, are unnerving, not just because they're uncivil. Natural creatures, as all Indians know, look *away* when they mean to be friendly. When a bobcat looks straight at you, leave. Take another case. Once in Wetherford they burned a witch. Kinsolving thinks much on this, but Knowles forgets it when the rape scene comes. Kinsolving's vengeance on the scapegoat—not the husband he hates but the wife—is an obvious parallel to witchburning as Knowles himself describes it, and burning, according to the newspapers, is a common abdominal sensation in cases of rape. Knowles either misses or avoids the parallel, either because it would undercut the melodramatic opposition of good and evil as Knowles understands them or because he does not understand that symbolic systems in good fiction are not allegorical plantings to instruct the reader but double-checks which help the writer to be sure of what he thinks. Only twice in *Indian Summer* does Knowles fall into writing like a novelist. He has a splendid scene in Kansas, in which Kinsolving takes up a crop-duster biplane and behaves gloriously like himself—doing stupid things, nearly killing himself, and smashing all the countryside; clumsily realizing it's stupid and dangerous but delighting in it anyway, making comically sober but ridiculous observations to himself which Knowles, in the ecstasy of honest inspiration, allows to stand. The other fine moment in the novel is one in which Kinsolving first meets his brother

Charley after four years. The little brother has grown huge, both brothers feel shy and awkward; then the little brother smiles, and to Kinsolving it is like finding Jonah safe inside the whale: "He was still alive inside after all, and Cleet immediately caught Charley around the shoulders in relief. . ." But again Knowles has missed the force of his symbolism (it slipped in by accident, no doubt). It may be that, trapped inside their Wetherford houses and religions and conventions, the other characters are still alive too, if Knowles would stop ranting and look.

The recent season I am discussing produced the usual quota of brainless sermons like Knowles's. There is a thing by William M. Hardy, *The Jubjub Bird*, which is supposed to be devastatingly funny but also profound, a book on the race problem which, as the jacket says, "lets no one off the hook." It is not funny, and the things on the hook are cardboard. There is another book by Ronald L. Fair, *The Hog Butcher*, which is, like his overrated earlier novel, an interesting contribution to sociology but a bad novel. It draws heavily on the tradition of pulpit rhetoric and makes the same easy distinction between the righteous and the ungodly. For example:

> Before long, moving vans are coming into the neighborhood every week [moving out the whites] . . . They didn't all want to move, but this thing they call Americanism takes guts to practice and they are gutless. This thing they call Americanism was only applicable when they were in line to receive packages of food. This thing they call Americanism only worked when it was applied to someone else. This lie they call democracy, this insidious myth they call fair play, this vicious thing called the-American-way-of-life was not meant for the black man.
>
> And rather than live with the black man, rather than live with their fellow Americans, they ran, and, without knowing it, without caring, they turned over another used section of the city to the black masses and at the same time increased their own burden with a heavier mortgage.

One sympathizes with Fair's anger, and his sermon is not irresponsible, like Knowles's; but the book lacks the total compassion and clearheadedness of art.

The only really disgusting book in the stack I have for review is Thomas Bledsoe's *Meanwhile Back at the Henhouse*. A celebration of sex which goes out of its way for gratuitous slime, hooked to a thoroughly slick plot, a great roar of symbols, and what looks like it must have been intended (but wasn't) as an obscene burlesque of the catastrophe in Greek tragic theater. The only thing interesting about the book is that it is part of our intellectual climate. Sensation, especially genitourinary sensation, has replaced God, and with God dead the universe becomes absurd, so that holy lovers end up murdered in their already bloody bed. Not that Bledsoe understands all this. When an idea becomes faddish enough, any fool can muddle through a demonstration.

The idea in question is the one I described earlier as the worst of the three great university doctrines at work in modern fiction—the idea that all men are clowns and tramps, that is, witless and valueless creatures of sensation who imitate the gestures of human beings and pick the moldering dumps of history. (This is not really Samuel Beckett's position; it comes from an oversimplification of Beckett.) It is the idea, I am glad to say, which Nadine Gordimer attacks in every clean-cut line she writes. Perfected style like Miss Gordimer's is the objective refutation of the whiner's thesis: it is an affirmation that absolute values are still there, if only as concepts in the stylist's mind, and can be reached. In *The Late Bourgeois World* Miss Gordimer tells of the breakdown of idealism to the hammerings of brute experience. (The values Miss Gordimer finds breaking down are in fact distortions of traditional values, or values misunderstood. The best comment is another novel on African problems, David Caute's *The Decline of the West*—to which we will return.) Max Van Den Sandt, the real hero of the novel, dead from before the opening page, was an idealist who, by the accident of his being born with only ordinary intelligence and forcefulness, could not succeed in the things he nevertheless bravely attempted. His wife lies awake at the close of the novel trying to decide whether or not she will do, in a relatively trivial way, exactly what her late husband did. If she chooses not to, we understand the reasons and sympathize; nevertheless, the affirmation of what one ought to do, even if it is absurd, is clear. The one great trouble with the novel is that it is slighter than a buttercup—simplified Jane Austen with occasional bedroom scenes introduced, scenes which are neither funny nor thrilling, merely there, like self-conscious little proofs that Miss Gordimer knows.

Another moderately good book, beefier than Miss Gordimer's but equally imperfect, is Paul West's *Alley Jaggers*. West's novel mocks the whining absurdist cliché by pushing it to its last logical extremity and there exploding it. West's epigraphs sum up the argument. The second of them reads in part, "but a man with a dungfork in his hand, a woman with a slop-pail, give him glory too." If human beings are limited, none is more limited than Alley Jaggers, plasterer, squashed by routine and poverty, saddled with an irritable mother and a fat, brainless wife (whom we accept in the end as lovable). If brute sensation has replaced God, Alley Jaggers is high priest (he makes a huge, fat idol, in fact). The novel is a tour de force of wallowing obscenity—copulation with an unwilling partner in a bathtub, later with a dead woman—and of frustrated spiritual affirmation: a tortuously and lovingly constructed glider smashed in an instant, a painstakingly fashioned religious sign which can get no further than PRAISE WE O, a vast, inarticulate love which turns to black-comic murder. In Alley Jaggers's world it is impossible to rise out of substance, but the people struggle nevertheless to defy and escape their limitations (for instance by baking a mean old woman's teeth in an oven), and when they are pushed back once and for all into the slime of their existence, they "give him glory" from there. West's language, like the world he creates, is insistently obscene yet poetic. Like Alley himself, West transmutes ugly reality into defiant, even joyful, art. There are a few brilliant scenes, for instance the one in which Alley makes love to the girl he's just killed—the girl he could not quite make it with while she lived.

But much as I like *Alley Jaggers*, I do not think it is of more than passing interest. In the first place, insofar as West's answer to the faddish whine that we're limited is legitimate, there is no good reason that the novelist should shackle himself to the brute sensations or brutish values of Alley Jaggers's world. West has done the best that can be done with his material; the trouble is that, holy or not, obscenity and brutishness are tiresome. The claim that human life is a stream of "dogsick," to borrow one of West's expressions, is a claim not worth answering. West has answered it in novel after novel, which shows that he isn't really concerned with answering anything, I've merely imputed that to him for the sake of my argument. The truth is simply that West is more attracted to the beauty in slime than to beauty anywhere else. That's fair enough; every writer has his favorite milieu, and to fake an interest one doesn't feel is death. But to grant the legitimacy of West's concern is not to say it will be of permanent interest to other people. Dickens too was interested in the obscene and brutish, but not exclusively. Moreover, West's intense concern with substance in any form—stained waterpipes, sawdust, feces, plaster, the noises people make, polite and otherwise (including language indifferent to sense)—imposes one serious aesthetic limitation on his fiction: profluence gets lost in the clutter of unvaried detail. Compare the work of any spare writer—Pär Lagerkvist, to take an extreme example—or any writer as much concerned with the process of reality as with the richness, or, finally, a truly poetic writer like William Gass, who makes a rich variety of details dance and sing—and you will see at once what I mean. In West there's no tension, no suspense, and getting through every single paragraph word-for-word requires a certain triviality of mind.

What is basically wrong with all the novels I have talked about so far is exactly this—they are trivial. Some because they are badly thought out (Knowles and Bledsoe, notably), some because they are thought out more or less carefully as far as they go but don't go very far. Janet Frame's *A State of Siege*, a ladies' book, in other words not serious fiction in the first place, turns out to be representative of the whole lot. An entertainment; more specifically, a psychological horror story which at least to some extent succeeds in what it sets out to do, which is scare you. Curiously enough, the material Miss Frame uses for building her effect is the same modern set of concerns which informs the novels of Knowles, Bledsoe, Gordimer, and West—the replacement of traditional values with sensualism and the idea of freedom. Miss Frame writes as if the whole modern question were easy and obvious—which it is. Drop out of all human commitments, according to Miss Frame, and all reality, outside and inside, will rise up and kill you. (Miss Gordimer's view is close, but she has less good to say of traditional values.) Miss Frame works out her thriller with ladies' book facility. The novel is awful, but I should like to talk about it for the sake of my point.

The central character, a spinster named Malfred, is at last freed by the death of her mother to do what she pleases with what is left of her life. Up to now she's taught art and has painted pictures of the sort people like, repressing her own wish in order to satisfy the needs and demands of her friends and family. The man she once more or less loved was killed long ago in the war, and the emotion she felt for him she has managed to transfer to a feeling for Nature—trees, flowers, weather. Free of all commitments now, belatedly granted the total independence she has long desired, Malfred joyfully moves to a tropical island. Her joy is dampened when she learns how isolated her cottage is, and it is shattered when a storm comes up and a strange, insistent knocking begins, now at her front door, now in back, and between knocks a padding of mysterious footsteps, an occasional bit of laughter. She lies in the dark terrified, clinging to sense by all the age-old devices of man—self-conscious and tortuous analysis of what the situation may mean, labored recollections, snatches of poetry, phone calls (on an unconnected phone) to the police. A rock smashes through her window, possibly a rock with a note wrapped around it (her perceptions are far from trustworthy), and Malfred dies of, apparently, a heart attack. She is found clinging to the rock.

Obviously, the novel "works" in that every detail has its neat thematic function. Malfred's conventional landscape painting (what she really wants to do is symbolic painting) reflects that excessively self-abnegating regard for traditional values, her "duty" to friends and relatives, which stirs Malfred toward rebellion and the longing for freedom. But if through distortion traditional values can have harmful effect, they can also save one's sanity, even one's life. Immersion in sensation—the beauty of Nature—saves Malfred from excessive grief when her beloved dies, but pushed to an extreme in Malfred's trade of friends and relations for a cottage in the tropics, it destroys. It is the cult of sensation in modern life which produces the savagery of the unknown knockers at the door. What happens to Malfred is in a way not worse than what happens to those who, unconstrained by social checks and urged on by the violence of Nature (a windstorm), lay siege to Malfred's house and mind. The rock in the dead woman's hand is real, and she is not the first to be murdered by terror in this house. The people who threw the rock—the clues suggest children—have been reduced by freedom and sensation to willful killers.

If mechanical neatness and sound doctrine were the guarantee of great fiction, Miss Frame's novel would be a major achievement. It is in fact just another book for ladies to scare themselves with. The characters and situations are stock, the action long-winded and predictable. An ideal book for serial publication in some magazine which carries, say, babycare tips from Dr. Spock and essays on SUICIDE: THE WARNING SIGNALS. My point is not that ladies' books should be outlawed by the Federal Government—though why people read them when they could be watching Bullwinkle Moose or Star Trek is not clear to me. My point is that the brilliant style of Nadine Gordimer and the wildman's eye and ear of Paul West have not yet hooked onto any great and significant intuitions but only to the stuff which makes plots for ladies' books. That's no crime, of course. Readers who compulsively read everything in sight—the jokes on the back of cereal boxes, the patent numbers on wallpaper seams—will be grateful to them for providing something better than the usual run. But anyone looking for really good fiction will be disappointed as usual.

Really good fiction has a staying power that comes from its ability to jar, turn on, move the whole intellectual and emotional history of the reader. If the reader is a house, the really good book is a jubilant party that spreads through every room of it, or else a fire, not just a routine visit from the mailman. This is not simply a matter of controlled complexity, and it is certainly not solely a product of perfected craft. *Moby-Dick* is one of the power touchstones, a book nobody has as yet been able to work out as a logical system. *Bleak House* is surely one of the worst-written books in English—a serious defect, God knows—but once you have read it you are stuck with it for life. To have this total effect on the reader, a book must be as wise as the reader is in his best moments, stripped of pettiness, prejudice, and obsession; it must urgently support the highest affirmations the reader is capable of making, penetrating—at least by implication—every nook and cranny of his moral experience; and finally it must have the weight of a reality which the reader, at least while he is reading, does not notice to be any less substantial than the world of fire engines, tables, and yellow house cats where he lives.

At least in theory, all this can be done in a relatively simple parable or in a book thousands of pages long. Consider Pär Lagerkvist's *The Holy Land*, part of a series of allegorical tales but one which can stand alone. Lagerkvist is one of the better novelists now alive, a man whose supremely disciplined art is impossible to imitate or even translate—though Naomi Walford has done an excellent job of translation. In the Lagerkvist world all the complexity and difficulty of modern life is charged, as if by some crushing force from outer space—or as if by abandonment by outer space—into a few stark and massive symbols in which all our experience and all human history are locked. His image of the world is like Beckett's except Lagerkvist's ruined and blasted planet is dignified and somber.

> All that could be discerned in that barren landscape were the ruins of some mighty pillars which, ancient and half-eroded, stood out against the tempestuous sky. These could offer but little shelter from the night chill and the fresh wind, but since there was no other place to make for, they set off towards them. With the blind man's hand in his, Tobias the pilgrim approached the ruined building which rose, ravaged and abandoned, on that limitless shore where nothing grew but thistles and tall, parched grass . . .

It is a world in which the traditional logic of events is dead; one goes on with the old gestures because they are all one has and because the mind clings to what it is, and rightly. Blind old Giovanni has a locket. Some shepherds ask about it and Tobias tries to explain:

> "Well, nothing very remarkable in itself, perhaps. But it can hold something very precious—something the wearer cannot bear to lose. Therefore one wears it at one's breast, close to the heart, and can't endure to be parted from it."
> "Oh."
> "What does it hold, then?"
> Tobias delayed answering.
> "We understand. It must be a secret."
> "Yes."
> "Empty. . ."
> "So it's of no value?"
> "It's his only possession, and I've often noticed that he's afraid of losing it. I don't believe he could live without it."
> "Although it's empty?"
> "Yes."
> "How strange . . . How can it be so precious when it's empty—when it doesn't contain what it ought to contain?"

> "We don't understand. Can't you explain it to us?"
>
> "Not everything can be explained. It just is so."
>
> The herdsmen were silent. Their grave, rather tired eyes looked at the thing hanging among the grey hairs of the old man's chest, but they asked no more questions.
>
> "Yes, yes," one of them whispered softly. "That's true. There are many things that can't be explained, but just are so."

When the locket is removed, Giovanni does indeed die, with a sense of peace and comfort. This is not something which can be explained (as a suggestion, for instance, that our characteristic human clinging is delusion, we would be happier if we let everything go); the idea and the image are indivisible. If a man has a locket he ought to keep it; that "just is so"; and when he loses it he is relieved, that is also so. In Lagerkvist, in other words, archetypal realities of feeling walk and talk and lie strewn and broken in the grass, demanding notice and assent. The *connection* between values has grown obscure, perhaps because God, who used to be the controller of connections, has died and heaven has burnt out and cooled to ashes; but the values of the heart, which meaninglessly live on, are not to be denied. In *The Holy Land* Lagerkvist does more than simply reheat the old values, however; he finds a new way of seeing. Partly by criminal intent, partly by chance, every man has a share in the indifferent cruelty of a universe gone adrift. Meaningful death is an atonement and sacrifice, repayment and gift, a return of energy to its source. Christ's death was a voluntary sacrifice, the death of the two thieves a repayment; the three together are the figure of every meaningful death. ("And yet—and yet. There the three crosses stood, all together: there was no denying it. Not just a solitary one—not just his. And not just the criminal's crosses. No. . .") If God is dead—no one in Lagerkvist's world knows for sure—there is not enough energy left in the world to overwhelm the meaningless plagues that strike the herds. (The sacrifice of an evil vulture and a cooperative lamb turns out to be in vain.) But each man can give up with his life what feeble energy he has. All this is of course pure event in *The Holy Land*; pure vision. Tobias, wearing the dead Giovanni's locket, talks with the girl whose death long ago he did nothing to prevent, knowing his effort would be futile:

> "There's nothing it it [the locket]. It looks as if there ought
> to be, but there's nothing."
> "No, there's nothing. . ."
> She closed it again. And gently, gently, she took it from
> him, lifting the worn chain from his neck and putting it about
> her own; she hung the locket at her own breast. At that
> moment it began to shine like the most beautiful jewel.

And Tobias dies. Allegory, which we so often hear dismissed as trifling
and insubstantial, is one of the ways in which significant intuitions
can be seized. To the extent that allegory is poetic logic rather than
some bottle of sugarcoated truths, it has staying power.

But I must add, at the risk of seeming impossible to please, that
The Holy Land is not a perfectly satisfying example. It is excessively
spare, and short. Lagerkvist is indifferent to what psychologists call
"Threshold." Powerful as his images are, he does not sit on them long
enough to allow their effect to come through. Lagerkvist is like a
stand-up comic who moves too quickly from joke to joke to give his
audience full experience of the humor. One of the most difficult problems a first-rate novelist has to solve is that of balancing movement
and static detail.

Black comedy, too, can have at least some measure of staying power
if it's worked right. The term may be vague, but I use it in a specific
sense. Black comedy occurs when what ought to be sad turns out to
be grimly funny, affirming through irony what could not otherwise
be affirmed. I will give an example from Samuel Beckett. In *Watt* the
title character longs to believe in the existence of Mr. Not but knows
better. Without really expecting success, he trudges to the house of,
he hopes, Mr. Not, gets closer and closer to the man, but, knowing
his Wittgenstein, does not presume to think he has found Mr. Not.
Watt's disappointment and frustration ought to be pathetic, but we
laugh. Watt has been turned into a robot by system, as all men are
in Beckett's view. The humor is exactly where it would be for Bergson
except that the contrasting fluidity or flexibility which makes mechanical
behavior funny is removed, in Beckett, to the realm of impossible ideals.
When we fail to try for the ideal we are ridiculous; trying, we rise
to the absurd. *Alley Jaggers* is black comedy with a new twist: West
goes beyond affirmation of Alley's attempt at flight to affirmation of

where he was in the first place. (If we tell the truth, the new twist is a degeneration: complacency.) In Anthony Burgess, on the other hand, the black comedy is straight. Burgess quotes Eliot's remarks that "The worst that can be said of most of our malefactors, from statesmen to thieves, is that they are not man enough to be damned." If we knew for sure that some god exists who damns and saves, then a novel full of people comically unable to make up their minds or get off their hind ends and assert themselves for heaven or hell would be satire. The same novel without the absolute base is black comedy.

Burgess's *Tremor of Intent: An Eschatological Spy Novel* is that kind of book. Poor Hillier, Burgess's central character, knows well enough what the absolute issue is. Commenting on his friend Roper, an English scientist who has defected to Russia, Hillier says:

> Here, in brief, is the peril of being a scientist brought up on a fierce and brain-filling religion. He starts, in his late teens, by thinking that his new sceptical rationalism (bliss it was in that dawn to be alive) makes nonsense of Adam and Eve and transubstantiation and the Day of Judgment. And then, too late, he discovers that the doctrines don't really count; what counts is the willingness and ability to take evil seriously and to explain it.

Hillier thinks of his mission to trick and bring back Roper, violating Roper's misguided but noble idealism, as his last move in the thoroughly dirty game of spy and counterspy. After this he will break out and turn honest. But Hillier is only a man; he cannot resist the force of truth drugs administered to him, and, once having assisted the enemy, however unwilling, he cannot escape. Limited in a thousand ways by their tragicomic humanity, Burgess's characters can get no farther than the tremor of their noble intent. What ought to be becomes increasingly urgent as it becomes increasingly remote.

What makes Burgess a good novelist is that the absolute ethic he proposes is clear, inclusive, and convincing, and that the people involved in the complex problems Burgess sets up are more or less convincing human beings, however grotesque, whose excuses for failing to measure up are as valid as our own and must therefore be overwhelmed by a shock of blind assertion by the reader, a kind of despairing laughter, a revolt. Infernal complications obstruct the ends the spirit reaches for—such complications as Freudian ambivalence of emotion and motive, the distractions of physical human need, the doubtful morality of available means. A typical dilemma:

> "Knowing God means also knowing His opposite. You can't get away from the great opposition."
> "That's Manichee stuff, isn't it? I'm quite looking forward to doing Mediaeval!"

The first statement, which is true, is immediately cut down by a flip statement which cannot be answered except by a tortuous scholastic argument on orthodox and heretic sides of a body of doctrine which is itself museum stuff. Laugh and grind your teeth and let it go.

Anthony Burgess is a good writer, as everyone knows, but not a great one. One reason for this is that Burgess's characters do not fight toward the impossible with the same demonic intensity as those of, say, Lagerkvist, and they are not as cruelly broken when they fall. This is why among writers of black comedy (in which class Lagerkvist has not recently made a bid), there is still only Beckett at the first rank. Burgess's basic limitation, however, is one he shares with all black-comic writers—which is why I have granted black comedy only a measure of staying power. Black comedy is narrowly pessimistic. Burgess, like Beckett, would say "Faw!" to this. An argument which is unanswerable. Still, the Faw is wrong; some things just are so. Let me explain.

The implicit argument of black comedians is that if men do at times achieve something like the ideal, it's by luck. (Hillier might not have had the bad luck to be given truth serum and thus might by chance have escaped.) Since luck cannot be counted on, a realistic and unsentimental depiction of life must focus on what happens when the meaningless variable is ruled out. We assent under duress. No one wants to be thought sentimental or, in his pleasure at his own good luck, indifferent to the patent bad luck of others. All the same, in the universe luck has *not* been ruled out. As a matter of fact, the odds in favor of luck are mysteriously high, and there are those who maintain that as centuries pass and social injustice is diminished they rise by leaps and bounds. All men who have not been totally crushed by bad luck know in their blood and bones that having children is worth the risk. When they are told that life is ultimately nonsense they assent but close off a corner of the mind, which whispers, *Nevertheless*...

Black comedy is the reflection of a degraded and beaten society— cruelly oppressed Ireland (Brendan Behan), cynical old France, or any crowded and brutalized big city—consider those New York and London writers who find the glowing essence of life in their toilet bowls. Black comedy does not reflect deep suffering (consider the concentration camp writers) but only spiritual poverty and despair, that is, neurosis. Black comedy is a passage too narrow and too thickly hedged to allow the flow of what must somehow shamelessly flow—that water of, God or no God, grace.

I am not expressing a touching, merely personal preference for spiritually uplifting books but a fact of experience, one which has proved an embarrassment to modern fiction. Given proper soil and watering, human consciousness thrives. Sometimes, given the worst soil possible, no water whatever, it endures. A thoroughly dark view of life is the view of a blighted spirit not to be trusted. This is merely to say that a man whose family has died in a house struck by lightning may not be a perfect judge of storms.

We blush at Victorian optimism and open sentiment, and we avoid such things by undercutting all we say, by enclosing each statement with qualifications like briar hedges and with apologies for having sunk to the awful indignity of speaking in the first place. Mind chokes heart. It's no worse than the heart's choking of brain—the kind of thing favored by the turned-on of California, with all their talk of "hypocrisy" and "love"—but it isn't enough. The most powerful fiction is that which finds a way of expressing openly and without distortion or limpness of mind the highest human affirmations.

Elie Wiesel's *The Gates of the Forest*, though not a great book, has power. It has the power of honest, hard-won thought and emotion which oversimplifies nothing of any importance. It is a novel impossible to criticize just as a truly just and kind man, whatever his faults, is impossible to criticize, because to do so would be shameful and crass. I know the arguments of psychologists who prove no man just and kind except for miserable reasons. I answer—knowing I am hardly the first—that here is where artists and scientists part. The reason art exists at all is that some things cannot be demonstrated, can only be felt and celebrated. The test of such things is not scientific but emotional. Read Wiesel and all Beckett's brilliance turns to a tasteless joke, a child purposely farting at a wedding or funeral. Black comedy is overwhelmingly convincing in isolation; at the first breath from a writer who believes in the holiness of life, it withers away to dust. To say that Wiesel's power is inherent in the subject matter—Nazi atrocity, the madness of the Jewish survivors—is true but not to the point. Finding an adequate subject and understanding it is the novelist's only business.

Better technique would make Wiesel's novel a good deal more forceful than it is, since bad writing robs the story of the reader's full attention; but the clarity and force of a very good writer's ideas and emotions can surmount some limitations of technique. To say this is of course to deny categorically the doctrine that ideas and emotions cannot be discovered or released except through technique. It is to insist again, with no proof except an appeal to the experience of reading certain books, that great fiction begins in the character of the writer, the poet as poem.

No amount of factual information, or technical ability, or skill at introducing people and places, or ear for rhetoric, or eye for the absurd, or head for wide philosophy can substitute for a truly good man's sane and profound affirmation. But the affirmation gains immeasurably when all the rest is present. The best book I have read lately, and the only one besides Lagerkvist's, which has a chance of surviving the century on its own merits, is David Caute's *The Decline of the West*. Caute too has faults (it is not true that all novels have faults: some "faults" work), notably a tendency to bank on the symbols in an essentially realistic novel, a bad habit of splitting elements of dialogue ("You ought," she said, staring at the pond, "to go back to the states"), a tendency to explain too much on an easy psychological basis. But Caute's virtues are impressive. Like such writers as Tolstoy, he makes history appear to make sense. He can deal convincingly with an amazing variety of times and places, psyches and events. He knows more than most people, not only about history (his professional concern) but about philosophy, art, and practical politics as well. If his technique is mediocre sentence by sentence—full of mannerism, never poetic—his control of larger structures—the manipulation of multiple plots, the significant juxtaposition of scenes—is enviable. He is one of those novelists who can make one believe that the novelist has personally experienced all that every one of his characters has experienced—Frenchmen, English-men, Nazis, Africans, Americans, and more. It all sounds like passion-ate autobiography, though one knows it can't be. One recalls Plato's remarks on the mysterious omniscience of Homer, or Tolstoy's remarks to Dostoyevsky: "You think you know what that horse is thinking, Fyodor. The difference between us is, I *know*." (I may have made that up.) Above all, I think, what Caute achieves in *The Decline of the West* is a vision of the ideal made actual, a vision meticulously figured out. Caute knows about absurdity but also about determination and luck. He moves the reader closer to the way it is, to the terrible and holy. To put all this another way, he has studied with a scholar's care and an artist's intuition the doctrines of our age, and he has seen through them and beyond them. What he has to say about master and subject races is applicable anywhere at any time—he makes that very clear—and the values which control the war against the West and within it, that is, personal faith and self-sacrifice, will govern the spiritual history of the world when all racial wars are over. They are the essence of history.

The Achilles' heel of *The Decline of the West* is—alas—its openness of sentiment. Part of the time one thinks of Hemingway's sentimen-tality through understatement—flat descriptions of gruelling torture, objective, almost scientific descriptions of passion; but more often one thinks, unfairly, of soap opera. A single example may at least suggest the weakness of the whole book:

> "I have served my country loyally for twenty-six years, through peace and war. I took part in the Ethiopian campaign against the Italians, sir, and I was mentioned in dispatches, twice, by Colonel Granger, who—"
>
> "What is the relevance of all this?"
>
> A tremor passed down his spine; suddenly the world whose rules and codes he had served and respected throughout a life-time had turned its back on him, had become deaf. Everyone was the same, yet strangely not the same, imperceptibly trans-formed as if by some invisible ray or gas...

Despite the half-hearted ironic detachment, Caute's sob of sympathy for wretched Deedes comes through and puts one off. The white man's inability to obtain justice here exactly balances—and echoes through verbal repetition—the situation of a central Negro figure earlier. Style openly and frankly reinforces this pathetic reversal—the piling up of appositional extensions of feeling expressed in opening clauses ("had turned its back on him, had become deaf"), and loaded suggestions of psychological state ("suddenly," "strangely," "imperceptibly"). The dramatic situation justifies the emotion; nevertheless, it does sound like something from Dr. Kildare. What is one to do? Deny true emotion because it sounds silly? Yet even apparent silliness is distracting. No wonder we retreat to mask, to irony, to constipated soul. Knowing Nietzsche and Freud, knowing what ludicrous figures they cut who speak with more sincerity than self-consciousness, we are turned into mutes. Caute has the courage to speak out anyway, but we sense the strain. This is one great technical problem which modern fiction has as yet found no way to break through. Melville for the most part leers and insinuates and brays, Joyce subtly assesses with icy Jesuitic eyes, and Faulkner howls or rapidly whispers, defiantly parading his huge emotion; and feeling, the heart of the novelist's business, sits waiting for the right incantation, nervous and bored.

Witchcraft
in *Bullet Park*

W HEN IN 1969 JOHN CHEEVER TURNED
from the lovable Wapshots to the weird creatures who inhabit Bullet
Park, most reviewers attacked or dismissed him. They were, it seems
to me, dead wrong. The Wapshot books, though well made, were
minor. *Bullet Park*, illusive, mysteriously built, was major—in fact, a
magnificent work of fiction.

One reason the book has been misunderstood is that it lacks a simple message. No man who thinks seriously about the enormous old
questions can reduce his thought to a warning sign like BRIDGE OUT.
Another reason is that Cheever is right about evil: it comes quietly,
unannounced by thunder or screeching bats—comes like the novel's
well-dressed man getting casually off a train ten minutes before dark.
Talking of the oldest and darkest evil, Cheever speaks softly, gently,
as if casually. Suspense is not something he fails to achieve in *Bullet
Park*, but something he has avoided. The novel moves as if purposelessly,
like its bland-minded, not very likable protagonist, and from time to
time gives a nervous start at the blow of a distant axe.

Cheever's subject is chance—but more than that. Chance is a vehicle
that carries the book into darker country. The opening lines present
a setting—a train station—designed to suggest the whole human condition in this mysterious, chance-filled universe. A temporary planet

whose architecture, like that of the station, is "oddly informal, gloomy but unserious"; a place of isolation where chance seems to rule even art. "Paint me a small railroad station then," the novel begins—as if any other setting would do as well. (But: "The setting seems in some way to be at the heart of the matter," says Cheever, sly. Art, like life, may start with chance, but chance shrouds something darker.)

The harmless-looking man who steps from the train meets a real estate agent named Hazzard—"for who else will know the exact age, usefulness, value and well-being of the houses in town." By chance, days later, the harmless-looking man will be standing on the platform with Eliot Nailles, the novel's hero, when another man is sucked to his death by an express train. The stranger has nothing to do with the accident; he's buried, at the time, in his newspaper. But the skin crawls. We learn later that by a series of accidents the stranger has become, unbeknownst to himself, a center of demonic malevolence.

We've been told repeatedly that the universe is gloomy and frightening, random. Brute existence precedes essence and also sometimes follows it, as it does in Nailles's good Christian mother, reduced by senility to a human doll in a nursing home. Ah, yes, ah, woe, we are tugged by cosmic strings, dolls all! Or are we? Cheever reconsiders the idea of chance, remembering psychic and psychological phenomena, the claims of good and bad witches. What emerges is a world where hope does exist (magic is real and can cure or kill), a world in a way even grimmer than Beckett's because here love and sacrifice are realities, like hope, but realities in flux, perpetually threatened, perishing.

The novel says yes-and-no to existentialists, who can account for all but the paragnost. Cheever, in other words, sees the mind in its totality—sees not only the fashionable existential darkness but the light older than consciousness, which gives nothingness definition. Partly for the sake of this wholeness of vision, Cheever in *Bullet Park* abandoned the fact-bound novel of verisimilitude, which is by nature impotent to dramatize the mind's old secrets, and turned to dependence on *voice*, secret of the willing suspension of disbelief that normally carries the fantasy or tale.

Cheever's voice—compassionate, troubled, humorous—controls the action, repeatedly calling attention to itself in phrases like "at the time of which I'm writing." Where his voice fades out, character voices come in. Without explanation or apology, he shifts, early in the novel, to the cry of an unnamed and never-again-to-be-heard-of adolescent, a cry against suburban hypocrisy. ("Oh damn them all, thought the adolescent.") Later, telling how Eliot Nailles nearly murdered his son, Cheever shifts to Nailles's own voice as Nailles goes over the incident in his mind. With similar abruptness he introduces the voices—or, sometimes, centers of consciousness—of Nailles's wife, neighbors, a zodiac-trapped French teacher, a Negro swami and the harmless-looking stranger, mad Paul Hammer.

Hammer decides to murder Nailles—at first Eliot, later his son, Tony. The decision is without explicit motivation, based mainly on "the mysterious binding power of nomenclature." Cheever could have explained the whole thing, black magic as psychosis (the magic of names), and would have done so in a Wapshot book. But how do you *render* a thing so strange? Instead of explaining, he inserts Hammer's journal. With a madman's objectivity, Hammer sketches the story of his life.

The coldness of tone (even when the scene is comic), the flat description of his enfeebled quest for relationship, his survival by flight into symbolism (yellow rooms, a dream-castle, pieces of string) explains magically what the fact-bound novel would turn to the dry unreality of a case study. The motive for the projected murder is coincidence—a correspondence of names, two pieces of string. We learn that Paul Hammer has murdered before, without knowing it himself, to get a yellow room. But the rendered proof of his demonic nature is his voice, a quiet stovelid on terror and rage.

As in all first-rate novels, the form of *Bullet Park* grows out of its subject. More here than in his earlier writings, Cheever depends on poetic (which is to say, magical) devices—rhythm, imagistic repetition, echo. Instead of conventional plot, an accretion of accidents. Far below consciousness, the best people in Bullet Park are mirror images of the worst: they live by magic, correspondence.

On the level of consciousness, Nailles lives by sugary, foolish opinions and declares his life "wonderful"—but he cannot ride his commuter train except drugged. Out of touch with his son, governed partly by ethical clichés and partly by the normal frustration of the blind—ruled in other words by chance—he throws out his son's beloved TV and starts the child on the way to mental illness. By the chance combination of his middle-class values, his son's slight willfulness, an argument with his wife, and an accidental meeting with black-jacketed boys whose faces he cannot see, Nailles tries—in what could pass for inexplicable rage—to murder his son on a miniature golf course. (The mechanistic universe writ small. The symbolism of place is always grim in *Bullet Park*.) Though Nailles's putter misses his son's skull, the black-magic selfish rage in his attack leaves the son psychologically crippled—in fact, dying of murdered will—savable only by a swami.

An accidental meeting with a man in a bar and a chance echo when Nailles returns home makes Nailles distrust his faithful wife—faithful because, by accident, her would-be seducers were confounded by, respectively, a fire, a cold, an attack of indigestion. In short, Nailles, a tragicomic fool, is simply lucky. By accidents of his childhood, he is in touch with Nature: he cuts down diseased elms with a comically typical suburban chainsaw and shoots, in his undershorts, a century-old snapping turtle (naked man against the dinosaur). Hammer, by accidents of childhood and bastardy, is cut off from Nature and himself. Nailles's blessing is that he is married to a good woman and has a son, whereas Hammer is married to a bitch and is childless. Nailles's luck means that he's faintly in touch with the higher magic of the universe—the magic of love, creative force—whereas Hammer is in touch only with lower magic, correspondence.

Magical coincidence, echo, repetition. When images recur or correspondences appear, they are causes, benevolent or harmful. From his psychic, wholly self-centered mother, Hammer gets his witchy idea of drugging and immolating some innocent victim to "wake up" drugged America. When Rutuola, the gentle swami, makes magic, the result is ritual. Both are attempts to draw in the power of the universe. Both work, sometimes. Both are crazy. ("I know it's crazy," Tony says, raised from despair by the swami's chant of *Love, Love, Love*, "but I do feel much better.")

Benevolent witchcraft, ritual, assumes that the universe contains some good and that men in groups can reach harmony with it. (Rain or shine, Nailles drives with his windshield wipers on, because that's his silly congregation's sign of faith in the resurrection.) Malevolent witchcraft, on the other hand, assumes cosmic forces attendant to the will of the witch. Neither side wins decisively. (Selfless men contain selfishness, and even Hammer has impulses toward love.) The mainly benevolent have their marginal advantage because in times of crisis they tend to work together. Out of lonely arrogance, Hammer spills his plan to the swami, and from love the swami warns Nailles.

But though Tony is rescued—Nailles rising to that strange trance-state in which nothing can go wrong (a dazzling piece of writing)—Nailles's existence is merely salvaged, not redeemed. Nailles at the start called his drab life "wonderful." When Rutuola brought Tony from despair, "everything was as wonderful as it had been." Now, when the murder has been blocked, with the help of that ridiculous chainsaw, Cheever closes: "Tony went back to school on Monday and Nailles—drugged—went off to work and everything was as wonderful, wonderful, wonderful, wonderful as it had been."

There, it may be, is the underlying reason that reviewers were annoyed by *Bullet Park*. The novel is bleak, full of danger and offense, like a poisoned apple in the playpen. Good and evil are real, but are effects of mindless chance—or heartless grace. The demonology of Calvin, or Cotton Mather. Disturbing or not, the book towers high above the many recent novels that wail and feed on Sartre. A religious book, affirmation out of ashes. *Bullet Park* is a novel to pore over, move around in, live with. The image repetitions, the stark and subtle correspondences that create the book's ambiguous meaning, its uneasy courage and compassion, sink in and in, like a curative spell.

Alice
in Wonderland

J OYCE CAROL OATES—WHOSE NOVEL *WON-
derland* reveals how deeply Lewis Carroll has influenced her—has a
passage in her short story "In the Region of Ice" where a nun who
teaches literature, Sister Irene, speaks with her friend of a brilliant mad
student. Since the exchange says things that ought to be said about
Lewis Carroll, let me begin with it and double back to it later.

> "I'm very grateful to have him in class. It's just that . . . he
> thinks ideas are real." Sister Carlotta, who loved literature also,
> had been forced to teach grade-school arithmetic for the last
> four years. That might have been why she said, a little sharply,
> "You don't think ideas are real?" Sister Irene acquiesced with
> a smile, but of course she did not think so: only reality is real.

Both of the two latest products of the Lewis Carroll industry began
as noble intuitions. One comes off badly, the other well. The idea of
Aspects of Alice was to assemble a "comprehensive" selection of essays
and poems on Carroll's Alice books, from the first delightfully obtuse
reviews to the most recent opinions, sane and otherwise. What splendid
writers a man could include: W. H. Auden, Virginia Woolf, Alexander
Woolcott, Walter de la Mare, Horace Gregory, Allen Tate, Robert

Graves, Harry Levin . . . All these and more Robert Phillips includes (not all are up to standard when writing about Carroll, but never mind); then he drowns the reader in a great quop of inanity.

The book is handsomely designed—plenty of white space, lovely paper that can accommodate both the type and the drawings by Carroll and Sir John Tenniel. Also included are some of Carroll's photographs of the real Alice, plus photographs of Carroll and Sir John. But the reader can tell from the front matter what a pudgy book this will prove in the end: a ponderously clever title, a dedication page too embarrassing to quote and a foreword that begins (with violins and French horns): "She has survived the Victorian age, several wars and depressions, the Age of Anxiety, and when last seen . . ." One feels one has stumbled on a book about Alice by the Water Babies.

Mr. Phillips's assumption is that the general reader need not be burdened with the more difficult philosophical and mathematical essays on Carroll, much less those arresting but heavy studies by specialists in linguistics. (He does include A. L. Taylor's famous piece on chess and theology—superb on chess.) On the other hand, he believes the general reader will want—though Phillips himself confesses their foolishness—Kenneth Burke's piece on how the Alice books are really all about bowel movements, along with over a hundred pages of Freudian and Jungian, not to mention psychedelic, fantasy.

Carroll's pleasure in the company of well-mannered little girls proves ominous, of course. As for the meaning of the books, Alice is a penis; or Alice is Carroll's oral trauma; or Alice is Christ Our Lord in drag: "As he was deserted, denied, taunted in His royal robes, crowned with thorns and humiliated, made to drink the bitter vinegar of man's scorn and lifted up on the cross as 'King of the Jews,' so she is deserted by her sleeping companions, mocked by the powerful, crowned with a very heavy, tight golden crown, made to drink 'sand [mixed] with cider,' 'wool [mixed] with wine'; starved at her own triumphal banquet." Such things may amuse up to a point and ought to be represented, I suppose, though not at any length. They prove what the Alice books everywhere say, that rigidity of system is insanity.

Heavy concentration on the roots and symptoms of Carroll's benign or malevolent lunacy (he was, of course, anything but mad) is perverse for two reasons: it's insidious even if we laugh at it, since it taints the mind; and it's out of date. It's a fact that Carroll liked little girls, and one in particular. He told them stories and frequently had tea alone with them in his college rooms. With self-righteous grown-ups and boisterous little boys, he stammered. This is merely to say that he loved the openness and innocence most commonly seen, in nineteenth-century England, in upper-class female children, and that he could not cope emotionally with harsher qualities—in other words, that Carroll, though a fine and gentle man (granted, he had two or three famous tantrums), was maladjusted, harmlessly neurotic. To go any further than that is plain unbalanced.

The psychoanalytical readings on which Mr. Phillips wastes a fourth of his collection are demonstrably based on doubtful, or anyway boring, suppositions (as eldest child in a large family, Carroll may have felt rejected), systematic errors (all lakes in fiction represent birth waters) and falsehoods (the joke, popular with his students, that Carroll was so paranoid he sent off the manuscripts of his *Sylvie and Bruno* in shuffled strips, and sent by separate post a code for reassembling the mess—a joke no one believed until the Freudians and Mr. Phillips).

Carroll's students, by the way, liked him, and one can easily see why. He solemnly drew cartoons as he lectured, and passed them around to the class at the end of the period. The purpose of his "Symbolic Logic" was to make hard matter teachable, and his enlivening approach is now standard in logic classes: "No kitten without a tail will play with a gorilla. . ." When psychoanalysts can write so well and so sensibly, they may speak again. (Did you know, by the way, that drum majorettes are penises?)

But the defense of Carroll against idiots has been presented many times, by W. H. Auden among others. Virginia Woolf got the heart of the matter: unlike most people, Carroll never lost touch with his childhood—a point so obvious that its implications are sometimes overlooked. The naughty, bossy, seemingly irrational (but in fact insanely rigid) Wonderland characters are the essence of childhood in one of its aspects, and so is Alice, minding her manners like a good little girl and trying to make sense of a crazy universe bristling with commands and admonitions that seem to make—and indeed do make—no sense. The discovery of nonsense, savagery and childishness at the core of things—the discovery that ends both *Alice in Wonderland* and *Through the Looking-Glass*—signals the child's emergence into adulthood.

All of which (and more) is explained in the best essay Mr. Phillips included, Donald Rackin's "Alice's Journey to the End of the Night," a piece that heroically labors up on dripping wings from the slough of essays a la Freud and Jung, hovers a moment, then crumples in a sad deliquium to be swallowed by mumblings on Lewis Carroll as Acidhead.

Donald J. Gray's textbook in the Norton Critical Edition series is more satisfying: authoritative, illustrated, annotated texts of the Alice books and "The Hunting of the Snark," with a rich and sensible selection from Carroll's diaries and letters, documents by people who knew him, and critical essays—a wise and balanced selection of essays, though one that might profit from expansion. Gray includes invaluable comments on Carroll's work as a photographer, mathematician and logician.

In mathematics and logic, as elsewhere, Carroll shows a quirky mind in which intuition and intellect war, and intuition wins hands down—with sometimes comic results. He was not in fact a very good mathematician.

His conscious opinion was that ideas are real. As his "New Theory of Parallels" shows, he doggedly followed the old school of thought, in which mathematics should be based on self-evidently true axioms—an opinion Wonderland would laugh at, as would any of those modern mathematicians who pretend to derive inspiration from Carroll. As for Carroll the logician, R. B. Braithwaite sums up superbly when he says, in an essay that should certainly have appeared in Phillips's book, that Carroll's mind "was permeated by an admirable logic which he was unable to bring to full consciousness and explicit criticism. It is this that makes his 'Symbolic Logic' so superficial . . . and his casual puzzles so profound."

Braithwaite's essay should be studied hard by all writers on Carroll, because it hints at something central. It is true, as George Pitcher shows (in an essay Gray includes), that Carroll profoundly influenced Ludwig Wittgenstein; and true, as Michael Holquist shows (also in Gray), that Carroll has influenced modern writers from the surrealists to Robbe-Grillet and Nabokov (who translated *Alice in Wonderland* into Russian). Carroll did seem to write, as Holquist says, a strikingly modern "depersonalized" fiction that "could be perceived only as what it was, and not some other thing." As Walter Kerr (not included) once pointed out, Carroll reached modern absurdism before anyone else.

But the truth, all the same, is that none of the things awed moderns say about Carroll would strike Lewis Carroll as true. He was the kind of genius that has baffled professors since Plato wrote the "Ion." He worked as great artists always do, pace the Profession of English, by pure feel—as he put it himself, "in a dream," or as James Joyce said, "by faith." It never occurred to him that Humpty Dumpty was (or was not) a linguistic nominalist, much less that "The Hunting of the Snark" was a formalist manifesto. The puzzles and games in the Alice books, rightly celebrated by modern thinkers, were to Lewis Carroll's conscious mind mere jokes, imitations of reality as seen by children.

The ringing last line of Holquist's essay, "A Boojum Is a Boojum," that is, fictional creature with no real-life referent, is thrilling but probably false. Though a Snark may be anything from a snake-shark to a snipe and spark ("you may serve it with greens, and it's handy for striking a light"), a boojum, as Edmund Epstein has explained to me, is a scary (boo!) gargantuan circus elephant named Jumbo whose wife was—that's right—"Alice."

To the end, that strangely beautiful child was Carroll's muse. His pure and holy love for her, and hers for him, freed his whole being as other pretty little girls freed his tongue. She made him a genius, gave the timid arithmetic teacher the courage to look straight at the real and overwhelm it with puns. Nothing could be less modern—or more constant in art. If we cringe at the thought that art is love, or hunt for nasty explanations in the potty, the whole history of mankind has been in vain.

Or put it this way: As the greatest photographer of children in the nineteenth century (his finest pictures were of Alice), Carroll worked totally by intuition: he took the picture when his set-up felt right. And as the greatest children's writer who ever lived, he did the same.

It was Alice who made Carroll's set-up feel right. On the day of that famous picnic when Carroll spun out his story for Alice Liddell and her sisters, the classicist Duckworth looked over his shoulder from rowing and said in pure amazement, "Dodgson, is this an extempore romance of yours?" Carroll answered that it was. And it was.

The Breast

"**B**ETTER THE BANAL THAN THE APOCA-
lyptic," Prof. David Alan Kepesh says—the central character in Philip
Roth's new novella, *The Breast*. For reasons not altogether clear to his
doctors—"the assault (some say) of a volcanic secretion from the pitu-
itary of 'mammogenic' fluid"—Kepesh has turned into an enormous
breast, round at one end like a watermelon, at the other end a nipple
that can hear and talk and feel sexual stimulation but never reach
orgasm, forever howling "more!" Perhaps it's a dream, Kepesh hopes.
Perhaps madness, an effect of having taught too much Swift, Kafka and
Gogol. But it's not; the transformation is real. So the professor rants
and reasons, or tells banal jokes to himself and those who visit him.

One of his visitors is his brave, banal father, who comes once a
week and, "seated in a chair that is drawn up close to my nipple,"
reports the dull adventures of people who were once guests at the
Kepeshes's Jewish hotel in the Catskills. Another is his loyal, banal
mistress, Claire. She has a nice girl's distaste for sexual experiment,
but when she learns that his nurse's washing him excites him, her
question and his answer parody and celebrate the bedroom conversation of all good, banal lovers.

> "Would you like me to do what she does?"
> "Would you—do it?"

The noblest and most banal of all the professor's visitors is his psychiatrist, Dr. Klinger, a stubborn clinger to reality, who for years has been doggedly ridding Kepesh of neurotic arrogance and self-pity, plain-mindedly, proving to him again and again that his troubles—even this recent transformation—are mere matters of fact, things to be taken for what they are, no more, so that now, going over his once exciting traumas, Kepesh, "citadel of sanity," can sigh, "My life's drama has all the appeal of some tenth-grade reader containing Maupassant's 'The Necklace' and 'The Luck of Roaring Camp.' "

Boring, yes, but a fine achievement, that acceptance, that ability to tolerate and even affirm the ordinary. Nothing could be further from the ideals of, say, Heidegger and Sartre, whose guilt-laden, mad notions have done so much in this century to make life and literature really boring.

Sensibly, casually, Roth plays the existentialist jive for laughs. Early in his ordeal, Kepesh complains:

> In the midst of the incredible, the irredeemably ordinary appears to remind me of the level at which most of one's life is usually lived. Really, it is the silliness, the triviality, the meaninglessness of experience that one misses most in a state like this; for aside from the monstrous physical fact, there is of course the intellectual responsibility I seem to have developed to the uniqueness and enormity of my misfortune. What does it mean? How has it come to pass and why? In the entire history of the human race, why David Alan Kepesh?

With a little help from his friends Kepesh comes off it. In the end he, though an odd form of life, achieves the ordinary, knows the foolishness of his supposed responsibility to ask grandiose questions, romantic evasions of Rilke's admonition ("which is not necessarily as elevated a sentiment as we all might once have liked to believe") that you must change your life, change it in the direction of the mundane, the banally committed, the merely honest. Good point. More and more novelists are coming to it. The 1970s may yet turn out.

The highest value in fiction (as everyone has always known except novelty freaks and, of course, the criticism industry) is moral stability, the ability to celebrate reality without distorting or evading it, though admittedly that's worthless, impossible in fact, without masterful technique and the ability to invent the right vehicle—realistic or, as in *The Breast*, fabulous. The truth of what you say is what really matters, and the only importance of technique is that when you say it badly you haven't said it. Sloppiness and self-indulgence, as in such earlier Roth novels as *When She Was Good* and *Portnoy's Complaint*, debase the vision, making it seem either false or silly. Feebleness of invention, as in some of his early stories, limits the vision to, at best, the merely touching.

Technically at least, *The Breast* seems to me Roth's best book so far. The humor and pathos (it has fair amounts of both) come from his solid grasp of how life is, his firm knowledge of the importance of strength of character and the will to live. Or, as Kepesh calls them in his meetings with his psychiatrist, "S. of C., and the W. to L." He explains: "These banal phrases are the therapeutic equivalent of my lame jokes. In these, my preposterous times, we must keep to what is ordinary and familiar."

The trick which is the heart of the book is brilliant: to celebrate the ordinary, the silly, the banal, create a grotesque and extraordinary banality—a huge detached breast with human consciousness and feeling. The trick is good, so obvious and easy and yet so rich with meaning, it's a little hard to translate from what it is, a piece of art, to reviewer's language.

Roth plays every possible game with his conceit. For instance, Kepesh mournfully and very touchingly (though I know that sounds ridiculous) compares his "real life" situation with the merely fictional situation of, among others, Kafka's Gregor Samsa, cockroach—a joke that gives Roth a chance to make fun of Freudian art and neurosis theories, to ape pompous and silly ideas of literary critics about "unique vision" and "genius," and to reconsider (lightly and slyly, of course) the whole theory of the non-realistic novel.

For another instance, the breast conceit allows Roth another confused and loving slap at Mom, also at mankind the wailing infant; a shot at the Playboy culture we're mired in; and a cunning metaphor for post-Christian, post-Sartrean man—blind, insatiable. "A joke. A grotesque." Or a joke and grotesque to some; not to the wise.

There are two secrets to pulling off such a literary trick, and Roth knows them. First, once committed to reporting the experience of a man turned into a breast, the writer must by powerful imagination immerse himself in the situation. What exactly would everyone involved feel, think, say, do? (You can get away with mistakes in the realistic novel. That's why one can write best-selling trash. In a world constructed out of thin air, impishness and childish joy, one little slip and you're a dead man.) Roth is on good terms with the hunchbacked muse of the outrageous. His dull, real people in an outlandish situation are hilarious. The spinster nurse who pretends not to hear the breast's obscene suggestions. Or the former English department head, now dean, at Stony Brook, whom Roth caricatures with relish and mad genius.

The second secret is that one must, all the time one writes, be so steeped in the meaning of the central conceit (more a matter of feeling than intellect) that nothing comes into the story just for laughs. Every event, every joke, must ambush the reader with reality while he laughs, and again Roth mostly pulls it off. He also does, I'm sorry to say, what I've always found tiresome and stupid in his writing, especially of late, and what's worse, he does it right at the beginning, which may prevent some readers from ever reaching the good parts. He talks too much—like a hung-up schoolboy or like the trendy popular novelist he is, for all his virtues—about taking down his trousers, studying his penis, moving his bowels, maintaining his sexual potency, and so on. He says, for instance: "...the flesh at the base of my penis had turned a soft reddish shade. I looked stained, as though a small raspberry, or maybe a cherry, had been crushed against my pubes, the juices running down onto my member, coloring the root of it raggedly but unmistakably red."

I know all the arguments that favor this claptrap (I mean the pun), including the argument at the core of Roth's book about banality, but I still say it's boring. As a rule of thumb I say, if Socrates, Jesus and Tolstoy wouldn't do it, don't. Or merry, dirty Chaucer, who does nothing like this, much less Swift who, anyway, was crazy. The banal may be wonderful subject matter, but it's lousy as a literary method. Gass, Elkin, Purdy and Fowles, among others, deal brilliantly with sex and defecation. In Roth, as in Updike, the stuff's embarrassing, unhealthy. (The sick, the self-regarding, is precisely what Roth attacks in *The Breast*. He shoots down all signs of it wherever he sees them. It seems to me he missed one.)

The fault's not enough to wreck the book; though for me, at least, it undermines the book's authority. And I may as well mention the symptom of what some may think another fault: The story doesn't linger the way the best writing does, imposing its own reality on the reader's way of seeing for days and weeks.

I think the reason is this: Roth doesn't chisel out sentences like a poet. He writes with intelligence and sophisticated cleverness, delightfully and lightly. Nowhere am I startled by a fine new idea, a turn of phrase that inclines my hair to stand up. These are matters of taste, no doubt. In matters of style, I personally prefer the mildly apocalyptic to the banal.

But I say all this merely for the sake of completeness. Roth is no Gogol—a comparison he boldly and jokingly invites—but *The Breast* is terrific for a thing of its kind: inventive and sane and very funny, though filthy of course, as I've mentioned. It's incredible, in fact, how smart he is for a man so hung up with his you-know-what.

The Way
We Write Now

EVERYONE SEEMS TO BE AGREED LATELY
that the serious novel in America is going through a change. The realistic novel is dead, one hears; and something exciting is rising from its ashes. I take a dimmer view, but I do think something is happening, and the decline of realism is a superficial part of it. What is happening is that after a period of cynicism, novelists are struggling—for the most part in ways doomed by indifference to novelistic form—to see their way clear to go heroic. Strange new worlds are in, cynicism and despair are out, replaced not by true affirmation but by psychological survival tactics.

Let me begin with some statements of the obvious. American novelists, even Americans by choice like Vladimir Nabokov or Jerzy Kosinski, can never get rid of the qualifying effect of American literary and cultural tradition—that is, the American character—as long as they write to or about Americans. I would say that this means, not so much historically as symbolically: the Transcendentalists, with their cult of the child, Indian or illiterate (Faulkner's Negroes, children, or idiots); "life-like" speech (the Jewish idiom is as good as Huck Finn's for cutting down soulless sophisticates); and Whitmanish quop by way of form—the optimistic expectation that the book will somehow pull through, like nature.

It means childlike faith such as Emerson's, which organizes reality's clutter and smashes through reason's discouraging howevers, but when forced to see facts gives way in a rush to petulant, childish despair like that of Howells or Twain-grown-old. If James and Fitzgerald, and in his own way Melville, got past the blithe and unsustainable innocence that is the heart of the American character, it remained their literary subject, as it remains the subject of their heirs, John Cheever, John Updike and William H. Gass. For Nabokov it's frequently the butt of the joke, as in *Lolita* and *Ada*.

Our experience of extremes (happy Emerson, black-hearted Melville, light and dark as simple as virtue and wickedness in a Congressman's election speech) makes all Americans radicals. Our normal view is that if everything isn't terrific, it stinks. Thus American self-doubts about Vietnam, race relations and ecology lead instantly to a conviction that life is unendurable, God is horror, and our wives and children all hate us. So in the sixties black humor came in—the Vonnegut shrug—and nihilism, as in William Burroughs, and smart-mouth satire of the kind third-rate novelists are still turning out, Brock Brower, for instance, in *The Late Great Creature*. Where not crushed entirely, the built-in American hunger for audacious affirmation went desperate and kinky, as in Norman Mailer's *An American Dream*, which tried to save the fat from the fire by witchcraft. Most critics assumed it was all some kind of metaphor, not yet having heard Mailer's theories on telepathy and the moon.

In the absence of any remotely tenable audacious suggestion (Faulkner, by now, was as dead as Captain Marvel), we began to get by in the late sixties on the merely audiculous, that is to say, the heroics of a strenuously encouraged mouse. It came to be generally understood—partly because of William Gass's tour-de-force novella *Willie Masters' Lonesome Wife* and his numerous articles (later collected in *Fiction and the Figures of Life*)—that though real existence may be senseless and painful, art makes up for it. And art, when the artist is unable to say anything helpful, means style.

Gass's own writing doesn't illustrate his theory. Some of Robert Coover's does, though not his best book, *The Origin of the Brunists*. All of John Barth's does. The "reality" of *The Sot-Weed Factor* or of *Giles Goat-Boy* is the words of the novel, nothing else. Giles finds that a librarian is reading the very book he's inside. Every novel is a funhouse, as Barth has it elsewhere, in which the novelist pulls the levers and the hayseed reader rides. The themes in Barth are the traditional American themes—there are even moral problems and thrilling solutions. But Barth is not so brazen as to recommend his solutions to humanity (if humanity exists).

The recent cult of style has the splendid effect of making novels more enjoyable, less sludgy; but the assertion that style is life's only value—that style redeems life—is false both to life and to the novel. Gass, in his own novel *Omensetter's Luck*, has nothing in his theory to protect him from a too-long middle section that is mostly the verbal acrobatics of an oversophisticated, exhausted character, and nothing to explain why the end of the novel, which involves moral affirmation and a change of heart—a typically American, totally convincing resurgence of innocence—is so profoundly moving.

Similarly, his own comments in the short works collected in *In the Heart of the Heart of the Country* have nothing to do with the moral and poetic power of the stories. "The Pedersen Kid" Gass describes as "an exercise in short sentences." Once watches in vain for the flicker of a smile. Gass isn't joking. He's Huck Finn grown up and teaching philosophy in St. Louis. In another age, an age not embarrassed by audacity, Gass might take pleasure in the fact that his books are moving affirmations, and he might consistently construct his fables around the search for value, rather than around language peaks. As it is, by the luck of good character, he surpasses and contradicts his age and, to a large extent, his theory.

Jerzy Kosinski, another celebrated stylist (*The Painted Bird, Steps, Being There*), is truer to both. The blood-curdling sketches and story fragments which make up *Steps* have undeniable effect—like falling from a silo and landing on a plow—except for the honest country reader who, not inexcusably, throws away the book. The obsessively dark vision is dedicated "to my father, a mild man" and has an epigraph on self-control from the *Bhagavadgita*. In other words, Kosinski isn't imitating reality but making up a world whose only real-life parallel is the life of the damned. Escape to purgatory and ultimate salvation are not, he seems to feel, his business as an artist. His business is not empathy and the analysis of moral and psychological process but strictly appropriate presentation of a morally static surface. His business is "style."

The purity of the experiment is revealing. Where style really is the whole concern, there can be no real drama—how people come to be damned or saved—and no "lesson." Like twelve-tone music, the technique can express only boredom and horror. Granted, boredom and horror are legitimate subjects. What makes Kosinski's triumph suspicious is that, to the disillusioned optimist (Twain too furious and heartbroken to make jokes, or Updike's Skeeter, the outraged idealist who delivers tirades in *Rabbit Redux*) *Steps* seems an accurate description of life, whatever dedication and epigraph may hint. The affirmations lay outside the book, which itself supports a gross oversimplification traditional with Americans. Needless to say, the unrelieved blackness readers find in *Steps*, though Kosinski may not mean it, is the whole bag of tricks in William Burroughs, who believes every groaned-out word. In *The Ticket That Exploded*, style is explicitly a cruel false hope to us soft machines, a thing we must destroy.

The antithesis to the search for salvation through style is the gospel according to Donald Barthelme. He avoids style at any cost, and also avoids psychological or moral analysis, escaping despair by America's oldest, still commonest trick: the childishness and befuddled innocence of Yankee Doodle, Huck Finn or Holden Caulfield—the childishness (in this case mad) that sneaks past oppressive reason.

"The intellect," said Thoreau, "is a cleaver." In a world whose findings drove Melville half insane, the Transcendentalists' ideal child indefensibly asserted convictions that felt right to basically sentimental and good-hearted, though often fierce and wrongheaded, Americans. In a world where the mechanics of DNA and RNA prove conclusively what Melville could only fear (it's DNA that makes Burroughs so furious) and where our noblest intentions have resulted in what some call genocide, our traditional optimistic feelings are, for some crazy reason, as intense as ever. To say we're wrong is like telling a lion to settle down and be a horse.

Barthelme's crazies can express and validate those romantic feelings, at the same time checking our cocksure tendency to meddle and preach and reform every passing jay. We laugh at his seven psychological dwarves in *Snow White*, since they're lunatics and fools; but their feelings about people and the puzzlement and ultimate wonder of things are exactly our own. It has nothing to do with black comedy—Beckett's *Happy Days*, for instance, which angrily laughs at brainless optimism.

(Barthelme's characters are not exactly optimists.) Like Ralph Waldo Emerson ("I contradict myself?"), Barthelme's crazies systematically evade the issue, and they encourage the reader to evade it too, with neurotically healthy vigor. They work like the Christianity of those Updike adults who have shucked religion but carry on from childhood a security ultimately untouched by their knowledge that it's groundless.

At times Barthelme himself becomes the sacrifice—when he says "baff" for "bath" and no one but Barthelme can be speaking (not some narrator or character). He flaunts his psychological weakness as Twain flaunts Huck's ignorance, and for the same purpose: to stay clear of the grown-up lies. Frequently the management of plot is the model of our evasion of what might wreck us. Notice, for instance, in the story "Prunella" in *City Life*, how neatly Barthelme slips every real-world difficulty. He distorts reality but he survives and (mostly) smiles. He stays with what feels important but can't be defended, reshaping the world to fit the soul and accepting the oddity caused outside, for example a father who's been run over and killed but is also, for some reason, sitting on the bed and weeping.

Barthelme's affirmation was never meant to have poetic power and has less first-rate humor than his admirers claim, but his work, slight or not, is mainline American—"innocent eye," non-analytical mind, faith over knowledge, celebration without irony of trifles that Americans love, like the phantom of the opera. Barthelme—and this is the important point—affirms not a value or system of values but a way of being. His choice rules out novelistic form (conflict, profluence, enlightenment) and is typical, or so I hope to show, of what is now going on, the rise of groundless, cautiously optimistic affirmation, the good as psychological survival tactic.

Superficially, no two writers could be more unlike than Stanley Elkin and Joyce Carol Oates. Elkin at his best is a mad barbarian turned stand-up comic (his favorite devices are the pun and the punchline) who answers all whining and pessimism with perverse assertions that whatever the whiner whines about is in fact a great good. In *A Bad Man* he praises, with incredible verbal energy, a bad man. In *The Dick Gibson Show* he turns that friend of midnight drivers, the trivial and dreary all-night talk show, to a fast, loud circus of bickering and outrageous, consciously Chaucerian tales. In his forthcoming novella collection he goes further, hitting lunatic magnificent heights—or maybe depths. Not that he avoids reality. His characters are forever arguing with themselves, with each other, or with the reader ("Perhaps you will say. . ."). But the purpose of each discouraging, sensible objection is to trigger an altiloquent, crazyman response.

Elkin's message, in fact, is in nothing he proclaims or pretends to proclaim, not even in the fancy symbolism, but in energy pure and simple. In his earlier writing (*Criers and Kibitzers* and *A Bad Man*) he sees all human relationships in terms of power. In *The Dick Gibson Show* (which is therefore a better book) relationships which begin as power-struggles soften toward understanding and appeals for love. Nevertheless, it's raw energy that Elkin loves—in prose and in characters. He's Ahab smashing through the mask with jokes, an eternal child whose answer to oppressive reason is to outperform it, outshout it. Grizzly reality is his straight-man.

I happen to know Joyce Carol Oates, the goriest writer in America, shuts her eyes during the bloody parts of Polanski's *Macbeth*. One knows from her best stories and from watching the gentle and humorous minor characters in her novels, that her values are Jamesian and that she possesses the razor-sharp intellect needed to make Jamesian distinctions. Nevertheless, she writes "gothic" novels and has described the genre as "a fairly accurate assessment of modern life." Unlike all the other writers I have mentioned, she is capable, I think, of doing what great novelists always do, which is to build tight form out of single-minded psychological and moral analysis.

She has occasionally done this in long stories (for instance, "Free") though not in her best or most typical stories ("In the Region of Ice" and "The Wheel of Love") which have, though the technical means are different, the effect of her novels. In novels she avoids analysis in a way that seems intentional, fragmenting the world (and the novel's rhythm) by a use of close, almost myopic examination followed by startling cuts—to another character, another era—that disorient the reader like the kick of a mule. Crisis situations arise and vanish before either the reader or characters can assess them, making fine intellect a useless tool (she writes repeatedly of the brilliant but mad) and producing an image of history, personal or public, as a track of machine-gun wounds. Value affirmations are as fleeting as destructions, and often as grotesque.

The result is that, as for Barthelme or Elkin, thought-out values— the solid foundations of character that Henry James or Jane Austen fictionally develop and recommend to the reader—are replaced by a philosophically groundless survival tactic: horror and uneasy compassion as a fixed state of mind. If her purpose is to "understand," say, the Detroit riots in *Them*, that is not, I think, her artistic achievement. The technique she chooses—like Barthelme's, in this one respect— makes the reader a certain kind of person for the moment, an innocent who, wide-eyed and trembling, survives.

Odd as the suggestion will no doubt seem, John Updike does much the same, though in another way. He is, in one sense, a realist—he has a keen, deadly accurate eye and a sure feeling for his time and place. His work makes nonsense of the theory that the realistic novel is dead. But his realism, like that of James, is rich in mythic and symbolic overtones, archetypal patterns. He writes repeatedly about children and grown-ups, country and city, past and present, often, as in *Couples*, the Arcadian past of nymphs and satyrs (in *Couples* they shape-shift to Merrymount revelers) and a present where Arcadia is sought in vain by people of psychologically arrested development. In fact, as the critic Larry Taylor has shown in his book on Updike, all of Updike's work can in a way be approached as a brilliant symbolic exploration of the pastoral tradition.

Updike's chief way of "understanding" a problem is to discover its symbolic equivalents. Symbolism is his way of thinking and hope of salvation, as perfected style is the hope of Gass or energetic affrontery the hope of Elkin. In *Couples*, again, he plays a good deal with (among a thousand such symbolic counters) the fact that in Christian tradition fate is represented by a circle, faith by a straight line, but that in hyperbolic geometry, all lines make circles.

Get the symbolic equations right, Updike says in effect (and include enough sex and precise description to keep the characters human), and the confusion will all snap clear. The most baffling and painful questions take on order once you find all the possible analogies between (in *Rabbit Redux*) copulation, religion, space exploration, Parkinson's disease, the war in Vietnam, and race relations. All writers use this method to some extent, but in Updike it becomes more important than plot, character or style, any of which he will alter for a symbol. Symbolism, in other words, is for Updike, as it was for Hawthorne and Melville, a good-luck piece.

The method is medieval, which doesn't mean wrong, and the hope is as groundless, philosophically speaking, as Elkin's clowning or Miss

Oates's widened eyes. In *Rabbit Redux*, his finest book so far, Updike finds in the method not only solace but a seemingly firm platform from which to launch further affirmations, and in these he goes far beyond most other writers in terms of value commitment. I honor him heartily for that, yet I wonder if even here the assertions stick. Even here he is relatively indifferent to what James believed was the real business of the novel, whether the novel is realistic or not.

Though Updike comes to some of his conviction through the experience of his characters, he never puts his money on psychological and moral analysis, drama, inevitably unfolding novelistic form. That process gives Updike his rough draft, I suspect—the lines of his plot and those many fine moments of insight, penetration. But given the draft, he stops thinking about the real, scientifically inexpressible mechanics of people and events. He begins juggling and ornamenting, working up his complex allegory and moving farther and farther from dramatic necessity. At the point of the main dramatic conflict in *Rabbit Redux*, the novel turns to tirade, a retreat from drama. What Rabbit really thinks about it all is left uncertain.

In short, as other writers lately are doing for other reasons, Updike abandons close analysis and dramatic inevitability in favor of, simply, a way of being—Huck Finn as ingenious equation-maker. There's the problem in all our finest contemporary fiction, I think. It's the reason for the thin, unglued quality in even the most dazzling technical performances. Whether you write about dragons or businessmen, it's in the careful scrutiny of cleanly apprehended characters, their conflicts and ultimate escape from immaturity, that the novel makes up its solid truths, finds courage to defend the good and attack the simpleminded.

Saint Walt

A FEW YEARS AGO WHEN YOU MENTIONED Walt Disney at a respectable party—or anyway this is how it was in California, where I was then—the standard response was a headshake and a groan. Intellectuals spoke of how he butchered the classics—from *Pinocchio* to *Winnie-the-Pooh*—how his wildlife pictures were sadistic and coy, how the World's Fair sculptures of hippopotamuses, etc., were a national if not international disgrace. A few crazies disagreed, and since crazies are always people to watch, it began to be admitted that the early Pluto movies had a considerable measure of *je ne sais quoi*, that the background animation in *Snow White* was "quite extraordinary," that *Fantasia* did indeed have one great sequence (then it became two; now everyone says three, though there's fierce disagreement on exactly which three).

Being a stubborn, intractable sort of person with no innate good sense, and having invested hours and hours of my life riding my chain-tread Roadmaster seven or eight miles every Saturday night to Walt Disney movies that came to the Star Theater in Attica, I held out—the way you'd hold out for a kind old uncle accused of child molesting—for Disney's absolute and total exoneration. With animus, mind you. The solemn generation had done me damage. Since *Snow White* was too frightening, bad for children's psyches (even now I hide under my seat when I think the witch is coming), they'd emasculated Captain Hook in *Peter Pan*; they'd even half-tamed the alligator (but a smile can be as scary as buzzards and a warty nose and thunder). They also took away our comics and Oz books—all about castration—and deplored those terrific crows in *Dumbo* as a sinister piece of racism. So I fiercely argued for the side of the unrighteous—"Disney is the greatest!" I said. "Compared to Disney, Michelangelo is a lowbrow, filthy-minded punk!"—ruining parties, ending old friendships. . . I will tell you God's truth: when I was in San Francisco, northern California seriously considered withdrawing from the part of the state Walt Disney lived in.

I fought on. The odds seemed overwhelmingly against me, and at times, I admit, I felt a little discouraged. But the outcome is history: Walt Disney is now universally recognized as the greatest artist the world has ever known, except for, possibly, Apollonius of Rhodes. There has recently been published, in fact, a huge, somewhat expensive, richly illustrated art book on Disney's work, *The Art of Walt Disney: From Mickey Mouse to the Magic Kingdom* (Abrams). It's a book well worth buying, written by a bona fide professional art critic, Christopher Finch. Except here and there, when Finch seems to me gratuitously and senselessly critical (he objects, for instance, to the "Night on Bald Mountain" and "Ave Maria" sequence which closes *Fantasia*, finding it a less sublime expression of Christian feeling than, say, Chartres Cathedral), Finch has exactly pinpointed Disney's greatness and appeal: Walt Disney was a man who wanted to please, a man who had a downright awesome faith in the ordinary. He was a celebrator of man-as-he-is. He had no grand programs for improving man's character, only programs for making man's life more enjoyable, more healthy. So, in an age when other people's animated cartoons were still jerking foolishly through vaudeville gags, Disney produced *The Band Concert*, his first Technicolor music short, featuring Mickey Mouse and Donald Duck and the best *William Tell Overture* you'll ever hear; and in an age when people were just beginning to worry about ecology, Disney was not only planning but building futurist cities, ecologically balanced, pollution free. (Finch closes his book with an essay by Peter Blake, practicing architect and former editor of *Architectural Forum*, on the profound significance of Disneyland and Walt Disney World for architecture and urban planning—in fact, for the very survival of urban man.)

Finch traces Disney's life from beginning to end—and beyond the end, since some of Disney's noblest projects, including the Experimental Prototype Community of Tomorrow, were still in the planning stage when Disney died of cancer—and in the process shows what it was about Disney that made him so nearly infallible. Disney knew what he liked, felt absolutely certain that other human beings were exactly like him, and went after it, cutting no corners. His assumption was absurd, of course, but it's an assumption every real artist makes, and the character Mickey Mouse alone would be enough to justify the assumption. Though Disney couldn't even draw Mickey Mouse—as Disney was always the first to admit (Mickey was the invention of Ub Iwerks, but every line, every pucker or sheepish grin was subject to Disney's never hasty approval)—Mickey was, in fact, Walt Disney. Only Disney could do Mickey's voice, a point more important than it may at first sound, since the voice controlled every flicker of emotion the animators gave that indefatigable, endlessly subtle mouse; and as Disney's character mellowed, so did Mickey's. From *The Band Concert*, where neither bee nor tornado nor even Donald Duck can interrupt his conducting, to *The Sorcerer's Apprentice*, where he takes on the powers of the universe, Mickey is the Artist, the Ordering Intelligence that will not be abashed by its littleness, at least not for long. There is, of course, more Christian feeling in late Mickey Mouse than in the "Ave Maria."

One could make much of this—the Midwestern Protestantism of Walt Disney, his comfortable certainty that all is well, that evil is a thing never to be taken very seriously: though the beautiful apple may tempt Snow White, it cannot really kill her; the Wicked Queen will be thrown down like Lucifer by lightning out of heaven, and around Snow White's casket, lighted as if by a stained window, the soundtrack will play, full of sorrow and devotion, "Some Day My Prince Will Come," which, praise heaven, he will indeed. These are not at all cheap appeals to stock Christian emotion; for the most part, they're probably not even a matter of conscious symbolism, merely an attitude so basic to all Disney's work, even his propaganda films during World War II, that he hardly understood what was there. Take his greatest film, *Pinocchio*. It opens with what Finch calls, rightly, "a stunningly effective shot—the camera pulling back from a large white star, panning across the tiled roofs of a sleepy European village, then closing in on the lighted window of Geppetto's cottage." Finch continues: "It is the kind of shot that has become familiar enough in live-action movies since the advent of power-operated zoom lenses, but taken within the context of its own period, and within the history of animation, it is innovative and spectacular. Nor is it just a piece of flashy showmanship. It serves to capture our imagination and draw us into the atmosphere of the story before a single word has been spoken." It does all this, Finch does not go on to add—perhaps because it's too obvious—because it's covertly Christian, as Christian as the angel-like blue fairy, or demonic Stromboli with the hell-fire eyes, the salvation through sacrifice in the belly of a whale, the final death and resurrection of Pinocchio.

If one wished to be tiresome, one could go through all Walt Disney's films and show, in every myth or legend that he treats, how he tends to transform it to the Christian one, or rather, the Christian one as understood by Methodists, Presbyterians, and the like—people who, in general, feel so confident that God has things well under control, so certain that "All shall be well, and all shall be well, and all manner of things shall be well," as the Angel told Dame Julian of Norwich, that they forget even to bother with religion, or, to put it a better way, they transfer feelings to everyday life. Whether in the hands of Mickey Mouse or Mary Poppins or the benevolent witches in *Bedknobs and Broomsticks*, magic is miracle in a Disney film—strictly Protestant miracle, thrilling but commonplace, exactly what we should have expected. The temptation is always to see such a view of life as evasive and simplistic—the standard charges against Disney. Perhaps it is (no one knows), but it is a view that has been held by some very complex minds, including Melville's. Profound and subtle as Melville may have been, he is closer in spirit to Disney than is usually recognized. If his "wickedly squinting whale" is no cartoon (as a whaler he must have known it was a little inaccurate), consider that caricature of evil, Cap'n Ahab, and those pigtailed heathen Chinese he uses as his oarsmen. Like the Wicked Queen, Stromboli, and the rest, Ahab challenges the universe as cosmic outlaw and finds he never had a chance. Ishmael survives, floating on a coffin, and unharming sharks glide by "as if with padlocks on their mouths"—all Disney images. In other moods, Disney was close to Poe—haunted houses, rotting castles, the unearthly beauty of innocent ladies—good and evil in stark, "simplistic" contrast.

But whereas Poe moved from the early comic tales to a vision increasingly dark and pessimistic, Disney grew increasingly certain that all would be well. More and more he made heroes of traditional villains—witches, mad scientists. More and more he turned his art to the improvement of so-called reality.

Disney's true works of art, of course, are the animated films and his few really good live-action films (*Treasure Island*, *20,000 Leagues Under the Sea*, *Mary Poppins*), not the television programs with which he advertised his studio's wares or the amusement parks and model cities they helped to finance; but the impulse behind both kinds of work was the same, that well-being the movies celebrate, the conviction that evil, rightly understood, is a threat no more serious than Cruella de Vil, in *One Hundred and One Dalmatians*, Shere Khan, the comically menacing tiger of *The Jungle Book*, or the great flunk-out villains of the animated *Robin Hood*. What is perhaps most interesting about Disney's new respectability is what it implies about the world that has grown respectful. What once seemed grave objections to Walt Disney's art seem now mere oddities of his character, like St. Francis's queer habit of preaching sermons to birds.

Take sentimentality. In the fifties, sentimentality was a terrible crime. Books on understanding literature grimly warned against it (Hemingway and Faulkner required apology), books on painting explained why the seeming sentimentality in early Picasso was an optical illusion. "Undercutting" and "irony" were very big words. Then came the Beatles, and that same afternoon everybody stopped looking at the extraordinary background in Disney's *Snow White* and started looking at Snow White, and behold, if she was a sentimental distortion of the way real girls are, if she was an absolute fiction, exactly like the Wicked Queen, it was nevertheless true that the way she moved—the way she floated on the extraordinary background—was a splendid thing to see, a thing worth the great plopping tears of the seven dwarves and the audience too. Why not? That is to say, American intellectuals were suddenly no longer afraid of seeming foolish and childlike (as Americans have always been, as American artists have always pointed out). Some may even have noticed that the former scorn of emotion "not adequately grounded in the probabilities of character and action" was defensive, tight-sphinctered immaturity. Dickens, too, was beginning to be reevaluated. Somebody was growing up—at least a little.

Or take Disney's way of dealing with animals in the wildlife series. He sets the mating tricks of birds to music; he emphasizes, by camera angle, selection, and soundtrack, the horribleness of the wolf pack's kill. Suddenly, for some reason, everyone understood that what had once been interpreted as a sometimes silly, sometimes sadistic streak in Walt Disney's character was an accident of moment. He had decided to do an Alaska movie, an adventure of some kind, and had hired a pair of Alaskan photographers to shoot him some footage which might trigger an idea for an adventure story. Along with other footage came some pictures of seals. Disney sat still, struck by the fact that he liked watching seals (therefore everyone must), and puzzling out what he might do with the discovery. He had invented, that instant, the Nature film, but when Disney thought of it, there was no way under heaven to sell such a film except by the creation of an illusion of plot and character—exactly the kind of thing his studio was best at, the presentation of animals as parodic human beings. It never occurred to him to do anything else, but as soon as *Seal Island* was on the storyboards, *Born Free* and the great documentaries were inevitable. His real feelings about animals he proved by building them safe environments and enormous sanctuaries and by his moralistic ecological pieces for television.

Or take Disney's attitude toward machines, from the flying car in *The Absent-Minded Professor* to the willful Volkswagen, star of *The Love Bug*, to the audio-animatronic creatures of the Hall of Presidents or the Country Bear Jamboree. I first saw Disney's robot Lincoln in 1964, at the Illinois pavilion of the New York World's Fair. It was a horrifying business—even I, his devoted admirer, would admit it. Like a group of Auschwitz Jews, the audience is moved into a large and plush auditorium, where the doors close automatically, almost silently, and you wait in blackness and unearthly hush for the sound of escaping gas. The stage lights come up, revealing funeral urns and sculpted drapery (Disney's chief notion of the classical came from mortuaries in Illinois and Missouri), and there's the huge, seated figure of Lincoln, obviously dead. Music, a cross between sickeningly patriotic and sickeningly religious—then more light, and then, slowly, the great dark corpse rises and speaks. Finch tells us, not that one wants to know:

> The sheer energy locked up in the hydraulic and pneumatic systems of any audio-animatronic figure is considerable, and

unless this energy can be precisely controlled, the figure can become quite violent. The Lincoln figure [just before its installation at the fair] was very complex and posed serious control problems. The President smashed his chair and threw mechanical fits that threatened the safety of the men working on him. But Disney was determined that the figure be ready in time, and eventually the power was harnessed.

What really made the figure seem horrible, of course—and would later make the Hall of Presidents more horrible yet—was the ghastly suggestion, which had never occurred to Disney and his people, that all religion and patriotism are a sham and a delusion, an affair for monstrous automatons. Or perhaps a suggestion even deadlier: that all of us are monstrous automatons, helpless Pinocchios dangling from the strings of Disney's computerized Muzak and mind-shushing "rides."

Lately we've learned to shrug off such suggestions. We see the Presidents—or the gross and tiresome Country Bears—as Disney saw them, merely as big, remarkable toys, desperate efforts (if I tell the truth) to amuse a corn-pone audience. To put it another way, nothing in Disney is threatening anymore. Those rides, for instance, in which you're given no choice but to stare straight ahead, and the car moves forward or turns side to side, forcing you to look at what they want you to look at—exactly as a movie editor or, say, an ancient poet chooses which scene you're to look at and in what sequence. Those rides once seemed a proof of man's helplessness in a mechanized, indifferent world of sales pitches, Styrofoam cake, and accordion music. But the impression was mistaken.

The computerized, impersonal, fully automated world that so terrified all men of sense—and that Disney so eagerly looked forward to—no longer threatens us because we've begun to survive it. His unspeakable lowbrow taste we wave off like a mosquito: his dancing hippos in *Fantasia*, his sculptures of hippos at the New York World's Fair, the innumerable obscenities at Disneyland, were never intended as a philistine assault on the citadel of art, and the reaction of anger, the feeling of important values threatened, now seems lunatic. His celebration of the ordinary was a celebration of all of us, even intellectuals, as we are; and the reason Walt Disney has gone up in our estimation is that we ourselves have gone up in our estimation. We have decided to admit

that we are sometimes a little simplistic and sentimental, that despite
dire predictions we are inclined to believe that life on earth will continue for a while—we're even willing to do things about it—and willing to admit, just between ourselves, that as stories go, well, *Finnegans
Wake* is a little hard to follow. Or to put it more soberly, in a way
that sounds less anti-intellectual, we have begun to doubt those great
dark visions of the forties and fifties and to be more nearly persuaded
by those optimistic innocents for whom nothing, in the end, is more
important than a first-class, relatively tasteful imitation of how real
human beings behave when no one's looking—men like Chaucer and
Walt Disney.

We have relaxed into admitting that Disney's villains and heroes—and
those he fathered indirectly, through former employees like Jay Ward
and Walt Kelly—are the people of our age: you and me, reader. Who
can expect real seriousness or dignity from the Road Runner or Pogo,
not to mention that maniac Donald Duck? Who can expect old-
fashioned artistic high seriousness from those middle-aged writers like
William Gass or Stanley Elkin, writers whose talents were licked into
shape by some clownish, dumb-eyed Disney bear? The whole reality
of such writers is a huge animation that shudders between extremes
of Geppetto's village and R. Crumb's john. It's futile, in short, to attempt any judgments of Walt Disney's art. We can no longer tell it
from so-called reality—which for all our sakes, and for the sake of
the future, is probably just as well.

The Adventurer

I T'S FREQUENTLY POINTED OUT THAT THERE
are no longer heroes in literature, only anti-heroes and spoof heroes
like 007, and that the reason for this is that writers and readers can
no longer believe that there are heroes in so-called real life. In a world
in which everything seems to have gone wrong, we long for heroes,
secretly wish we could be heroes ourselves—that by some incredible
act of intelligence and daring we could make everything noble, as it
used to be—and on the slightest provocation we turn some quite ordinary moral mediocrity into a godly ideal: Dr. Kissinger, for instance,
before we learned of his involvement in the murder of Chile. Hope
springs eternal, but we know better now; and so the novel really is,
in a certain sense, dead, and civilization has died with it. We wanly
smile at the last-gasp humor of Barthelme, we laugh out loud at the
outrageously engaged, cartoonish romantic heroes of Elkin, or, like
Cato whiling away his last hours, we sniff out the tortuous windings
of philosophical Gass.

Optimists tell us our general despair is an effect of Vietnam and
the Nixon Administration, but Paul Zweig's important book, *The Adventurer*, suggests that the trouble is much deeper. The idea of the true,
unselfconscious hero—"the adventurer"—went hollow long ago, and
went hollower and hollower, stage by stage. The object of his study is

to trace and explain those stages. Even when he's wrong about particulars, his argument—for me at least—throws startling light on where
we are and where we've been and provides what every first-rate theory
is supposed to provide, a new way of seeing not only the books and
men he chooses to talk about but also those he passes over in silence,
from the late Roman odes to, for instance, Wallace Stevens.

He begins with the shamanistic element in epic poetry, mainly
Gilgamesh and the *Odyssey*—tells how the adventurer (in this case the
shaman) went away to such places as the country of death and brought
back wisdom and power, helps to humanity; how the heroic adventurer was half maniac wild man, as dangerous to his friends as to his
enemies, not yet shackled by ethics or common sense, an elemental
force; how the adventurer-shaman brought health to the whole community, gave life meaning. All this Zweig elaborates with talk of the
Iliad, *Beowulf* and *Sir Gawain and the Green Knight*. Throughout this
discussion of things ancient and medieval, Zweig's thesis is somewhat
harmed, I'm afraid, by his fairly complete misunderstanding of the
poems; but distracting as Zweig's misinformation may be, the thesis
is a sound one, and a true argument badly argued may nevertheless
be significant.

When he turns to the adventurer in modern times, Zweig's book
takes wings. In a series of brilliant analyses which touch on most of
the important modern European and American writers but focuses
mainly on Defoe's *Robinson Crusoe*, Casanova, the gothic novelists, Edgar
Allan Poe, Nietzsche, Malraux and Sartre, he traces what happened
to us: how the adventurer's flight and fight turned inward, so that where
once monastic or castle walls held out the dangerous wilderness the
adventurer brought news of, there were now the thicker, far solider
walls of Protestant morality, Defoe's code of "due and regular con-
duct," so that even on Crusoe's island, potential paradise of the adventurer, we find that (as Zweig quotes Virginia Woolf as saying), "There
are no sunsets and no sunrises; there is no solitude and no soul. There
is, on the contrary, staring us full in the face nothing but a large earth-
enware pot." Adventure, to Crusoe, is a dumb idea. It leads to being
captured by headhunters. Better to tame one's patch of land, fence it in.

But alas, the walls of decency themselves become a prison, and as
that fact began to be recognized clearly, new forms arose—the gothic
novel of impotent evil and bungling good, the frivolous attempt at

escape in Casanova, the monstrously stupid transvaluations of the Marquis de Sade, as well as things healthier, what Zweig describes as "the new mythology of adventure" in Edgar Allan Poe, and the transvaluations of Nietzsche. On all these Zweig writes, with splendid originality and insight, such a set of analyses as we haven't seen in years. To report his conclusions, it seems to me, would be like giving away an earned surprise ending. Part of what's surprising about Zweig's book, in fact, is that he can think of so *much* that's new and true to say about so *many* old chestnuts. His piece on Poe is the best, maybe. Someone has finally managed to explain why the mysterious ending of "The Narrative of A. Gordon Pym" is so terrifying.

Zweig closes with Malraux and Sartre. He points out the well-known terrible paradox in T. E. Lawrence's *Seven Pillars of Wisdom*, "the paradox of our culture: its longing for great acts, combined with a sense of their irrelevance," and shows that Malraux and Sartre divide that paradox between them: "Malraux's adventurer is locked into a solitary combat with the viscous elements of the jungle, with the fever of decay which saps his body, with the irreducible solitude which constitutes *la condition humaine*"; for Sartre, fighting even a jungle is absurd: "The trees floated, more like a collapse; from minute to minute, I expected to see the trunks become wrinkled, like weary rods, shrinking and falling to the ground in a soft, black, folded heap." Out of this come, among others, Beckett, Borges and Norman Mailer, on all of whom Zweig speaks shrewdly.

In the end Zweig leaves the reader—wisely, perhaps—to write his own final chapter, a chapter that would get down beneath the surface of one interesting remark in Zweig's introduction: "We are faced with an interesting paradox. Oriental traditions discourage adventure because they consider the vigorous individuality of the adventurer to be an illusion, a trick of Maya. Modern traditions in the West have been even less hospitable to the adventurer. . .Yet vigorous individuality is precisely what our culture has come to value most."

Zweig's explanation of our present state is that we in the West have gone inward completely, to drug literature, anti-realistic "fabulation" and so on. That sounds like a grim and terrible *finis*, but I wonder if it is. The shamans took drugs and created fabulations. Out of their discoveries and symbolic tales writers like Homer made highly conscious, social and religious works of art like the *Odyssey*, the story of a man (not a shaman but a man) who fights his way back to the duties he loves, his kingship and family, and purges his island of people who scorn "hospitality" in the highest sense—ordered community, glory of Zeus and the Chinese. Both in the *Iliad* and the *Odyssey*, Achilles is a splendid half-divine animal who's vastly admired and ultimately judged wrong—inferior to Odysseus, who lies and cheats and, with Penelope's help, survives.

I might never have noticed if it weren't for Zweig's book, but it seems to me that as far back in time as we can trace the mind of man, the idea of the hero has always rung hollow—for all its appeal—and that the stages of the adventurer's decline are nothing other than alternative ways, after old ways have failed, of desperately snatching at the heroic ideal we stubbornly refuse to live without.

Beyond
the Bedroom Wall

IT'S NOT EXACTLY COMMON, IN RECENT years, to run across a clearly first-rate novel that traces the generations of a family. The last really good ones, if memory serves, were Wallace Stegner's *Big Rock Candy Mountain* and John Cheever's two Wapshot books. There are all sorts of reasons such novels don't get written, and one way of dramatizing Larry Woiwode's achievement in his huge new novel, *Beyond the Bedroom Wall*, is to spell out some of those reasons.

We still have a foolish prejudice against what Henry James called, in annoyance at Tolstoy, "windy, baggy monsters." Even as we admit the foolishness of the prejudice, we must grant that the problem of really controlling the mass of material necessary for a family saga is monumental. By nature, life sprawls; and the sprawl involved in four or five generations can lead only, one would swear, to soap opera.

For another thing, the "serious novel" has become, in our time, self-conscious. Whereas the eighteenth- or nineteenth-century novelist talked comfortably and (it seemed) knowledgeably about doctors, fishermen, prime ministers, marriageable ladies and madwomen, more recent novelists have tended to doubt their omniscience and narrow their domain. Turn-of-the-century novelists stuck to what they knew by writing about the artist—usually a painter—or by writing about the sensitive young man who may eventually become a novelist. Later (with major exceptions like, sometimes, Faulkner) one wrote directly about the novelist trying to write a novel, revealing all his cards, asking for advice.

What has made the self-conscious novel fashionable is not, I think, its great honesty and wisdom. Even in the best hands, such as Samuel Beckett's, this fiction is pretty paltry stuff intellectually. Its advantage over the more old-fashioned kind of "realistic" fiction is that it suits our for the most part childishly petulant contemporary mood—our self-congratulating self-doubt, our alienated, positivistic pessimism ("Can one man feel another's toothache?"). And it suits, also, a nobler quality in contemporary life: our delight in discovering how things work, our pleasure in seeing objects for themselves, enjoying their colors and textures. In our age, magicians explain their tricks, even print them in magazines, and our admiration soars. Hence, the movement in literature from realistic self-consciousness to "fabulation": we no longer pretend to be omniscient authorities on doctors, fishermen, prime ministers, etc. We tell grand lies with gusto, flaunting our art and trickery (I am thinking of Pynchon, Nabokov and the like), making up, almost wholly from imagination, rocket-men, dragons and also postal clerks. The construction of a novel, once hidden from view like the machinery on a film set, becomes part of the pleasure (like the exposed machinery in a Fellini film). How is Galsworthy, I ask you, to compete with *that*?

But on the other hand how can such gim-crackery compete with Galsworthy? When self-doubt, alienation and fashionable pessimism become a bore and, what's worse, a patent delusion, how does one get back to the big emotions, the large and fairly confident life affirmations of an Arnold Bennett, a Dickens, a Dostoyevsky? After Woody Allen's fairly funny but unmistakably dreary film, *Love and Death* (has even Woody Allen begun to doubt his doubts?), how is one to get back to plain, grown-up talk about love and death?

Beyond the Bedroom Wall: A Family Album is a brilliant solution to these aesthetic problems. It seems to me that nothing more beautiful and moving has been written in years. I was reminded, as I read, of a friend's prediction that the next great movement in literature will be an unashamed return to Victorian copious weeping. That's overoptimistic, probably; but it's a wonderful thing, it seems to me, to laugh and weep one's slow way through an enormous intelligent novel tracing out the life of a family.

The story begins with Otto Neumiller, who emigrated to Mahomet, N.D., from Germany in 1881, and in Mahomet, because of his intelligence and absolute integrity, made and then lost a small fortune. The narrative moves on to become the story of his children, mainly Charles, a dedicated, upright carpenter whose finest piece of work, perhaps, is the coffin he builds for his father. The story then gradually becomes that of Charles's son, Martin—school principal, handyman, artistic dreamer—and Martin's schoolteacher wife, Alpha. They move with their several children to Illinois, where Martin's father has already gone, and the move helps bring on Alpha's death. Martin's children grow up—one becomes a doctor, one an actor, one a poet and so on (they are all in some sense poets)—and the family disperses, drifting away from the emotional-geographic center of their lives, the plain and solid, religious Midwest. Martin marries again, his second wife dies, and the narrative focus shifts to the problems of his children and (briefly) some of his grandchildren.

Such a summary of the plot can hardly suggest the richness of detail, keenness of observation, and insight into the inter-relations of time and place and character in *Beyond the Bedroom Wall*. Woiwode is marvelously convincing, generation after generation, family branch after family branch, yet manages, incredibly, to find a focus for it all in one character, Martin Neumiller, of the novel's middle generation, a man fascinated by his life and loves, one who longs all his life to write a book about it all but knows no such book could possibly be written—reality is simply too vast, is, indeed, "man's most powerful illusion."

From the beginning to end of this novel, Woiwode's dramatization of getting a hold on reality—the problem of fully realizing what lies out there at the edge of dreams and memories, "beyond the bedroom wall"—is simply brilliant. He tells, slowly and elaborately, the story of the love of Martin Neumiller and his first wife, Alpha—how they met and fell in love, how they married and raised children, how Alpha died young (an episode of unbelievable sensitivity and power)—and then he shows, with a strange mixture of tenderness and disheartening objectivity, how little of all that story was grasped and fully understood, even by Martin. The children of Martin and Alpha are all intelligent and inquiring, all fascinated by the lives of their parents, and all profoundly influenced by the character and experience of parents, grandparents, cousins, family friends; the children love one another and love their parents, love their father's stories, and do everything they can to understand; but to each of them many parts of the family picture are a mystery, a source of bafflement and frustration driving them more urgently to love.

This frustration is heightened, for the reader as well as for the characters, when Woiwode turns to Martin's second wife, Laura. We get her only in flashes, now from one child's point of view, now from another's, occasionally, only for a moment, from Martin's, and the result is a fragmented image in which the fragments don't fit: there is no doubt of her reality—all the images have full authority, absolute conviction—but her character, her beauty and goodness, her streak of bitchiness are all left, quite intentionally, uncertain. The evidence is contradictory, opinion is divided, and as we try to understand her—try to grasp the parallels between her life and Alpha's (repeatedly hinted, repeatedly taken back), her figure retreats, beckoning, unredeemed by art or loving detailed memory, farther and farther into the meaningless darkness beyond each dreaming, remembering character's bedroom wall.

In the same way, the children of the last generation become increasingly mysterious—though we know them intimately, by sudden flashes. They move farther and farther apart, the world of family experience zooming out from the old family home in North Dakota as stars and planets have been zooming out since the time of the big bang. Only love, partly shared experience and mutual faith can keep the separating parts linked, and by the end of the novel Martin's children seem hardly to know each other. Yet the links hold, or are holding for now, supported by each family member's faith in the others' love.

Ultimately, by devices of which some readers will disapprove, the link of love, fragmentary shared experience, and faith links all humanity together in *Beyond the Bedroom Wall*. One of these devices is a verbal trick that draws the reader into the family. In an introductory chapter, or "Prelude" as Woiwode calls it (echoing Proust, purposely, I suppose), a half-dreaming, half-remembering character speaks to his sleeping wife as "you," and the pronoun rings outward to include the reader, and all readers, so that the Prelude can end: "But now I'm asleep beside you in bed, and for right now, dear one, loved one, loved ones, and friends, that's enough." The language is patently sentimental, of course, but by the end of the book it seems to be belatedly justified. (It is true, by the way, that in going unashamedly for emotion, Woiwode sometimes slips into the embarrassing. To take large risks is to fail sometimes.) And at various points throughout the book, especially in Martin's final lines to his son, the reader is similarly taken into the family. At least for a while—which is all art can hope for—the metaphysic of this novel, the exploding universe held together by love, is totally convincing.

Beyond the Bedroom Wall is old-fashioned in many ways—its large cast of characters, all carefully developed, its devotedly reported courtships and funerals, its landscapes, houses and weather, its lyrical flights (unabashed prose-poetry that only now and then slips), its moments of super realism (Peggy Lee happens through, with the high school she went to and real-life family name)—but it is also, emphatically, a contemporary novel. Time leaps backward and forward in an original and spectacular yet fully controlled way; people's memories collide and fail to match; points of view shift suddenly. We get no single omniscient narrator but rather a kind of narrative collage, what I've sometimes described as narration by ventriloquy. As in every hip novel of the 1970s (and some from well before), the technique is an essential part of the meaning. Partly by the brilliance of his storytelling, partly by the beauty and fundamental goodheartedness of the story he tells, Woiwode nails the dramatic truth summed up abstractly in his epigraph from Erik Erikson: "Reality, of course, is man's most powerful illusion; but while he attends to this world, it must outbalance the total enigma of being in it at all."

Amber (Get) Waves (Your)
of (Plastic)
Grain (Uncle Sam)

A MONTH OR SO AGO I HAD AN ALL-NIGHT, relatively drunken conversation (I was drinking, not he) with an eleven-year-old about Patriotism. He, I should mention, is one of your more brilliant eleven-year-olds, a promising philosopher.

My friend told his mother the following day, "You know, John Gardner's a *patriot*!" She consoled him and heroically defended me.

But how queer that a love of one's country should require defense! Even I, I confess, endure a shudder of revulsion when I go into some foul, white hamburger hole and find gritty Bicentennial placemats all cluttered up with flags and idealized portraits of the Founding Fathers— George Washington with his teeth in, Samuel Adams looking honest, Ben Franklin with his clothes on (among other crank opinions, you may recall, Ben Franklin held that it was healthful to go around bare-naked), or that huge drunken ox Ethan Allen looking as sober as a church.

Even I, I confess, go pale with rage when I see bumper stickers say-ing, "This Is My Country," implying, of course, "Not Yours." My skin crawls when Presidents speak affectionately of "God" or car salesmen speak of "This Great Country of Ours." I get hot flashes when the American Rifleman's Association, number one defender of the vote by assassination, writes in antique italics, "O'er the ramparts we watch."

But I get equally hot flashes when I hear on every side, not just from children but from intelligent, sophisticated adults—as they'll tell you themselves with full confidence—that the American Dream is dead.

The American Dream, it seems to me, is not even slightly ill. It's escaped, soared away into the sky like an eagle, so not even a great puffy Bicentennial can squash it. The American Dream's become a worldwide dream, which makes me so happy and flushed with partly chauvinistic pride (it was our idea) that I sneak down into my basement and wave my flag.

People all over the world have decided they have a God- or Allah- or Buddha-given right to a more or less decent existence, here on earth, right now. To Richard II of England, who had the God-given right to kill any man he pleased, as long as he was English, and no questions asked (not even Chairman Mao can do that with impunity), or even to the noblemen who wrung from King John the over-famous Magna Carta, the "self-evident" idea of the American Founding Fathers would have seemed flat-out insanity.

That idea—humankind's inalienable right to life, liberty, and the pursuit of happiness—coupled with a system for protecting human rights—was and is the quintessential American Dream. The rest is greed and pompous foolishness—at worst, a cruel and sentimental myth, at best, cheap streamers in the rain.

Two great pseudopatriotic movements are gathering their coils to strike, these days, inspired by Bicentennial fervor. One is a movement to celebrate and canonize without mercy or thought all that's foul and mindless in the American heritage. (The serpent on the Right.) The other is a movement to "demythologize" those eighteenth-century heroes who've been foully, mindlessly adored, and supplant their myth with a new myth, America as trash. (The serpent on the Left.) I come, flag covertly waving, to expose those frauds—expose, I mean, both frauds.

When the Liberty Bell rang out victory for America's revolutionary forces (that "filthy rabble," as their Commander in Chief, George Washington, called them), the noise did not mean victory for the American Dream but only victory for those hoping to pursue it. The success of the idea of government "of the people, by the people, for the people," in Lincoln's phrase, meant in fact the success of government by *flawed* people—even, occasionally, *terrible* people—because there have never been, anywhere on earth, perfect human beings.

The first principle of American democracy is that, given the basic freedoms, majority rule is right even when it's wrong (as often happens), because it encourages free men to struggle as adversaries, using established legal means, to keep government working at the business of justice for all.

The theory was and is that if the majority causes too much pain to the minority, the minority will scream (with the help of a free press and the right of assembly) until the majority is badgered or shamed into changing its mind. To put it another way, most people are indifferent most of the time, and rightly so, to what government does; on any given issue, only those citizens who are really hurt, one way or another, are likely to write articles, make speeches, crowd in force to the polls, or set fires in taverns. (The most vulgar and unpatriotic thing you can do—worse even than putting on a three-cornered hat—is indiscriminately "get out the vote," making every citizen pull his voting-booth lever, whether or not he gives a damn.)

It's true that the system pretty frequently doesn't work. For decades, pollsters tell us, the American people favored gun control by three to one—law-enforcement officials have favored it by as much a nine to one—but powerful lobbies and cowardly politicians have easily thwarted the people's will. Nevertheless, the American democratic adversary system clearly beats kingship from across the Atlantic, and surely beats the system in modern China, which achieves efficiency and unanimity by the destruction of something like "sixty million bandits"—the entire Chinese middle class.

The grand promise of the American Revolution was that people here (except for slaves and women, who were legally defined as moderately subhuman) should have the right, guaranteed by law, to live, to be free, to struggle for happiness. Once that incredible promise was made, people everywhere began howling for their rights. The French, Russian, and Chinese Revolutions were direct results.

If none of these later revolutions was as successful as ours, the reason is that, for all its faults, the American system, pitting pressure group against pressure group (Nader and the consumer against Volkswagen, city against country, women against men) came close, at least sometimes, to keeping the revolutionary promise. Life, liberty, and the pursuit of happiness (as well as the flotsam of the American Dream, wealth, abundant sex, and the all-white neighborhood) took root in this country and flourished.

These are not the truths of the fast-food patriot, with his flag-cluttered placemats and idealized portraits. Someone has been telling that patriot lies. There was never unanimity. Hundreds of the wealthiest New Englanders shipped off, in 1775, for Canada and King George, and the Founding Fathers spent their whole lives fighting down citizens' revolts like the Farmers' Rebellion and the Whiskey Rebellion.

"Murder will out," as Chaucer wrote. That may be optimistic, but nevertheless it's a bad idea to tell sentimental lies about America's Founding Fathers.

George Washington was a man passionately devoted to a philosophical ideal, the notion of a society of reasonable men; but it is also true that he once got so angry at his soused, grubby, disorganized, noisily disrespectful troops that he stood stammering in rage, unable to speak, for a full thirty minutes.

Thomas Jefferson, the greatest idealist of them all, and a man who tried to make slavery unconstitutional, was nevertheless a slaveholder and, in all probability, a man tragically compromised by his love for "dusky Sally." There has always been such conflict. Abraham Lincoln, for all his good humor and lofty idealism, did not in fact free all the slaves, only the ones in the Confederacy.

It's right to demythologize those heroes, as long as we remember those rough, contradiction-filled idealists were, for their time and in some ways for any time, heroes. It's right to insist that when we talk about "the good old days"—when we gaze up in awe at those Yankee demigods—we should remind ourselves that it's partly illusion: Things were not as good then, and are not as bad now, as we sentimentally maintain. The American dream of justice for all is only an ideal—a thing we strive for and must continue to strive for but a thing we have never, at least so far, completely achieved.

But the myth of the mindless patriot is not worse than the myth of the cynic who speaks of America with an automatic sneer. Because America has committed crimes against humanity—against blacks and American Indians, against Mexicans (long before Chicanos were invented), and recently against some of the Vietnamese—mainly, it may be, the Vietnamese on our side—the cynic claims the American Dream was a lie from the beginning. If someone has been lying to the cream-puff patriot, someone has also been lying to the American left.

We believe in fairness, an American obsession, and our belief in fairness makes us cringe in embarrassment when any foreign government, no matter how repulsive, is compared unfavorably with our own. ("Well, we're not so perfect ourselves," we say. Which lets off *Uganda?*) The result is that we're sometimes inclined to forget, and our children may never hear, that our nation is one of the most decent this planet has ever known.

Comparisons may be odious, but it's important that we make them, now and then—quietly, not vulgar Bicentennial grandstands draped in bunting and half-naked girls. Only by making comparisons can we measure—or even notice—worth. Knee-jerk fairness, in fact, is unjust: Détente's all very well as a business proposition, but it need not imply that we've forgiven Russia for her tanks in Hungary, or China for the rape of Tibet.

The lie to the American left is this: that the American theory promised such-and-such and has sometimes not delivered, whereas We Deliver. The truth—a metaphysical truth, in fact—is that *nobody* delivers. Each group struggles, in whatever way it must, to achieve what is at least fair. Since unfortunately everyone wants more than what's fair, there's no foreseeable end to the struggle.

But the American system provides, at least as a visionary goal, fair and legal means of fighting. And fighting to capture or keep what we've learned to call our natural rights is what this country—and now all the world—is about.

The fight for the basic human freedoms is a continuing, intensely serious business, and theoretically at least, the occasion of America's Bicentennial might be a sensible time to pause and take stock of where we're coming from and where we're bound.

That's happening, to some extent. But serious discussion of what America has meant—and should mean more purely to future generations—is mostly drowned out by obscene commercial chatter about "America's 200th Birthday Party," with clowns and cupcakes, rock-and-roll versions of "The Star-Spangled Banner," and a trashy-carnival eyesore of a train which carries authentic documents and a simulation of the "historic" baseball Hank Aaron hit.

A hundred years ago, at the time of the Centennial—and the Reconstruction—no one had the nerve to have a Birthday Party. America was in trouble, as an honest democracy always is. They let the great occasion slide and got on with the labor of trying to fix things, each group putting the screws on every other, insisting it had certain inalienable rights, struggling (to some extent by legal means) for life, liberty, and the pursuit of happiness.

It's a tedious and fairly discouraging process, and in the days of Reconstruction, as we all now admit, it was a ghastly failure and a colossal bore—not at all like watching some grocer fall off his horse while galloping hell-for-leather down a roped-off highway, playing Paul Revere.

But the jockeying for rights, the continual process of trying to make things fairer—despite such impediments as drunken Congressmen and bawling mobs, despite the sly drone of the unspeakable rich and the penchant for murder in the innocent, blue-eyed Central Intelligence Agency—in short, the as-yet-unabandoned pursuit of the dream of liberty and justice for all, is a thing worth sneaking down cellar and waving a flag at.

JR

W E MAY EXPECT THAT SUCH A LONG AND
long-awaited book as *JR* will fall into one of two categories: either
some work intellectually and emotionally gargantuan, like *Don Quixote*,
War and Peace, *Remembrance of Things Past*, or *The Magic Mountain*,
or else some huge and magnificent, generous, ingenious, and memorable
entertainment, like *Our Mutual Friend* or *Old Wives' Tale*. If one judged
by the reviews that have appeared so far, one would imagine *JR* to
be the former kind of work: obscure and full of boomings, perhaps
even a true work of genius, which normally means pretentiously exclusive, turgidly self-indulgent, and awesomely unreadable, like *Finnegans
Wake*. According to George Steiner in *The New Yorker* (and there are
signs that Gaddis would like to think it's true), *JR* is indeed that fashionable monster "the unreadable book." Steiner scornfully quotes some
passages, and to anyone who hasn't read *JR*, they're persuasive. But
if one *has* read the novel, one can only hop on one foot, spluttering
in confusion and rage (like young JR), yelling "Crazy! holy shit!"—
because Steiner's right in a way. *JR* is, finally, bad art, but despite what
Steiner thinks, it's wonderfully and easily readable.

Except for the last two hundred pages or so, where the novel takes
a turn toward rant—filling the reader with an indignation he would
never feel at a writer's betrayal of some lesser fiction—*JR* is a delightful,

large and various, technically brilliant entertainment. But it is also false, in the end, because the novel's self-righteous, emotionally uncontrolled last movement poisons what went before it, casting suspicion on what seemed at first basically generous and fair-minded, genially satiric or justly sardonic.

In all fairness, Gaddis was apparently uneasy about bringing out *JR*. One of the characters in his novel wails, talking of his own difficult, long-unfinished book:

> —Sixteen years like living with a God damned invalid sixteen years every time you come in sitting there waiting just like you left him wave his stick at you, plump up his pillow cut a paragraph add a sentence hold his God damned hand little warm milk add a comma slip out for some air pack of cigarettes come back in right where you left him, eyes follow you around the room wave his God damned stick figure out what the hell he wants, plump the God damned pillow change bandage read aloud move a clause around wipe his chin new paragraph. . .

And a little later in the same monologue:

> —God damned friends getting indignant tell you bring him out, tell you bring him out like he is a little crippled maybe don't give a God damn, quick and dirty just dress him up a little bring him out anyhow go back waiting, plump the God damned pillow move a clause around. . .

Well, the invalid *JR* is out, more than a little crippled, though the trouble comes not from any faltering of clauses but from deeper forms of moral and aesthetic confusion.

For five hundred pages, give or take a few, Gaddis tells a crazy but interesting, tightly plotted story full of fascinating characters and caricatures, all of them more or less outrageous but viewed sympathetically or with comic detachment. The plot is implausible, and meant to be, shot through with coincidence and misunderstanding as in an old-time farce. But the tone is always right, and as in all good farce the characters are sufficiently rounded to make the foolishness important. And anyway,

Gaddis is going for meaning in Ben Jonson's way, not Aristotle's. Events—however comically jerked around, however blatantly staged by the novelist-trickster—force values and ideas into collision. This is of course a technique that only works if the novelist has the sense to take no side, or at least to take none openly, and indeed for something like five hundred pages Gaddis does take no side.

True, he mimics the language of so-called educators, bankers, Wall Street brokers, PR men, and the like; and true, the reader generally sides with the artists in this novel mostly about money versus art; but on the whole, the language and activities of the artists are as comic as anything the moneymen say or do. Both artists and moneymen can be clever or stupid, generous or selfish; and in two of the novel's symbolically focal characters, the sixth-grader JR and his composer friend Bast, the two inclinations—money versus art—are mixed. (To a greater or lesser extent, they're mixed in all the characters.)

It's obviously impossible to summarize the plot of an intricately plotted, concisely written, intelligent, and enormously compressed work of fiction that runs 726 pages; yet since Gaddis wastes nothing, neither actions nor words—since here as in *The Recognitions* everything hangs on repetitions, parallels, juxtapositions, mirror images—the plot must somehow be suggested. Very well then, this: One plot concerns a school where the chief administrative official, Mr. Whiteback, is also a banker and has his bank phone (among others) on his desk. He deals in PR, educational machinery, politics, and finance, and has terrible worries about meddlesome taxpayers, elderly citizens (who watch, in horror, his school's "packages" on TV), teachers, and students. He and his toadies speak a wonderful gibberish—"tangibilitize our goals"—and books, for him, are always quite naturally and rightly the first things to go.

Among his mad teachers are a scientist-technician who makes machinery lively by making it sound like sex; two struggling artists—Edward Bast, composer, and Jack Gibbs, novelist—who make more trouble, for others and themselves, than art; and beautiful Amy Joubert, daughter of a brilliant and vicious Wall Street broker. All the characters who are old enough are either falling in love, miserably married, or fighting for divorce.

The trouble begins—or some of it—when Amy Joubert takes her sixth-grade class, including our more-or-less hero JR, to Wall Street to "buy a share in America," that is, buy a few dollars' worth of some miserable, foundering stock. Half by brilliance, half by luck, JR, who has partly the soul of an artist (also sneakers, a runny nose), turns that stock—without consulting Mrs. Joubert or the class—into an empire. He is ambitious, generous, and humane; but the results are bad. To free his friend Bast to write music as he'd like (though JR has not the slightest understanding of music), and because Bast, in turn, can help JR with his schemes, JR makes timid, always well-meaning Bast the company's one visible executive (JR is, himself, too young to show his face) and thus accidentally drowns Bast in laborious trivia, throws his life into even more than usual chaos, and unwittingly forces the composer to write music he hates. JR's energetic idealism—along with other forces—has further bad results: a suicide, some murders, some careers destroyed, some deaths by economic pressure—above all the debasement of JR himself.

JR's moral ruin is one of the few things still moving in the novel's diabolical, dogmatic close. JR, who has tried to free Bast for composition, who has also tried, at least in his own view (partly rationalization), to advance not only himself but also the stockholders and workers in the companies he buys, is trying to catch up with outraged, sick, and demoralized Bast—JR tripping on the laces of his sneakers, calling to Bast through sleet and darkness, half-furious, half-crying, defending the change of policy he's imposed on a recently acquired FM station:

> —Look is it my fault if this here symphony takes like half an hour to play it! And I mean you say cheapen [Bast has accused JR of cheapening and debasing all he touches] boy this whole deal it's like two million dollars in it and I mean like who wanted to buy their lousy station anyway! I mean this here Pomerance's agency they go around there for us where all we want is like this one hour a night to get our message acrost so they tell us how much and then they get real snotty and say they still control the program content which that's these here symphonies and all so I mean how many messages are you supposed to get acrost in this here hour where it takes this band half of it to play this one symphony for these here people which aren't hungry where this other crap takes like three minutes each, I mean what do I care what they play there! Like we're paying them for this here whole

hour aren't we? I mean if they could get through these here symphonies in like five minutes where we're getting this bunch of messages in we're paying for I mean what do I care what they play! I mean who's paying them to play all this here great music these people which aren't hungry like at Russia? where the government makes everybody listen to it? Like I mean this here station it's losing so much money it can't hardly last anyway so I mean we have to buy it to help them out I mean what am I suppose to do!

Everyone in the novel howls about or suffers the unfairness of things—finally the unfairness of an unbalanced universe (as the novelist manqué Jack Gibbs points out), not merely the good and evil in capitalism. That vision, if Gaddis had been true to it, might have made *JR* a fine novel.

The intricate, seriocomic plot, the glorious plethora of vividly imagined characters, and the bite of the social criticism could have set *JR* on a level with the best of Dickens. And these leave out of account the brilliance of technique. Gaddis introduces the reader by easy stages to his method, narrative through dialogue. He opens the novel with a classical scene from farce, two dotty, chattering old ladies and their frustrated lawyer. Notice how quickly, guided almost exclusively by dialogue, one catches on to the comic characters and situation:

> —Money. . .? in a voice that rustled.
> —Paper, yes.
> —And we'd never seen it. Paper money.
> —We never saw paper money till we came east.
> —It looked so strange the first time we saw it. Lifeless.
> —You couldn't believe it was worth a thing.
> —Not after Father jingling his change.
> —Those were silver dollars.
> —And silver halves, yes and quarters, Julia. The ones from his pupils. I can hear him now. . .
> Sunlight, pocketed in a cloud, spilled suddenly broken across the floor through the leaves of the trees outside.
> —Coming up the veranda, how he jingled when he walked.

—He'd have his pupils rest the quarters that they brought him on the backs of their hands when they did their scales. He charged fifty cents a lesson, you see, Mister. . .

—Coen, without the *h*. Now if both you ladies. . .

—Why, it's just like that story about father's dying wish to have his bust sunk in Vancouver harbor, and his ashes sprinkled on the water there, about James and Thomas out in the rowboat, and both of them hitting at the bust with their oars because it was hollow and wouldn't go down, and the storm coming up while they were out there, blowing his ashes back into their beards. . .

Thus by half the first page, Gaddis has his themes going (art, money, education, and value), his heightened, comic reality established, and the voices of his characters carrying the story. He can do nearly anything with voices. Characters who appear for only a moment (a crazy rock musician, a train conductor) become solid presences, and slapstick events (people stepping on one another's toes, comically symbolic) are made instantly vivid through dialogue alone. The wit seems inexhaustible—in the farcically symbolic names, for instance: Bast, phloem, related to Greek *phallos*, and short for bastard (child of opposing values), and a cheated African leader named Nowunda, to mention only two. A marvelous novel for pages and pages—one frequently laughs aloud—and then something goes awry.

Dark satire is not an easy literary game. Melville managed it in *The Confidence-Man*; Swift managed it several times; so did Ben Jonson. It requires active control over the reader's outrage—otherwise the satire turns to melodrama. Gaddis is fine while the satire remains light; but in the later pages of the book he is determined to go dark—black-hearted and terrible as Swift, or Melville at his angriest. It's a worthy enough ambition, but he fails to pull it off. He gradually seems to distrust his material, begins to force it, loses his ironic detachment, gets too angry. Feeling life's pressure as Jack Gibbs might say, Gaddis stops studying the invalid to discover what it needs, begins, instead, to ram down pills, demanding that the invalid get up, try to walk. The wildly cluttered mail- and machinery-filled office where Bast tries, comically, to work, begins to be unfunny, especially after Jack Gibbs moves in, trying to write his novel.

Everything begins to be the fault of the moneymen, a crass world's stupid imposition on intelligent and decent artists. Bast has in a sense deserved his troubles; through weakness and misguided gentleness he went along with JR's schemes; but Gibbs is not to blame for the fool- ishness all around him, keeping him from work—JR's phone calls and mail, the sponging of fake artists, his estranged wife's viciousness. We begin to hear more often, at higher and higher pitches, the novel's refrain line, "believing and shitting are two different things"; and though Gaddis makes an effort to keep the forces balanced—Bast's "father," a musical conductor, was as selfish and unloving as Amy Joubert's father, a Wall Street broker—the balance is at best intellectual. Bast and Gibbs become simply sentimental victims.

The mask falls, the writer is mad as hell. Whereas Gaddis could earlier legitimately jerk his plot around, since he was then still faithful to his characters' emotions and ideas (however lunatic), his piling up of coincidence aims now at driving home a skewed, self-righteous argu- ment: true artists "believe," false artists and moneymen (the two can be the same) merely "shit."

Jack Gibbs speaks of the values of true art, and Bast explains them, more or less, to JR when he tells the boy that in listening to true music one is raised to selflessness: "you weren't supposed [i.e., expected or required] to hear anything. . ." True art one sees or hears with one's own godly, dispassionate, and compassionate eyes and ears. (The Wall Street broker, Amy Joubert's father, sees and hears with eyes and ears that are transplants. His wife says of him, quite rightly, that he should be declared null and void.) True art, to put it another way—Bast's way—never plays to win.

But Gaddis himself plays to win. Despite all he knows, Gaddis joins the enemy he himself has identified: he manipulates, brays, whines, refuses to risk writing the book Jack Gibbs at one point says he would like to write, one that boldly runs the risk of being misunderstood. This charge is a hard one to prove, short of a line-by-line analysis of the last two hundred pages, but some of the ways in which Gaddis overloads his argument can be perhaps suggested.

When Bast has been all but crushed by catastrophes largely brought on by money people and phony artists, we get a scene in which, feverish and delirious after a train ride and painful conversation with JR, Bast talks with the lawyer, Coen. Bast rambles, echoing one of the novel's refrain lines after another, page after page—his father's line, "believing and shitting are two different things," several lines spoken earlier by other characters, especially lines spoken by JR, "Not pissed off at me are you. . .?" "I mean why is everybody always getting mad at me?" "Get to start over right?" and so on.

The scene is unconvincing, for two reasons. First, delirious speech, like dreams, can rarely be made convincing in fiction: either the character speaks nonsense, which is convincing but boring, or we feel the authorial manipulation. And second, refrain lines in fiction always have a special emotional charge, and when touching, symbolic, or otherwise significant refrain lines are presented page after page, one after another, the reader can react in only one of two ways, with strong sympathetic emotion (because the poetry has worked) or with revulsion (because the writer's attempt at poetic effect has failed). In this scene, the writer's manipulation is painfully obvious, and can only have one purpose, to bully the reader into feeling pity for Bast and (to some extent) JR, and make him hate all those wicked capitalists.

People are not very loving in the world of William Gaddis. The generous reader can imagine JR as a young man who, though he uses people, does honestly intend to do them good at the same time, so that the fact that his work has the opposite effect is no proof of malevolence. Gaddis sets up that possibility, but he doesn't seem to believe in it. Notice how misanthropically he rigs things. The music teacher, Bast, forces JR to listen to a snippet of Bach's twenty-first cantata. Almost violently (because of his feverish condition) Bast demands that JR tell him what he's heard. JR answers literally and according to his lights:

—Okay okay! I mean what I heard first there's all this high music right? So then this here lady starts singing up yours up yours so then this man starts singing up mine, then there's some words so she starts singing up mine up mine so he starts singing up yours so then they go back and forth like that up mine up yours up mine up yours that's what I heard! I mean you want me to hear it again?

Bast raves in furious righteous indignation—and because he forces it, the voice seems not Bast's, but mainly Gaddis's own—and eventually says, in answer to JR's "is it my fault if. . ."

—The minute you get your hands on something the power to keep something like that going [the FM classical station] you couldn't do it you couldn't even leave it alone for a few people still looking for something beautiful, people who'd rather hear a symphony than eat who can still, who hear a magnificent soprano voice singing ach nein when you hear this here lady singing up mine you can't get up to their level so you drag them down to yours if there's any way to ruin something, to degrade it to cheapen it . . .

It is true that JR cheapens things—his favorite expression is "holy shit" (often repeated pay-off to the often repeated tag-line, "believing and shitting are two different things")—but it is also true that JR is an eager, energetic student, by no means stupid, and none of the supposedly enlightened people in the novel has made the slightest effort to teach him anything at all—with one exception, Amy Joubert, who fails because she makes sentimental mistakes. Bast and Gibbs, and others of their kind, are so cynical, arrogant, criminally self-centered, and cheaply enraged at "mechanization" and other modern evils that they never notice for an instant that a student like JR might need them. No evidence anywhere suggests that Gaddis thinks them wrong in this regard.

Except for his inarticulate ranting and raving at the end, Bast gives only one lecture in the course of the novel: asked to deliver a TV lecture on Mozart, and given an idiotic script which speaks of the composer as "this little Peter Pan of music who never really grew up" and so forth, Bast departs from the script, vituperatively mocking the script in his hands and whining about the victimization of artists by the rich and crass—never recalling for a moment that he is being listened to by people who might learn something from him.

Still reading from the script Bast says: "His wife's name Constanze means constancy, and she was constant to her dear childlike husband all the rest of his"—then Bast begins to stumble, furious—"of his, his cheap coffin in the rain that . . ." Now Bast goes crazy:

> —the um, constant yes she, she constantly spent what little money they had on luxuries and she, she was constantly pregnant and she, finally she was constantly sick so you can see why she, why Mozart burst into tears when he married her.

He was always the, this little darling of the gods [the script earlier translated Amadeus] he'd supported his whole family since he was a child being dragged around by his father and shown off like a, like a little freak...

And after more rant,

and oh yes this mysterious stranger dressed all in gray who Mozart thought was a messenger of death, it was really just a messenger from a crackbrain count named Walsegg who wanted to hire Mozart to, and then pretend he'd written it himself. What else could Mozart do? He's sick, worn out, used up, he's only about thirty-five and he's been supporting everybody in sight for thirty years...

Well, you will say, artists are temperamental. (Gaddis returns as if obsessively to van Gogh's chopped-off ear, conveniently forgetting a number of things as, above, he forgets Mozart's kidneys.) But temperamental or not, Bast has shown only contempt for JR and his fellow students, and given them nothing. Or worse: he has presented the artist as a weakling and financial sucker who ought to get his silly wife in line and start entering his checks. This does not, of course, prove Bast a bad artist—he's the book's one survivor. But since Gaddis seems to side with Bast, it leaves the reader with a legitimate objection: how are the values Bast drubs JR for not possessing to be passed on?

Though I've pointed to signs of it—the writer's manipulation of a delirious character, and the writer's attack on so-called educators whom he hates without noticing the failure of those he approves—it's not possible to prove here that Gaddis loads the dice. But page after page through the novel's last movement, the reader gets a stronger and stronger sense of the writer tilting the machine, not following the argument to see where it leads or where the characters want to go, forcing, bullying, like a trial lawyer or a Marxist in debate with an innocent.

One leaves the novel, or anyway I do, annoyed and frustrated, wishing that Gaddis might have been less arrogant in his scorn of all things crass and more in favor of the artist's pursuit of truth—wishing that he might have abandoned his own fierce and fashionable prejudices (which every reader he gets will share anyway) for the sake of learning what would make the invalid whole and well, a wise and balanced work. It is easier to imitate Proust the bitchy man than to imitate his careful and judicious art, easier to imitate Poe as Griswold understood him, or Beethoven as all but his best friends understood him, or Goethe the real-life monster, than it is to do justice to their full and finally humane vision.

Jack Gibbs, the character closest to Gaddis himself, is at work on a virtually endless book about art and mechanization. He takes pride in his knowledge that his book will not "communicate," that is, it will be full of big words, hard to read. When another character remarks that the book sounds "difficult," Gibbs says smugly, "Difficult as I can make it." One is reminded of the remark William Gass made not long ago (in Joe David Bellamy's *The New Fiction: Interviews with Innovative American Writers*): "I began *The Tunnel* in 1966. I imagine it is several years away yet. Who knows, perhaps it will be such a good book no one will want to publish it. I live on that hope." The difference is that for a man as conscious of nuance as is Gass—a man preternaturally sensitive to language, and a master humorist when he chooses to be—the rhetorical *I live on that hope* can only be comic self-mockery, a joke at the expense of exactly that posturing misanthropy which seems to lesser men the proper mark of genius, and which ruins Gaddis's book. It pays, of course, that scornful sneer; people love to be told everything stinks. It sounds so intelligent.

The Acts
of King Arthur
and His Noble Knights

W HEN JOHN STEINBECK WAS AT WORK ON
his *The Acts of King Arthur and His Noble Knights* in the middle and
late 1950s, he hoped it would be "the best work of my life and the
most satisfying." Even in its original form, the project was enormous—
translation of the complete *Morte d'Arthur* of Sir Thomas Malory;
and the project soon became still more difficult, not translation but
a complete retelling—rethinking—of the myth. Steinbeck finished only
some 293 uncorrected, unedited pages, perhaps one-tenth of the original. Even so, the book Steinbeck's friend and editor Chase Horton
has put together is large and important. It is in fact two books, Steinbeck's mythic fiction on King Arthur's court, and a fat, rich collection
of letters exchanged between Steinbeck, Horton and Elizabeth Otis,
Steinbeck's agent. The first is an incomplete but impressive work of
art; the second, the complete story of a literary tragedy—how Steinbeck
found his way, step by step, from the idea of doing a "translation"
for boys to the idea of writing fabulist fiction in the mid-1950s, when
realism was still king.

Part of the story told by the letters is Steinbeck's discovery that
the *Morte d'Arthur* is a great and difficult work of art. He had expected
to translate from Caxton and expected the work would go very fast, but
when he dipped into the more authentic, recently published Winchester

manuscript, longer and linguistically much more difficult, he quickly discovered "lovely nuances in the Winchester which have been removed by Caxton" and, eventually, real and deep mysteries in the work. As he puts it in one letter, "Somewhere there's a piece missing in the jigsaw." Steinbeck became fascinated, began to work much more slowly and carefully—as well he might, since virtually all he had available was Eugene Vinaver's superbly edited text. No critic had yet shown the coherence and overall structure of the *Morte d'Arthur*, and as for the light biography might throw on Malory's epic, Prof. William Matthews had not yet published his evidence that scholars were studying the wrong Sir Thomas Malory—that is, studying not the educated aristocrat kept in genteel house arrest, surrounded by his books, but the rapist, church-robber and thug by the same name. Steinbeck soon realized that, as he puts it in one letter, he "must write the writer as well as the *Morte*." He stopped translating and began studying still harder, soaking up the Middle Ages, trying to get a clear impression of the writer he must make up.

By January 9, 1957, when he writes to Chase Horton, Steinbeck is reading slowly. "I literally move my lips." He has a meeting set up with "Adams of the P.M. Library" and with Dr. Buhler "whose name you will know from his Medieval and Renaissance work." He's read history and critical books and pored over Malory and is "getting many glimmerings" but is still holding fire. By August 7, 1957, he has met repeatedly with Vinaver, has inspected Caxton's first printing at the Rylands Library in Manchester, has visited many of the places associated with the Arthur legend, and can speak of what he still calls his translation as the largest and most important work he has ever undertaken. By July 7, 1958, he can speak of "the hundreds of books bought, rented and consulted, of the microfilms of manuscripts unavailable for study, of the endless correspondence with scholars in the field, and finally the two trips to England and one to Italy. . ." By April 9, 1959, he is learning to make medieval axes ("With the old axe you can practically carve wood because of the small area of impact") and carving kitchen spoons out of oak.

Some of the most interesting passages in the letters have to do with translation in the highest sense. At one point, having studied the beauty of Malory's language and feeling something like contempt for his own and the language of his fellow modern writers, Steinbeck swears off even letter writing. "I want to forget how to write and learn all over again with the writing growing out of the material. And I'm going to be real mean about that" (October 25, 1957). Later, more optimistic now, he says of American English:

> This is a highly complicated and hugely communicative language. It has been used in dialogues, in cuteness and perhaps by a few sports writers. It has also been used by a first person telling a story but I don't think it has been used as a legitimate literary language.

And a moment afterward:

> The American language is a new thing under the sun. It can combine all the erudition of which I am capable with the communication of our own time. It is not cute nor is it regional. The frames have grown out of ourselves but have used everything that was there before. But most of all it has an ease and a flow and a tone and a rhythm which is unique in the world. There is no question where it comes from, its references, its inventions, its overtones grew out of this continent and out of our twenty generations here. It is English basically but manured and seeded with Negro, Indian, Italian, Spanish, Yiddish, German, but so mixed and fermented that something whole has emerged.

The sentiment sounds old and familiar, but as Steinbeck means it I think it is not (though Walt Whitman understood it). The point is not that when we drop into American we feel a slight impulse to put it in quotes (as in "drop into American") but the plain American might be *assumed* to have grandeur and nobility and so used, so that it might express for us, without apology, what we do in fact respect. Steinbeck ends this particular meditation on language with a brilliant metaphor: "My looking is not for a dead Arthur but for one sleeping. And if sleeping, he is sleeping everywhere, not alone in a cave in Cornwall."

At about the same time he came to see Malory's full relevance to our times. Steinbeck writes:

Malory lived in as rough and ruthless and corrupt an age as the world has ever produced. In the *Morte* he in no way minimizes these things, the cruelty and lust, the murder and childlike self-interest. . . But he does not let them put out the sun. Side by side with them are generosity and courage and greatness and the huge sadness of tragedy rather than the little meanness of frustration. . . There is nothing in literature nastier than Arthur's murder of children because one of them may grow up to kill him. [Many writers] would stop there, saying "That's the way it is." And they would never get to the heartbreaking glory when Arthur meets his fate and fights against it and accepts it all in one. How can we have forgotten so much?

Steinbeck is well beyond translation now. In March 1959, he writes to his agent that his work is "no more a translation than Malory's was." He writes more and more surely about what he is doing and his excitement in the work. Then he sends his agent the first section of the manuscript.

The letter collection does not include Elizabeth Otis's reaction, but clearly she was troubled by what she read. Steinbeck's answer is formal, careful, polite. In apparent response to something she has said, he praises T. H. White's delightful piece of cotton candy, *The Once and Future King*, but tells her he wants to write "a permanent book." A few days later he writes sadly, "I am moved by your letter with the implied trust in something you don't much like," then, still later, "As for my own work—I am completely dissatisfied with it." And the project dies.

Steinbeck's Arthurian fiction is indeed "strange and different," as he put it. The fact that he lacked the heart to finish the book, or even put what he did complete into one style and tone, is exactly the kind of petty modern tragedy he hated. The idea was magnificent—so is much of the writing—though we see both the idea and the writing changing as they go. In the early pages he follows Malory fairly closely, merely simplifying and here and there adding explanation for the modern young reader.

As he warms to his work, Steinbeck uses Malory more freely, cutting deeply, expanding generously. In the passage on Merlin's defeat by

Nyneve he writes like a man retelling a story from his childhood, interpreting as he pleases and echoing hardly a line. Merlin tells King Arthur
what he must guard against and says he, Merlin, must go to his doom.
Arthur is astonished that the wizard would go to his doom willingly,
but Merlin does so nonetheless, because, as he says, "in the combat
between wisdom and feeling, wisdom never wins" (Steinbeck's addition). He travels off with the young woman he loves, fated and knowing it. With only an occasional glance at his source—sixteen cool lines
(in tight modern English they could be written in three)—but keeping
the formal old sound, for the most part, Steinbeck writes:

> Nyneve was bored and restless and she left Ban's court with
> Merlin panting after her, begging her to lie with him and stanch
> his yearning, but she was weary of him, and impatient with an
> old man as a damsel must be, and also she was afraid of him
> because he was said to be the Devil's son, but she could not
> be rid of him, for he followed her, pleading and whimpering.
>
> Then Nyneve, with the inborn craft of maidens, began to
> question Merlin about his magic arts, half promising to trade
> her favors for his knowledge. And Merlin, with the inborn
> helplessness of men, even though he foresaw her purpose, could
> not forebear to teach her. And as they crossed back to England
> and rode slowly from the coast of Cornwall, Merlin showed
> her many wonders, and when at last he found that he inter-
> ested her, he showed her how the magic was accomplished
> and put in her hands the tools of enchantment, gave her the
> antidotes of magic, and finally, in his aged folly, taught her
> those spells which cannot be broken by any means. And when
> she clapped her hands in maidenly joy, the old man, to please
> her, created a room of unbelievable wonders under a great
> rock cliff, and with his crafts he furnished it with comfort
> and richness and beauty to be the glorious apartment for the
> consummation of their love. And they two went through a
> passage in the rock to the room of wonders, hung with gold
> and lighted with many candles. Merlin stepped in to show
> it to her, but Nyneve leaped back and cast the awful spell
> that cannot be broken by any means, and the passage closed
> and Merlin was trapped inside for all time to come.

Here there are still Malorian elements—sentences beginning with "Then" and "And," formulaic repetitions, archaic diction—but all the rest is modern. For instance, it is novelistic, not mythic, to speak of Merlin's "panting," "pleading and whimpering," or of "the inborn craft of maidens" and "the inborn helplessness of men," novelistic to speak of riding *slowly* from the coast of Cornwall (a quick touch of verisimilitude), novelistic to show Nyneve clapping her hands with pleasure, or later, leaping back. By the time Steinbeck reached "The Noble Tale of Sir Lancelot of the Lake," he had his method in full control. He makes authorial comments of a sort only a novelist would risk, cuts pages by the fistful, and at the same time embellishes Malory's spare legend with a richness of detail that transforms the vision, makes it no one but Steinbeck's. Here is a passage with no real source in the original:

> A man like Lancelot, tempered in soldiery, seasoned and tanned by perils, lays up supplies of sleep as he does food or water, knowing its lack will reduce his strength and dull his mind. And although he had slept away part of the day, the knight retired from cold and darkness and the unknown morrow and entered a dreamless rest and remained in it until a soft light began to grow in his cell of naked stone. Then he awakened and wrung his muscles free of cold cramp and again embraced his knees for warmth. He could see no source of light. It came equally from everywhere as dawn does before the rise of the sun. He saw the mortared stones of his cell stenciled with patches of dark slime. And as he looked, designs formed on the walls: formal rounded trees covered with golden fruit and curling vines with flowers as frankly invented as are those of an illuminated book, a benign sheltering tree, and under it a unicorn glowing white, with horn and neck lowered in salute to a maiden of bright needlework who embraced the unicorn, thus proving her maidenhood. Then a broad soft bed shivered and grew substantial in the corner of the cell...

There is nothing at all like this in Malory. What we have here is myth newly imagined, revitalized, charged with contemporary meaning, the kind of thing we expect of the best so-called post-modernists, writers like John Barth. Steinbeck creates a lifelike Lancelot, a veteran soldier who knows his business (how to grab sleep when you can and so on); shows, in quick realistic strokes, how the soldier wakes up, wrings his muscles against cold and cramp; and how magic starts to happen to this cool, middle-aged realist. The falsity of the magic is emphatic—"as frankly invented as [the designs in] an illuminated book."

The paragraph encapsulates Steinbeck's whole purpose at this stage—a purpose close to Malory's yet utterly transformed—to show in the manner of a fabulator how plain reality is transformed by magic, by the lure of visions that ennoble though they ultimately betray. It's a theme we've encountered before in Steinbeck, but a theme that has here the simplicity and power of myth.

The Acts of King Arthur and His Noble Knights is unfortunately not Steinbeck's greatest book, but as Steinbeck knew, until doubt overcame him, it was getting there.

Lancelot

THANKS TO *THE MOVIEGOER*, *THE LAST Gentleman* and *Love in the Ruins*, readers have come to expect a good deal of Walker Percy. His virtues, in this age of mostly terrible fiction, are notable. Though he cares about plot and character, making fictions that easily translate into movies, he is a serious, even moderately philosophical novelist not at all ashamed of his seriousness. Nor should he be: the familiar philosophical questions he raises, and his ways of raising them, are as interesting as his characters and plots, or anyway they would be if he had any idea of how to answer them. He cares about technique, enough so that—as is often the case in the very best fiction—technique is one of the things we watch with interest, though here sometimes with dismay. He's clever, witty, efficient, concerned, and his fictions pass one of the two or three most important aesthetic tests: they're memorable. All this I say without much reservation, which is to say I think he's a novelist people ought to read, as they will anyway, since he's caught on.

Lancelot is the story of a man, Lancelot Andrews Lamar, who, after years of happy marriage, learns that his beautiful, voluptuous wife has been unfaithful to him. The wife is Texas rich, low-born, a bad movie actress, originally attracted to Lancelot because he is of an old Louisiana family, owner of a huge declining mansion. She took on his class as she takes on accents. From the beginning there was no hope that she would be faithful. Out of his disappointment and jealousy—and out of his sophisticated modern sense that perhaps there are no evil acts, no good acts either, only acts of sickness, on one hand, and acts flowing from unrecognized self-interest, on the other—Lancelot turns his wife's sexual betrayal into a central philosophical mystery. Question: Is all good mere illusion?—in which case, seemingly, there can be no God—or can we at least affirm that evil exists, so that (as Ivan Karamazov saw) we see God by His shadow? This question sets off Lancelot Lamar's "quest," as he tells his old school chum, now father-confessor, Percival. (The whole novel is Lancelot's "confession," though it reads like writing, not speech.) Lancelot says, "We've spoken of the Knights of the Holy Grail, Percival. But do you know what I was? The Knight of the Unholy Grail. In times like these when everyone is wonderful, what is needed is a quest for evil." A good start for a philosophical novel. One begins to read more eagerly.

In his pursuit of evil, Lancelot first tries voyeurism, making absolutely certain of what he already knows, that his wife—and nearly everyone around him—is betraying all traditional values, turning life to garbage. Predictably the proofs do not satisfy, and Lancelot takes the next step. He turns himself into a monster to find out how evil feels—if it feels like anything. Even as he commits his most terrible crime, Lancelot feels nothing, so for him as for Nietzsche there can be no such thing as good or evil in the Christian sense, only strength, on one hand, and, on the other, "milksopiness."

The events that dramatize Lancelot's transformation are typical of the Southern gothic novel at its best, grotesque but sufficiently convincing to be chilling. They flow from the potential of character and situation with deadly inevitability, supported by brilliant descriptions of place and weather—the climax comes during a hurricane, or rather two hurricanes, one real, one faked by a film crew—and supported by the kind of intelligence, insight and wit that make the progress of the novel delightful as well as convincing. A quick example: Lancelot's huge Louisiana mansion is full of people who are making a typically stupid modern movie about, in fact, promiscuity as freedom. Nearly all of them are slightly crazy, in the way many movie people really are, and Lancelot, eagerly on the watch for evil, catches precisely what's wrong with these new Californians. On the night of the hurricane, one of them, an actress called Raine, talks mystically about "fields of force":

> "I feel the convergence of all our separate minds of force. Can't you feel something changed in the air between all of us?"
> "Well . . ."
> "There's a force field around all of us, waxing and waning," said Raine absently, suddenly waning herself, losing interest. She spoke a little more, but inattentively.
> "Maybe you're right, Raine." I could never figure out the enthusiasm of movie folks. It was as if they were possessed fitfully by demons, but demons of a very low order to whom one needn't pay strict attention.

I've said that technique is one of the things one watches with interest as one reads *Lancelot*. Percy uses, throughout the novel, the conventional device of regular rotation from motif to motif, incrementally building toward the dramatic and intellectual climax. Lancelot tells, for a while, the story of his wife's unfaithfulness, then breaks off to speak of Elgin, the brilliant young black who turns out to be, in effect, a modern slave (without a moral second thought he covertly films the novel's betrayals for his "master"), then shifts to talk of Anna, the raped girl in the hospital room next door—the true "new woman," Lancelot thinks, violated back into innocence—then turns to direct address to his silent confessor, Percival, then to elaborating one or another of the novel's central symbols, or to wonderful rant on what's wrong with the modern world. All this is well done, and the rant—much of it true, some if it intentionally crazy—gives the novel rhetorical oomph. For instance, Lancelot rails at his confessor:

> Don't speak to me of Christian love! Whatever came of it? I'll tell you what came of it. It got mouthed off on the radio and TV from the pulpit and that was the end of it. The Jews knew better. Billy Graham lay down with Nixon and got up with a different set of fleas, but the Jewish prophets lived in deserts and wildernesses and had no part with corrupt kings. I'll prophesy: This country is going to turn into a desert and it won't be a bad thing. Thirst and hunger are better than

jungle rot. We will begin in the Wilderness where Lee lost.
Deserts are clean places. Corpses turn quickly into simple pure
chemicals.

Convinced that Percival's meek Christianity and faith can have no
effect and incensed, rightly, by the modern world's obscenity—summed
up in the trashy illusions of the film maker, Merlin—Lancelot decides,
slipping into madness, to start up, somehow, a new revolution and,
like Christ Triumphant, either purify the world or destroy it utterly.
We're encouraged to believe that he and others like him might really
pull it off. He's a competent murderer. Lancelot's decision is not quite
firm, however. He would like to be answered by his priest-confessor,
though faith, we're told, has never been sufficient to answer reason.
Percy is content to leave it at that. He suggests in his final line that
some answer is possible, but he doesn't risk giving it to Percival. Certainly no answer can be deduced from the novel except Kierkegaard's
consciously unreasonable "leap of faith"—a blind, existential affirmation of the logically insensible Christian faith. But surely everyone
must know by now that Kierkegaard's answer is stupid and dangerous.
Why Abraham's leap of faith and not Hitler's? Lancelot himself makes
that point.

The reader has come all this way in critical goodwill—ignoring
Percy's errors of scientific and mythic fact, though important arguments
hang on them (human females are by no means, as Percy thinks, the
only ones that make love face-to-face, and Malory's Guinevere was
by no means indifferent to the betrayal). And from interest in the story
and argument the reader has put up, too, with quite gross aesthetic
mistakes on Percy's part. Even granting the funny way Southerners
name their children, the allegory is too obviously contrived; it distracts
us from drama to mere message. Also, as I've said, the "confession"
sounds written, not spoken—a bad fault, since it shows that the writer
is not serious about creating a fictional illusion but is after only a moderately successful "vehicle," like the occasions of Chairman Mao's verse.

From interest in the drama and argument, we blinked all this, but
when the end comes and we see the issue has been avoided and evaded,
as it nearly always is in our stupid, whining, self-pitying modern novels,
we hurl away the book. When everyone's talking, as Lancelot does,
about the world having no values, it's not a good time to rehash *The*

Brothers Karamazov (Is there evil? Does it imply God?) or offer a sniveling version of Ayn Rand, that is, "Maybe—just maybe—Lancelot is right." Everybody, these days, is thinking and feeling what Walker Percy is thinking and feeling. Lancelot rages, at one point, "I will not have my son or daughter grow up in such a world...I will not have it." Paddy Chayevsky's mad TV news commentator and his disciples say the same—only better—in the movie *Network*. Everybody says it. Over and over, film after film, novel after novel, people keep whining about the black abyss and turning in their ignorance to Nietzsche and Kierkegaard, as if no one ever answered them (George Sedgwick, Brand Blanshard, Roman Ingarten, Paul Weiss, dozens more).

Fiction, at its best, is a means of discovery, a philosophical method. By that standard, Walker Percy is not a very good novelist; in fact *Lancelot*, for all its dramatic and philosophical intensity, is bad art, and what's worse, typical bad art. Like Tom Stoppard's plays, it fools around with philosophy, only in this case not for laughs but for fashionable groans. Art, it seems to me, should be a little less pompous, a lot more serious. It should stop sniveling and go for answers or else shut up.

Falconer

JOHN CHEEVER IS ONE OF THE FEW LIVING American novelists who might qualify as true artists. His work ranges from competent to awesome on all the grounds I would count: formal and technical mastery; educated intelligence; what I call "artistic sincerity," which implies, among other things, an indifference to aesthetic fashion, especially the tiresome modern fashion of always viewing the universe with alarm, either groaning or cynically sneering; and last, validity, or what Tolstoy called, without apology, the artist's correct moral relation to his material. I will not spell out in detail what all that means, especially the unspoken premise here that some opinions on life are plain right and some plain wrong, nor will I waste space explaining why nearly all the rest of our respected novelists seem to me either mediocre or fake. I will simply try to explain why Cheever's *Falconer*, though not long or "difficult," not profound or massive, devoid of verisimilitude's endless explanations on the one hand, and of overwrought allegorical extension on the other—though in fact merely a dramatic story of character and action accessible to the most ordinary sensitive reader—is an extraordinary work of art.

Falconer is a prison. The novel tells the story of one man's imprisonment there, and of his quietly miraculous escape. The man is Zeke Farragut, a college professor and heroin-methadone addict who accidentally, and for good reason, has killed his brother, a man who was truly murderous, but the kind you can never put in jail because although he cruelly persecutes his family and friends and causes attempted suicides, he does it all legally.

Structurally, the novel is a set of Browningesque monologues by prisoners, guards, and passing strangers, along with a few dialogues, some funny (as when the prisoners play dumb), some chilling (as when Farragut's wife comes to visit). The novel moves like an opera built almost entirely of arias and comic, tragicomic, or tragic duets. Cheever has a gift for catching the emotional nuances in the speech of murderers, drug addicts, petty larcenists, pious and deadly "good" people, people full of contradictions—like the killer guard who means no harm and loves his plants—like all of us.

Everywhere, the writing is convincing, more authoritative than any tape recording, and it shows us what is wrong with Philip Roth's notion that literature can never hope to compete with the craziness of life. One of the things a great writer can do, in a mad time, is simply write things down as they are, without explanation, without complicated philosophical, sociological, or psychological analysis of motivation, simply trusting the authority of his voice, because he knows that all he's saying is true, that his ear is infallible, and that in a world bombarded by "communications" he can trust the reader's experience and sensitivity—or can at least trust the best of his readers.

Such writing is of course risky, but that's the wonder of it. All true art takes risks, and all true fiction assumes a reader of intelligence and goodwill.

Farragut has a wife, Marcia, who wanted to be a painter but was no good—an infuriating fact she refuses to face. She is a beautiful, intelligent woman who once loved Farragut but loves him no more, since in her view his drug addiction, casual philanderings, and, now, imprisonment have ruined her life. The things she says when she visits Farragut in prison are unbelievably cruel and could come from no one but an injured wife, though many readers—lucky people—will surely cry, in the face of such cruelty, "Impossible!" Cheever simply copies down reality at its fiercest, making no excuses—sets down as unjudgmentally as any machine the crackle of fire in the angry woman's voice, the fake disinterest and specious objectivity, the undying murderous jealousy toward a girl with whom Farragut had long ago had a brief, sweet affair:

> "So tell me how you are, Zeke. I can't say that you look well,
> but you look all right. You look very much like yourself. Do
> you still dream about your blonde? You do, of course; that
> I can easily see. Don't you understand that she never existed,
> Zeke, and that she never will? Oh, I can tell by the way you
> hold your head that you still dream about that blonde who
> never masturbated or shaved her legs or challenged anything
> you said or did. I suppose you have boyfriends here?"

One could write for pages on the terrible cunning and cruelty in
that speech. No one, I think, has ever written down a more deadly
wife than Farragut's.

Yet for all her unutterable viciousness, Marcia comes off in *Falconer*
as an understandable human being, not a mere bitch, yet also not—as
she might have been in someone else's novel—one of those pitiful people
"more sinned against than sinning." We simultaneously despise her
and understand why Farragut once loved her, even loves her still. The
achievement—the mature nonsentimentality of it—is remarkable, for
Marcia, like Farragut's brother, is one of those true murderers the law
cannot punish. It's pure accident that she hasn't killed her husband.
Cheever writes:

> At a rehabilitation center in Colorado where Farragut had
> been confined to check his addiction, the doctors discovered
> that heroin had damaged his heart . . . He must avoid strenu-
> ous changes in temperature and above all excitement. Excite-
> ment of any sort would kill him . . . Farragut flew east and
> his flight was uneventful. He got a cab to their apartment,
> where Marcia let him in. "Hi," he said and bent to kiss her,
> but she averted her face. "I'm an outpatient," he said. "A salt-
> free diet—not really salt-free, but no salt added. I can't climb
> stairs or drive a car and I do have to avoid excitement. It seems
> easy enough. Maybe we could go to the beach."
> Marcia walked down the long hall to their bedroom and
> slammed the door. The noise of the sound was explosive and
> in case he had missed this she opened the door and slammed
> it again. The effect on his heart was immediate. He became
> faint, dizzy, and short-winded. He staggered to the sofa in

the living room and lay down. He was in too much pain and fear to realize that the home-coming of a drug addict was not romantic.

No two ways about it, Marcia has become a terrible human being. But Farragut, though we grow immensely fond of him for his sensitivity and wit, above all for his suffering, is no angel either. We get only glimpses, since the novel is mostly from Farragut's point of view, of how painful it is to live with him. But Cheever hints at the evidence—Farragut's many mistresses, his neurosis and floating detachment from his family and work, his own disgust at his more blatantly cruel brother, who, in the socially acceptable way, cuts out and kills by means of vodka.

No one is simply good in *Falconer*; the novel convinces us that in point of fact no one in the world is really good. Yet *Falconer* has nothing in common with the typical contemporary novel about how life is garbage. Life, for Cheever, is simply beautiful and tragic, or that's how he presents it, and both the beauty and the tragedy in *Falconer* are earned. Cheever finds no easy enemies, as William Gaddis would, no easy salvation for the liberated penis and spirit, as Updike would. He finds only what is there: pathos and beauty, "the inestimable richness of human nature."

The pathos can strike surprisingly, as if from nowhere. There is a minor character known only as "Chicken Number Two," a petty thief and killer who bullies and brags and makes trouble throughout the novel, a creature of bottomless stupidity who at the time of Falconer's minor riot demands that visitors be allowed to sit with their prisoner friends at a table, not separated from them by a counter. A guard points out that Chicken hasn't had a visitor in twelve years, nobody out there knows or cares about him. Cheever writes:

> Chicken began to cry then or seemed to cry, to weep or seemed to weep, until they heard the sound of a grown man weeping, an old man who slept on a charred mattress, whose life savings in tattoos had faded to a tracery of ash, whose crotch hair was sparse and gray, whose flesh hung slack on his bones, whose only trespass on life [now, Cheever means] was a flat guitar and a remembered and pitiful air of "I don't know where

it is, sir, but I'll find it, sir," and whose name was known nowhere, nowhere in the far reaches of his memory, where, when he talked to himself, he talked to himself as Chicken Number Two.

It is familiar theory that people outside prisons are as bad as the people inside, but Cheever makes the argument stick, and in his statement of the old opinion there is nothing liberal or slogany. He does not pretend that the prisoners are really wonderful people and the outside citizens, all hypocrites. He says what is true, that we're a miserable pack, yet a pack capable of vision, like Farragut, who "even in prison . . . knew the world to be majestic." Throughout the novel, in one prisoner's story after another, and in the continuing story of Farragut's life, evil falls on evil—in flat, sometimes half-comic prose, disaster on disaster, shot by shot. Here, for instance, a mere parenthesis in a larger disaster: "Mrs. Farragut was not an intentionally reckless driver, but her vision was failing and on the road she was an agent of death. She had already killed one Airedale and three cats." No one who has not happened to live unluckily—many people have—will believe such a catalog of small and large disasters; except for the maniac who believes life "wonderful" (as Nailles used to, in Cheever's *Bullet Park*), Cheever's catalog, because of the authority of his writing, will convince.

What is more, the catalog of disasters here is tolerable, not inconsistent with an affirmation of life and love. What redeems this miserable, ghastly world is miracles—the small miracles of humor and compassion that we may without lunacy extend to universal principle, even to a loving though somewhat feeble God. *Falconer* contains numerous minor miracles (the occasional, half-unwitting generosity of prison guards, the prison humor that gives brutalized men dignity) and two major miracles—two escapes from prison. In the first major miracle, a friend and homosexual lover of Farragut's escapes in disguise as a priest and is—for no reason—helped by the local bishop. Tolstoy would give us the bishop's reasons, but that is unnecessary in Cheever's kind of novel. Mostly, the world is inexplicably bad, bad beyond all probability: children die, or even purposely cause others to die. (Farragut's brother once casually tried to kill him.) But also, on rare occasions, the world is mysteriously good. That is enough. To emphasize the miracle of the friend's escape and the bishop's whimsical assistance, Cheever breaks

point of view, shifting from Farragut's consciousness to the friend's—
it's the only time he does it in the novel, and the effect is like a wall
magically opening, letting in light.

The second major miracle is Farragut's own escape or, rather, resurrection. A prison friend dies, either of influenza or from the new vac-
cine being tried out on the prisoners. Farragut takes the place of the
corpse in its death sack, gets carried out through the prison gates, and
walks away.

The novel's end is a masterpiece of poetic prose, not only stylistically
but also because it rings true. Farragut has nowhere to go—his wife
hates him, his heart is bad. Nevertheless, Farragut escapes prison, joyfully breathes free, garbage-scented air, and meets, in bald-faced miracle,
a generous, odd creature who gives him a coat and offers him a place
to stay. Habitual cynics will scoff at such miracles, as the sentimentally
optimistic will purse their lips on hearing of the misery inside and
outside Falconer. But that is how it is, Cheever says. Cheever proves
what we are always forgetting: that great art is not technical trickery,
novelty of effect, or philosophical complexity beyond our depth, but
absolute clarity: reality with the obfuscating wrappings peeled away.
The reason Cheever is a great writer—besides his command of literary
form, impeccable style, and unsentimental compassion—is that what
he says seems true.

The Castle
of Crossed Destinies

A LTHOUGH NOT YET AS WELL KNOWN AS
he deserves to be, Italo Calvino is one of the world's best living fabulists,
a writer in a class with Kobo Abe, Jorge Luis Borges and Gabriel García
Marquez. He is most famous for his dazzling, astonishingly intelligent
fantasies—*The Nonexistent Knight*, *The Cloven Viscount*, *Invisible Cities*,
The Baron in the Trees—but his mastery is equally evident in what might
be called, loosely, his whimsical science fictions on the history of the
universe—*Cosmicomics* and *t zero*—and in his more-or-less realistic fictions, for instance, *The Watcher and Other Stories*. In the realistic stories
and in *The Baron in the Trees*, Calvino creates substantial, moving characters and fully elaborated, thoroughly convincing fictional worlds.
In all his books, but especially in *Invisible Cities*, he has moments where
the prose turns into pure, firm lyric poetry. In the science fictions he
brilliantly translates modern scientific and mathematical theory into
fictional emotion; and everywhere his final pursuit is metaphysical.
His strange new production, *The Castle of Crossed Destinies*, uses all these
talents, rises directly from the worldview he has been developing all
these years, yet is like nothing Calvino has done before.

The book is, in a way, a collection of tales. The framing story concerns a group of pilgrims who, after traveling separately through an
enchanted forest, come together at a castle or, perhaps, a cavern (no

one is sure) and, trying to tell each other their stories, discover that they have lost their ability to speak. The tales are worth hearing, we know in advance. The hair of all the pilgrims, both young and old, has been turned white by their adventures. One of the pilgrims hits on the idea of telling his tale by means of tarot cards. He selects the cards which best represent himself, he thinks, then adds a line of other cards, and, with the aid of grimaces and gestures, tells his tale.

His actual story may or may not have much to do with the tale we are reading since we get only the narrator's interpretation, and the narrator is by no means sure of himself—an annoying, unsatisfying business, the narrator will readily admit. But the cards are all the pilgrims have, and they decide to do their best with them. Another pilgrim chooses his cards and tells his tale; then other pilgrims follow, compressing their narrative lines with those of other pilgrims when they need to make use of some card already played. By the time all the cards are on the table, the interlinking of tales—or the narrator's interpretation of the cards laid down—is incredibly complex and subtle: a history of all human consciousness through the myths of Oedipus, Parsifal, Faust, Hamlet and so on, and a history of Calvino's career as a novelist, since the pilgrims' tales repeatedly allude to Calvino's earlier fiction.

The Castle of Crossed Destinies is an ambitious, "difficult" book, though short, and one's first inclination may be to make top-of-the-head judgments: "overly ambitious," "annoyingly complex," "lacking in sentiment." Like Kafka—or Chaucer—Calvino makes plodding comedy of our scholastic need to explain things. Like those writers, he uses a squinty, insecure narrator who's forever searching out answers, mostly getting wrong ones, or raising intellectual obstacles in his own path. Such comedy inevitably slows the pace. Again, one may feel that Calvino's review of his own career as a writer is a touch self-regarding, even coy. (Tolstoy would never have stooped to such a thing.) Or, thinking of the emotional power of books like *The Baron in the Trees*, one may complain *The Castle of Crossed Destinies* is lacking in warmth.

Those objections—and others—may have at least some validity, but to register them, even in the timid way I've done, is to feel oneself squeaking like a mouse. Cranky, self-conscious, confusing and confused, *The Castle of Crossed Destinies* is a shamelessly original work of art. Not a huge work, but elegant, beautiful in the way mathematic proofs can be beautiful, and beautiful in the sense that it is the careful statement of an artist we have learned to trust.

All Calvino's philosophy is here, subtly reassessed: the idea of existence as an act of will confirmed by love (*The Nonexistent Knight*), the tragicomic mutual dependence of reason and sensation (*The Watcher*), Calvino's usual fascination with chance, probability and will and his theory of value (mainly worked out in *The Cloven Viscount, Cosmicomics* and *t zero*). What comes through most movingly, perhaps, is Calvino's love for the chance universe we are stuck with. It comes through in the physical appearance of the book—the elegant binding, dust jacket and type design and the publisher's reproductions, in actual size and full color, of fifteenth-century tarot cards.

But Calvino's celebration of things as they are comes through still more durably in the central allegorical images, the tales and the structure of the whole. The place where the pilgrims meet—our world—is perhaps a castle fallen on hard times, becoming a mere inn, perhaps a tavern doing splendidly, becoming a castle. The meeting of minds and hearts we all hunger for, as pilgrims, is impeded by difficulties—language and interpretation, our differences of background (adventures in the woods), and the infuriating fact that no pilgrim's story is entirely unique: we need each other's cards, yet the cards never carry exactly the same meaning twice. ("Each of us," Calvino remarks elsewhere, "is a billion-to-one shot.") But despite the problems, the pilgrims tell their tales, each mixing his destiny with the other's destiny and thus helping to evolve (as the universe evolved in Calvino's science fictions) a total providence, so to speak—an enveloping work of art.

Art is a central theme here. Like the universe, it is partly brute substances in random combination. Studying the cards on the table, wishing to tell his own story, dear to him simply because it is his own, the narrator complains that he has lost his story in the stories of others. Thinking toward despair, he remarks: "Perhaps the moment has come to admit that only tarot No. 1 honestly depicts what I have succeeded in being: a juggler, a conjurer, who arranges on a stand at a fair a certain number of objects and, shifting them, connecting them, interchanging them, achieves a certain number of effects." But through a fiction he learns that his deterministic philosophy is wrong. The tale of St. George and the Dragon shows him that "the dragon is not only the enemy, the outsider, the other, but is us, a part of ourselves that we must judge." Art cannot preserve our passing moments, make us live forever, but it can help us to live well.

Calvino has made his narrator both writer and reader (interpreter of the cards), both creator and victim of creation. In the metaphor of the cards he has exactly described the process of art as concrete philosophy, how we search the world for clues as a gypsy searches the cards, interpreting by means of our own stories and a few unsure conventions. Finally, he claims, the search is moral and potentially tragic. Despite the permutations tale by tale, we always learn the same tale of man: we celebrate and cleanse or we die, destroyed by our betters. So it was, according to the cards, with "the legitimate heir of the throne of Scotland usurped by Macbeth. His [chariot] advances . . . and finally Macbeth is forced to say: I 'gin to be aweary of *The Sun*, and wish the syntax o' *The World* were now undone, that the playing cards were shuffled, the folio's pages, the mirror-shards of the disaster."

Like a true work of art, Calvino's *The Castle of Crossed Destinies* takes great risks—artificiality, eclecticism, self-absorption, ponderousness, triviality (what, yet another interpretation of the world's great myths?)—and, despite its risks, wins hands down.

Daniel Martin

SINCE PUBLICATION OF *THE FRENCH LIEU-tenant's Woman* (1969), and certainly since *The Ebony Tower* (1974), it has seemed that John Fowles is the only novelist now writing in English whose works are likely to stand as literary classics—the only writer in English who has the power, range, knowledge, and wisdom of a Tolstoy or James. He is a master stylist, we've known since *The Collector* (1963), and he has the talent, much underestimated these days, for telling suspenseful, interesting stories.

Storytelling—the rigorous attention to plot that characterized the nineteenth-century novel and that characterized, also, *The French Lieutenant's Woman*, Fowles's superb fictional exploration of the philosophical background and moral implications of the nineteenth-century novel—is not prized by some of our serious writers because in their rather too easy, too fashionable commitment to existentialist notions of human freedom, they underestimate the force of the past. If it were true that we are free to change our ways and that human history can at any moment take an abrupt, unpredictable turn for the better or worse, then we might take seriously those writers who ignore the past or play literary games with it, as do E. L. Doctorow in *Ragtime*, Nicholas Meyer in his two books about Sherlock Holmes and famous men, and John Barth in *The Sot-Weed Factor*.

But existentialism tells a half-truth. It is true that we must make choices, change our lives; but it is not true that we can ignore the inertial power of all that has brought us to where we are. This is a theme John Fowles has treated before, especially in *The Magus* (1966) and *The French Lieutenant's Woman*; it is the central dramatic problem in his new novel, *Daniel Martin*, Fowles's best book so far. Here, as in all his work, Fowles explores the problem partly by analysis of the ways in which the arts—especially the art of fiction—can limit or liberate our emotions and ideas (that is, our lives) and partly by brilliant close analysis of lifelike human beings.

The central character, Daniel Martin, is a successful playwright and movie scriptwriter who feels that he has lost touch with his past, his "real" self. When the novel opens, he has been divorced for some years, has drifted from one casual arrangement to another, living always in the present. Daniel Martin's buried past centers in one incident, the long-ago time when he made love to his best friend's fiancée, Jane, sister of his own fiancée, Nell. The moment was real, a true act of love. All that followed has been false: a bad marriage between Daniel and Nell, ending in divorce; an unhappy "good" marriage between Jane and Daniel's best friend, Anthony, who is a practicing Catholic, a philosopher, and an Oxford don.

Through the intervening years all four have lied in subtle ways about the situation. Jane tells Anthony what happened, but does not admit the truth that she was and is in love with Daniel. Anthony guesses her true feelings, but does not admit to anyone, least of all himself, that he is hurt. Nell, who has only her suspicions, makes Daniel's mask of silence a pattern for her behavior in their increasingly unhappy marriage: she tries to talk, at first, and tries to help Daniel with his work, but gradually withdraws into icy silences and convention. As for Daniel himself, he clumsily distorts the truth in a stage play, making himself the enemy of the other three. In response, Anthony writes a coldly analytical letter leading syllogistically to the conclusion that he and Jane must break off all relations with Daniel. The estrangement, notice, comes as a result of two misuses of thought's age-old devices: truth-seeking art untempered by compassion (the will to love that prods and clarifies imagination—Dan's play) and truth-seeking philosophy untempered by compassion (Anthony's cold-blooded analysis of the facts).

Then, dying of cancer, in hopes of atoning and correcting history, the philosopher forces a reconciliation and charges Daniel with the almost impossible job of resurrecting Jane's true, buried self—as well as Daniel's own buried self, the self that should have married Jane. Having won Daniel's promise, Anthony seals it in a way tragically fitting for a Christian who believes in ritual acts, benevolent coercion, and miracles. He nails the promise to the unalterable past, giving up not only his life but, according to his beliefs, perhaps the afterlife as well by committing suicide. The rest is the novel: Daniel's gradual discovery that he does indeed love Jane, though they disagree on almost everything from politics to art—a discovery that brings him back to life—and Jane's even more painful, equally miraculous resurrection.

Fowles's novel is about more than the search of a cast of beautifully rendered individuals for an authentic past and future. As Daniel and Jane search out where their lives went wrong, so the novel as a whole seeks an understanding of where our whole Western civilization went wrong and how we who carry the burden of history can redeem our age, find a future worth living. As individuals can forget or deny their beginnings, so humanity as a whole can forget its Eden, sliding into the persuasion—now popular with novelists and philosophers—that from the start the universe has been a dung heap. Fowles shows that both philosophers and writers are engaged in the same effort: serious writing about reality aimed at preserving what is of worth in human life. The true novelist, like the true philosopher, uses words as tools, not playthings. If both sorts of thinker use symbolism, it is the symbolism that rises out of life itself, not the symbolism imposed by the dogmatist who knows in advance what he will say.

Fowles nails the false novelists of our age who feel guilty about presenting the cautiously optimistic view of life most of us live by in spite of our fashionably gloomy language. He nails them partly in Dan Martin's reflections on the state of the modern novel:

> It had become offensive, in an intellectually privileged caste, to suggest publicly that anything might turn out well in this world. Even when things—largely because of the privilege— did in private actuality turn out well, one dared not say so artistically. It was like some new version of the Midas touch, with despair taking the place of gold. This despair might

sometimes spring from a genuine metaphysical pessimism, or guilt, or empathy with the less fortunate. But far more often it came from a kind of statistical sensitivity (and so crossed a border into market research), since in a period of intense and universal increase in self-awareness, few could be happy with their lot.

A profoundly moral man, as sensitive as anyone else to human suffering, Daniel Martin decides he will tell in the novel he means to write—the novel we are reading—the truth: "To hell with cultural fashion: to hell with elitist guilt: to hell with existential nausea; and above all, to hell with the imagined that does not say, not only in but behind the images, the real."

Daniel Martin is a masterpiece of symbolically charged realism: every symbol rises, or is made to seem to rise, out of the story. This is true even of those symbols that would seem in another writer's work to be most obviously message-laden. On that crucial long-ago day when Jane and Daniel made love, the emotions that led to their act were charged partly by their discovery, while out punting with other Oxford students, of a drowned woman. That she represents the "drowned" Jane of the novel, and the lost Daniel as well, is obvious; but the vividness of the scene, the precise observation of details (both external and internal), transmutes the allegory. Snipped-out quotation can only hint at the effect:

> Mark kicks off his shoes and climbs down into the reeds, parts them, then takes a cautious step forward. His leg sinks. He feels for footing farther out. Daniel looks round. Jane is standing now in the long grass, watching from forty yards away. Andrew walks toward him, holding out the flask. Daniel shakes his head. The reeds close behind Mark, half-masking him, as he sinks above his knees. Daniel stares at a tuft of purple hyssop on the bank. Two shimmering blue demoiselle dragonflies with ink-stained wings flutter over the flowers, then drift away. Somewhere farther up the cut a moorhen croaks. All he can see now is little interstitial glimpses of Mark's blue shirt between the dense green stems that have closed behind his passage; the susurrus, the squelches and splashes.

Beside him Andrew murmurs, "Bet you a fiver she's a tart.
Our gallant American allies again." Then he says, "Mark?"

"Roger. I've found it."

But Mark says nothing more. He seems to spend an inexplicable time hidden there in the reeds, silent; occasionally
a reed-head bends sideways. In the end he comes heavily back,
then clambers up on the grass, wet to the loins, his feet cased
in black mud, a stench of stagnancy; and something sweeter
in the air, hideous. He grimaces at the two others, glances
back toward where Jane is, speaks in a low voice.

"She's been dead some time. Stocking round her neck. Her
hair's full of maggots." He reaches down and tears off a handful of grass and brushes the worst of the mud away.

Incredibly, every vivid detail here works symbolically, as does nearly
every detail in Fowles's huge novel. Mark, representative of the World
War II serviceman's values, will all but vanish from the novel and historical consciousness as he vanishes in the reeds. The young Andrew,
who will marry Nell after her divorce from Daniel, holds out conventional comforts (the flask and a joking snobbery that does not express,
we will later learn, his real feelings as an aristocrat, carrying the in-
escapable burden of his class). Jane, whose psychological arrest will
approach psychosis, stands "in the long grass . . . forty yards away," behind the others. Daniel, who will for a long time evade life's seriousness
by a surface aestheticism, "looks round" about him, noticing bright
surfaces, the call of a bird.

By the end of *Daniel Martin*, the daring of Fowles's symbolism
will become downright awesome: a false and shoddy resurrection of
history's buried life in the raising of a temple that would otherwise
perish behind the Aswan Dam (the dam itself a symbol here, a masterpiece of technology that, like the atom bomb, threatens the civilization it serves and at the same time prevents total war, since an Israeli
bomb on the Aswan Dam would destroy most of Cairo and shut down
modern Egyptian civilization); an accidental assemblage, on a Nile touring boat, of vividly individualized representatives of Western history's
alternative "empires"—British, French, American, East European—
while on the banks stand impoverished and diseased fellahin, the detri-
tus of ancient Egypt; or, most stunning of all, the terrible desert

desolation of ancient Palmyra. "What an extraordinary place," Jane says. Dan comments: "End of the world." But they are not quite right. Fowles writes:

> It was the weather, they decided; it took all the serene aura out of classical antiquity, reduced it to its constituent parts, its lostness, goneness, true death . . . and the contrast of the reality with the promise of the name: Palmyra, with all its connotations of shaded pools, gleaming marble, sunlit gardens, the place where sybaritic Rome married the languorous Orient.

The "weather" not only in a literal sense but in psychological and philosophical senses as well: bad emotion and bad philosophy have reduced antiquity to "its constituent parts." Jane and Daniel—modern humanity—have lost the ability to see life whole. Like Rome and the Orient, like male and female, reason and emotion, opposing principles must marry. And in a sense, miraculously, in the waste of Palmyra, Jane and Daniel do.

At the end of the novel, looking at a self-portrait of Rembrandt as an old man, Dan sees, and Fowles spells out, the secret: *No true compassion without will, no true will without compassion.* It is through culture, through the arts' gropings of history, that we learn to see who we are, where we are, where we can go and cannot go. Without will, the artist's—or any other person's—conscious determination to love and to save (the impulse stirred in Dan by his philosopher friend's coerced promise and self-sacrifice), we cannot rise to compassion. And without compassion, without real and deep love for his "subjects" (the people he knows and, by extension, all human beings), no artist— no person—can summon the will to make true art or a true life. He will be satisfied, instead, with cynical jokes and too easy, dire solutions, like those in shallower novels about individuals and history, such as John Barth's *The End of the Road.* In *Daniel Martin,* Fowles defines what art requires, what life requires. It is the first line, and the implied last line, of the novel: "Whole sight; or all the rest is desolation."

The Silmarillion

T HE POWER AND BEAUTY OF J.R.R. TOL-
kien's *The Lord of the Rings* guarantees in advance the importance and
interest of *The Silmarillion*, his account of all that happened earlier
in his imaginary kingdoms of towers, dwarfs, elves and men. The longer
we look at it, the more impressive *The Lord of the Rings* becomes; and
the more we see of Tolkien's other work, the more miraculous it seems
that the powers should have granted him that great trilogy.

He was, in many ways, an ordinary man. As a scholar, he was a
good, not a great, medievalist. His famous essay, "Beowulf, the Monsters and the Critics," stands out mainly because it lacks the pedantic
stuffiness common in this field and because it gave early support to
a way of reading *Beowulf* that more rigorous critics were already pursuing to their profit. His edition of *Sir Gawain and the Green Knight*
was a good, trustworthy edition, not brilliant—curiously weak when
it comes to interpretation—and his modernizations of that poem and
also of *Pearl* and *Sir Orfeo* were loaded with forced inversions, false
rhymes and silly archaisms like "eke" and "ere." Tolkien's original story-
poems, like "The Adventures of Tom Bombabil," were even worse,
yet *The Lord of the Rings* looms already as one of the truly great works
of the human spirit, giving luster to its less awesome but still miraculous
satellites, *The Hobbit* and now *The Silmarillion*.

Tolkien's new book, edited by his Oxford medievalist son Christopher, is a legend collection of which the long tale "The Silmarillion" makes up the main part. The collection begins with the "Ainulindale," a creation myth, proceeds to the "Valaquenta," an elven account of the Powers (Valar and Maiar), then to "The Silmarillion," and finally to two short pieces, the "Akallabeth" and a short legend bridging this collection and *The Lord of the Rings*, entitled "Of the Rings of Power and the Third Age."

If *The Hobbit* is a lesser work than the Ring trilogy because it lacks the trilogy's high seriousness, the collection that makes up *The Silmarillion* stands below the trilogy because much of it contains only high seriousness; that is, here Tolkien cares more about the meaning and coherence of his myth than he does about these glories of the trilogy: rich characterization, imagistic brilliance, powerfully imagined and detailed sense of place, and thrilling adventure. Not that those qualities are entirely lacking here. The central tale, "The Silmarillion"— though not the others—has a wealth of vivid and interesting characters, and all the tales are lifted above the ordinary by Tolkien's devil figures, Melkor, later called Morgoth, his great dragon Glaurung, and Morgoth's successor Sauron. Numerous characters here have interest, almost always because they work under some dark fate, struggling against destiny and trapping themselves; but none of them smokes a pipe, none wears a vest, and though each important character has his fascinating quirks, the compression of the narrative and the fierce thematic focus give Tolkien no room to develop and explore those quirks as he does in the trilogy.

Character is at the heart of the Ring trilogy: the individual's voluntary service of good or evil within an unfated universe. The subject of "The Silmarillion" is older, more heroic: the effect on individuals of the struggle of two great forces, the divine order and rebellious individualism that flows through Morgoth. Standing in the crossfire of these two forces, dwarfs, elves and men barely have room to move and, often, no dignity but their defiance. Their vows become curses that hound them to the grave, and often the only payment for their suffering is the fact that—soaring up into the clashing music of good and evil in the universe—they live on in the song of their exploits. Music is the central symbol and the total myth of "The Silmarillion," a symbol that becomes interchangeable with light (music's projection). The double symbol is introduced at once in the creation myth, "Ainulindale." The Father of All, Ilúvatar, gives a theme to the Powers (the Ainur) and says to them, "Of the theme that I have declared to you, I will now that ye make in harmony together a Great Music. And since I have kindled you with the Flame Imperishable [life and will], ye shall show forth your powers in adorning this theme, each with his own thoughts and devices, if he will. But I will sit and hearken, and be glad that through you great beauty has been wakened into song."

Melkor, Tolkien's Lucifer figure, of course makes trouble, trying to untune the cosmic jazz, and a battle of the musics, reminiscent of Walt Disney's *Fantasia*, develops. After Melkor's first wrong notes, Tolkien writes:

> Then Ilúvatar arose, and the Ainur perceived that he smiled; and he lifted up his left hand, and a new theme began amid the storm, like and yet unlike to the former theme, and it gathered power and had new beauty. But the discord of Melkor rose in uproar and contended with it, and again there was a war of sound more violent than before, until many of the Ainur were dismayed... Then again, Ilúvatar arose, and the Ainur perceived that his countenance was stern; and he lifted up his right hand, and behold! a third theme grew amid the confusion, and it was unlike the others. For it seemed at first soft and sweet, a mere rippling of gentle sounds in delicate melodies; but it could not be quenched, and it took to itself power and profundity. And it seemed at last that there were two musics progressing at one time before the seat of Ilúvatar, and they were utterly at variance. The one was deep and wide and beautiful, but slow and blended with immeasurable sorrow, from which its beauty chiefly came. The other had now achieved a unity of its own; but it was loud, and vain, and endlessly repeated; and it had little harmony, but rather a clamorous unison as of many trumpets braying upon a few notes. And it essayed to drown the other music by the violence of his voice, but it seemed that its most triumphant notes were taken by the other and woven into its own solemn pattern.

Now Ilúvatar takes the Powers into the Void and there shows them the visible projection of the contending musics: The world in all its confusion—joy and sorrow, peace and war, beauty and ugliness, and the evolving agony recall history. That history, down to the Great Destruction, is "The Silmarillion."

As the passages I have quoted above should make clear, Tolkien's vision in this book is a curious blend of things modern and things medieval. What is modern is for the most part the tawdriest of the modern—not that one cares, since Tolkien's vision transforms and redeems it. Walt Disney is everywhere, though his work may have had less influence on Tolkien than did that of equally childlike artists, such as Aubrey Beardsley. Tolkien's language is the same phony Prince Valiant language of the worst Everyman translations and modernizations— things like: "Death you have earned with these words; and death you should find suddenly, had I not sworn an oath in haste; of which I repent, baseborn mortal, who in the realm of Morgoth has learnt to creep in secret as his spies and thralls." But one pushes aside all such objections, because the fact is that Tolkien's vision is philosophically and morally powerful, and if some of the fabric in which he clothes the vision is bargain-basement, he has greatly elevated it by his art.

What is medieval in Tolkien's vision is his set of organizing principles, his symbolism and his pattern of legends and events. In the work of Boëthius and the scholastic philosophers, as in Dante and Chaucer, musical harmony is the first principle of cosmic balance, and the melody of individuals—the expression of individual will—is the standard figure for the play of free will within the overall design of Providence. This concord of will and overall design was simultaneously expressed, in medieval thought, in terms of light: the foundation of "music" was the orderly tuning of the spheres. Other lights—lights borrowed from the cosmic originals—came to be important in exegetical writings and, of course, in medieval poetry: famous jewels or works in gold and silver were regularly symbolic of the order that tests individual will, tempting man (or elf) toward greed and selfishness—the wish to own the beauty of the universe and, instead of sharing it, keep it in a box. Hence Tolkien's "Silmarils," the splendid jewels, now lost, which led to the fall of elves and men and to the Great Destruction.

As he borrows the organizing principles and symbols of medieval poets and philosophers, Tolkien borrows the standard legends of characters tricked by fate, characters damned by their own best (or worst) intentions, characters who found proper atonement. His characters are of course new, but their problems are standard, archetypal. There is Feanor, the great artificer who makes the Silmarils—borrowing light from the original shining trees—then wrongly lays claim to the jewels and becomes a great betrayer, putting a curse on all his race. There are the immortals who fall in love with mortals, and vice versa; the accidentally incestuous lovers who in flight from destiny find their destiny; and so on. In all these stories there are splendid moments, luminous descriptions of the kind that enrich the Ring trilogy, moments of tenderness, though rarely moments of humor.

But in "The Silmarillion" what is most moving is not the individual legends but the total vision, the eccentric heroism of Tolkien's attempt. What Tolkien lacks that his medieval model possessed is serene Christian confidence. Despite the affirmation of his creation legend, Tolkien's universe is never safe like Chaucer's. The Providential plan seems again and again to hang by a thread above bottomless pits of disaster. Tolkien, in other words, has taken on the incredible task of seeking to rejuvenate the medieval Christian way of seeing and feeling, although—as all his legends reiterate—we can no longer see clearly (the songs of the elves are now all but forgotten, as was the First Age in the Ring trilogy) and our main feeling is now tragic dread.

Strange man! Strange mind! Why would anyone do it, we keep asking as we read. Why create a whole Christian-like religion, a whole new creation myth to set beside those of the Greeks, the Jews, the Northmen and the rest? Why write a mythic history, a Bible? Nevertheless, he has tried to do just that, and apparently—so Christopher Tolkien tells us—we have more of this mad-in-the-best-sense enterprise yet to come: ruminations on the languages of ancient times, theological meditations, more stories.

Art, of course, is a way of thinking, a way of mining reality. In the Ring trilogy, Tolkien went after reality through philosophy-laden adventure. In "The Silmarillion," for better or worse, he has sought to mine deeper.

The Stories
of John Cheever

J OHN CHEEVER, DEAN OF THE CONTEMPO-
rary American short story, has just brought out, by way of proof, a
generous collection of sixty-one stories spanning three decades and
pretty much the complete range of human situations and responses,
from the earth-shattering to the mundane. Though some of these stories
are distinctly products of their time—the sort of thing one wishes were
planted in time capsules—not one can be called dated. This is partly
a result of perfected craftsmanship, partly an effect of Cheever's un-
wavering eye for beauty, elegance, and accuracy.

Though Cheever is self-disparaging of his early work, the book—
which is arranged chronologically—offers magnificent stories in all periods of Cheever's career, whether early ("The Summer Farmer,"
"Clancy in the Tower of Babel"), middle ("The Bella Lingua," "The
Wrysons") or late ("The Angel of the Bridge, "The Swimmer," and
"The World of Apples," among others). Like all collections of short
stories, the book is uneven and isn't meant to be read cover to cover—
perhaps no book of stories this large and various is. Certain sections,
like the Shady Hill stories of suburban life in the middle, create a slump
for the reader when read end to end, but stand as gems of workman-
ship when read alone.

Cheever writes in the preface to the collection: "The constants that I look for in this sometimes dated paraphernalia are a love of light and a determination to trace some moral chain of being. Calvin played no part at all in my religious education, but his presence seemed to abide in the barns of my childhood and to have left me with some undue bitterness."

This love of light leads to moments of glorious transformations, as when in "The Angel of the Bridge" a middle-aged man is miraculously cured of his middle-aged terrors; magical visions as in the famous last line of "The Country Husband": "Then it is dark; it is a night where kings in golden suits ride elephants over the mountains." But at least as often Cheever's "undue bitterness" renders us powerful and grim scenes of avarice, broken promises, bad fortune, love gone bad, and (to quote one story title) the sorrows of gin.

Cheever seems most at home when inverting our accustomed ways of looking at the world, continually doing battle with our favorite notions of the happy housekeeper, the doting grandmother. (Paradoxically, the reversals themselves may become predictable.) "Clancy in the Tower of Babel" is perhaps the most cheerful story in the book, and it emerges, of course, from a morass of bigotry, poverty, and confusion. Similarly, Cheever's recent novel *Falconer* achieved glorious affirmations and hairbreadth escapes within the cheerless environment of a state prison.

In many of the stories in the collection, the premise is a happy, stable suburban world, and Cheever's inversions show a dark vision of things. But he is at his best, I think, when he combines the comic and the tragic, the hopeful and the despairing, as when the narrator cries out in "The Death of Justina": "How can a people who do not mean to understand death hope to understand love, and who will sound the alarm?" Cheever's insistent presentation of an alarming mixture of the dark and the light is beyond mere rhetoric, beyond mere technique—it is deliberate, in fact philosophical.

> Fiction is art and art is the triumph over chaos (no less) and we can accomplish this only by the most vigilant exercise of choice, but in a world that changes more swiftly than we can perceive there is always the danger that our powers of

selection will be mistaken and that the vision we serve will come to nothing. We admire decency and despise death but even the mountains seem to shift in the space of a night and perhaps the exhibitionist at the corner of Chestnut and Elm streets is more significant than the lovely woman with a bar of sunlight in her hair, putting a fresh piece of cuttlebone in the nightingale's cage.

Cheever's stories are realistic in the best sense of the word, anchoring the dream in the concrete example, nailing the reader to the page with ruthless attention to detail, character by character, scene by scene. But within his own mode—generally speaking, something recognizable as "a *New Yorker* story"—there is considerable diversity. Some of the stories are tight, "well-made boxes." Others sprawl. There are distinctly postmodernist experiments, for instance in the abrupt authorial interruption in "A Boy in Rome," the so-called "crot" format of "Three Stories." Cheever's undermining self-appraisal in "Characters That Will Not Appear" is nonetheless a witty self-parody in which a desperate author, Royden Blake, becomes the alter ego for Cheever.

We can, for reasons of convenience, divide his work into four periods. First there were the bitter moral anecdotes—he must have written a hundred—that proved that most of our deeds are sinful. This was followed, as you will remember, by nearly a decade of snobbism in which he never wrote of characters who had less than sixty-five thousand dollars a year...When he had finished with snobbism, he made the error I have mentioned in Item 4 ("explicit descriptions of sexual commerce"), and then moved on to his romantic period...He was quite sick at the time, and his incompetence seemed to be increasing.

Fortunately, typically, it is a gross simplification of Cheever's career as writer. He has reached a stature where he must be reckoned with as one of the major figures in contemporary American letters. Both his novels and stories have been potent enough to cause one distracted woman to cry out at Breadloaf this year, "Isn't he the man who gave suburbia a bad reputation?'' Though it has been in his power to do so, he has done a great deal more. This collection of stories ought to be seen and will be seen, I think, as a celebratory milestone in a great writer's career. Like all perfect things, these stories ought to be taken in small doses. They are meant to be apportioned over a period of days and months, for they represent nearly a generation of artistic striving.

Dubin's Lives

BERNARD MALAMUD'S NEW NOVEL *DUBIN'S Lives*, years in the writing, is, as everyone expected it would be, a major work, comic, philosophical, and poetic; a book no reader of either serious literature or books of prurient interest will want to miss.

The subject is "middle-age crisis." William B. Dubin, biographer, has come to that time of life when surgeons suddenly wish to be circus clowns, and husbands fall in love with younger women. Except for the ending, on which more later, the plot is so familiar it needs no summary: extramarital relations, psychological struggle. But this is not to say that Malamud has written a commonplace, predictable book. *Dubin's Lives* has the same fundamental plot as all those other books because, like all significant writers, Malamud is interested in what everyone else his age, and of his Age, is interested in. The difference is that Malamud develops the subject with brilliance and almost Melvillean doggedness, leaving no philosophical or psychological stone unturned.

Nothing in *Dubin's Lives* exists to serve plot, character, setting, or philosophy alone: every detail serves doubly, triply. Sooner or later almost everything one might think of to say about spiritual or physical identity—one's own and that of others—Malamud finds some concrete, dramatic way to say. Dubin is not just any man in middle-aged life crisis but a biographer, a professional explorer of other people's lives (he has written on Thoreau, Twain, etc., and is now at work on D. H. Lawrence, a man as passionate and confused as William Dubin). Dubin falls in love with not just any more-or-less beautiful young woman but one desperately trying to find herself, discover who she "is." Dubin's father was a lifelong "waiter" in both senses; his mother, after the early death (truncated biography) of Dubin's brother, was a schizoid madwoman. Though Dubin is in a crisis of search-for-the-self, the self he has appeared to be has to some extent defined and wrecked his two children (whose natures he struggles in vain to understand).

The novel's symbolic richness is all but inexhaustible. Like Einstein's bent universe, circling endlessly on its self and possessing no center— and like Dubin's life, meditations, and mistakes—Dubin's daily walks in pursuit of health, youth, adventure, and Thoreauvian oneness with nature are circular; Malamud compares the walks to the movement of an often-played record on a turntable. (In the final scene, music by one of Dubin's subjects, Mozart, everlasting spokesman of youth, is on the record player.) All of the biographies Dubin reads and writes are carefully chosen to throw light (and dazzling quotations) on the central identity question. Needless to say, the names of Malamud's characters, like everything else, work symbolically. For instance: Will-I-am (Dubin's pun) B. ("be") Dubin ("ich bist Du-bin," Dubin quips). It should also be needless to say, I imagine, that on one level—not the most profound—*Dubin's Lives*, like *Pictures of Fidelman* and almost everything Malamud has written since, is an exploration of art and the artist.

Trying to summarize the "ideas" in a novel like *Dubin's Lives* would be madness: they fly up like partridges, and, more important, they are novelistic ideas, urgently explored but never fully resolved, usually because they can't be. The end of the novel is ambiguous, unsettled. Dubin is faintly toying with living three days each week with his mistress, four with his wife (we strongly doubt that he will do it; he'll go on as he is, getting away with things); his mistress, who has suggested the idea, calls out her window as Dubin runs toward home, "Don't kid yourself!" What she probably means is, "You love me more than you love her"; but we know he loves both and neither, and, more important, we are reminded that it is Dubin's nature to kid himself: for all his will and intellect, he's a man almost infallibly wrong—at times, in fact, a swine. As Dubin runs home in these final

lines, the man who really loves Dubin's mistress, and has every right
to be loved in return, stands spying from the trees, watching other
people's lives like a biographer (Roger Foster is his name, foster child
of the universe, peeking helplessly from behind a double phallus, "a
long-boughed, two-trunked silver maple" [boughed and bowed].) Dubin,
running home—completing the usual circle of his walk—is like a con-
quering hero, but his victory is comic, even slightly repellent: "Dubin
ran up the moonlit road, holding his half-stiffened phallus in his hand,
for his wife with love." Some love! But Dubin partly knows it. Asked
by his mistress if he loves his wife, he has answered, "I love her life."
If he's a hero as well as a fool it's because, though he knows better,
he refuses to let go of the delusion that a man can live multiple lives.
Early in the novel Malamud writes, "Dubin in his heart of hearts
mourns Dubin." Now at the end, Dubin in his life-greed celebrates
Dubin: I am because you were. One might perhaps do worse.

No living American writes better than Malamud at his best, and
much of *Dubin's Lives* is Malamud at his best. We get in this novel
not only masterful realistic scenes but also some of the finest dream
sequences, scenes of mistaken perception, and mad scenes anywhere
in recent fiction. Early in the novel, Dubin looks out with pleasure
and sees his wife unexpectedly dancing below him on the lawn. (She
once studied dance, he remembers.) "Hap-pee!" he hears her cry up
to him. "Wonderful!" he shouts back. It turns out she had a bee inside
her blouse and was yelling to him for help. Later, in wintertime, a
man, a total stranger, mysteriously joins Dubin on his walk, and for
no clear reason, walks close to Dubin, sometimes bumping his elbow.
The man will not talk, and Dubin, somewhat baffled, decides to put
up with it. When birds fly over, the man raises an imaginary gun and
says "Bang bang." After a while, two crows fly over, the man drops
to one knee with a grunt and raises his arms as though sighting up
a gun barrel, and roars "Boom boom." Malamud continues:

> To Dubin's astonishment one of the black birds wavered
> in flight and plummeted to the ground. The stranger let out
> a hoarse shout and plunged into the white field to retrieve
> the crow. Holding it up for Dubin to see, he pressed the dead
> bird to his chest and awkwardly ran, kicking up snow, diag-
> onally across the field in the direction he had come.

Can a crow have a heart attack?
One of us is mad, the biographer thought.

I think it should be added that no one in America writes worse than Malamud at his worst. Not too much need be made of this, perhaps. Very serious novelists (Tolstoy, Melville) can afford to make mistakes not permitted to novelists of the second rank, that is, masters of elegant style and construction but no deeply booming thought. One typical Malamud mistake is easily forgivable. He frequently abandons verisimilitude and psychological credibility because he cares more about ideas than about how people really talk. Dubin can spin out off-the-cuff lectures (mostly to his mistress) so elegant and bookish, so logical, tightly constructed, to the point, that Dr. Johnson himself, if he could hear them in real life, would fall on his rear end in astonishment. No serious reader will much object. When the argument is interesting, reality be damned.

Other Malamud mistakes are less excusable. Though he can write like a master, he can also turn off his ear and write (speaking of a cat): "It was a long-bodied lithe almost lynx-like male, with an upright head and twitching tail." One section of the novel—a brief slump in the middle—is written in an arch, coy superliterary style reminiscent of the early style of Malamud's neighbor and Bennington colleague Nicholas Delbanco. (Delbanco, after passing the disease to Malamud, got better.) Dubin's wife frequently talks pure early-Delbancoesque: "And I feel that in her death I am diminished." None of Malamud's characters dares to speak such ordinary American as "I don't know many"; they say, prissy and fancy, "I know few." The omniscient narrator does the same, especially when he gets on the weather. One winces and hurries past. Ever since Joyce, mannerism has been the leaky valve in the heart of our serious fiction, but Malamud's particular mannered style suggests a character fault: like Dubin, he kids himself.

It ought to be said in Malamud's defense that no one who dares as much as Malamud does can expect to move as surely as the stylist who keeps watching his feet. The imagination behind *Dubin's Lives* is, like Stanley Elkin's, awesome, downright eager to take risks. We get one crazily original scene after another: fifty-nine-year-old Dubin peeking in through his mistress's window, a man terrified to near-madness by dogs, fighting off his mistress's dog; Dubin, having slipped off his circle, helplessly wandering in a magnificently realized blizzard, a mile from home but close to death; old Dubin in a tree while an angry farmer shoots blindly into the night, heart set on ending his biography. The novel is rich and intelligent, entertaining on many levels. Yet it leaves me uneasy. Because Dubin is in certain ways courageous, also because Dubin tries hard to be honest, though he can't be, Malamud seems to admire him more than he deserves. Though he treats Dubin as a comic hero, a deluded man, one keeps suspecting that Malamud is solidly on Dubin's side, not loving him though he laughs at him, but instead, winking and leering at the audience, faking ironic detachment as he sneaks William Dubin onto the pedestal, a moral sex-hero, Falstaff with a face-lift, so that everyone will think he's Prince Hal.

Sophie's Choice

*W*HEN HIS 1979 NEW YORK TIMES BOOK Review *piece on* Sophie's Choice *was chosen to be reprinted in* Critical Essays on William Styron *(Casciato and West, eds., 1982), John Gardner requested that the following statement precede the original text.*

Book reviews are necessarily written under pressure; at most one has a matter of days to figure out what one thinks and feels about a book that may have, like *Sophie's Choice*, taken years to write. After this review, I received a good deal of angry mail from Polish Americans, which makes me sorry I was not more careful to show my sympathy with the Polish and my large dependence on Mr. Styron's carefully documented and immensely sympathetic account. But what I regret most of all was my review's disservice to Styron himself.

Though I recognized the power and beauty of *Sophie's Choice*, I did not guess, at the time I wrote, the novel's staying power. Scene after scene comes back now, long after I last read the book, with astonishing vividness—perhaps the most obvious mark of a masterpiece. I think the reason is not solely that one of the novel's important subjects is the holocaust. Very few writers have been able to deal with the red-hot subject without in the end being burnt up by it. In retrospect I would say Styron succeeded where many failed, and, more than that,

that among the few who succeed he stands alone—if one does not count personal diaries or memoirs—as a writer who could fully dramatize the horror, the complexity, and something at least approaching the full historical and emotional meaning of the thing. He found the connections between the vast historical horror and the psychological equivalents in ordinary life, not to mention the eerie connection between what happened in Germany and what happens in these divided United States. But as I was saying, it is not just this subject matter that makes *Sophie's Choice* memorable. His descriptions of Brooklyn life and scenery have a vividness just as uncanny, and his analysis of the young writer's anxieties (any young writer's, not just Stingo's), to say nothing of his psychologically original and convincing analysis of Nathan and Sophie, make one look at people—and oneself—in a new way.

I regret, too, that I did not mention the novel's humor. I suppose I was overawed by the horror; but the fact is that one of the reasons Styron succeeded so well in *Sophie's Choice* is that, like Shakespeare (I think the comparison is not too grand), Styron knows how to cut away from the darkness of his material, so that when he turns to it again it strikes with increasing force.

Another of my regrets is that I read the book with a somewhat bigoted Yankee eye. I will say the inevitable: Some of my best friends are Southerners. Nevertheless, I reacted with disbelief and distaste to some extremely Southern material—for instance Stingo reading the Bible with an old black woman. If Styron had been faking the scene, I would have been right. But I am now convinced he was not; he was simply reporting real experience of a kind foreign to me, and, given my own Yankee reserve, embarrassing. Though none of my best friends are ancient Greeks, I am much fairer to Homer (who had some *very* odd opinions) than I was to my fellow American and contemporary. What makes the matter worse is that the scene is in fact not only authentic but symbolically crucial. Rightly understood, it negates my criticism that the "moral" of the novel is inadequate, the idea that all those people died so that Stingo might become a novelist. (I should mention that I write this without the review in front of me, and I'm not sure I voiced this objection. I remember thinking, at the time I wrote, that *Sophie's Choice* was faulty in the way Wallace Stegner's masterpiece, *Big Rock Candy Mountain*, was faulty, explaining away tragedy as a thing of value to the writer. I hope I decided not to say this, in the end, since in Styron's case at least, it's wrong. But whether or not I said it, other reviewers did. I hope they will join me in apologizing for the mistake.)

I'm not sorry to have pointed out that *Sophie's Choice* transmutes the old "Southern Gothic" to a new, universal gothic, and I'm not sorry to have claimed that the Southern Gothic is an inherently inferior form. But I would like to take this opportunity to say that the general implications of my remarks were ill-considered. What I suggested, I'm sure, was that, in following the gothic formula, *Sophie's Choice* was a castle built on sand. What I now think is this: Most great American art is an elevation of trash. New Orleans tailgate funeral jazz was (or so I think on this particular Friday) aesthetically mediocre stuff, but out of it came the high art of Ellington, Gershwin and the rest. Out of trash films, including Disney at his worst, came writers ranging from William Gass and Ishmael Reed to (forgive the self-congratulation) myself. Styron did not simply use the gothic formulae, he transmuted them. What is wrong with the gothics is not wrong with *Sophie's Choice*. When Dostoyevsky published *Crime and Punishment* (I think it was), somebody important—I forget who—made a long trip to him (I think) to tell him, "You are the savior of all Russia!" After *Sophie's Choice*, I wish I had said, instead of what I did say, or at least in addition to what I did say, "You are the savior of all America!"

JULY 3, 1981

The original text of the review follows:

Early in William Styron's new novel a character named Nathan Landau tells the narrator, an aspiring young Southern writer, "I admire your courage, kid...setting out to write something else about the South." And Landau adds a moment later, "you're at the end of a tradition." The aspiring writer is a virtually undisguised William Styron at twenty-two (we get allusions, from the now mature narrator, to his earlier fiction, easily recognizable as *Lie Down in Darkness, The Long March, Set This House on Fire* and *The Confessions of Nat Turner*); and what Landau says to the young Styron is clearly very much on the mature Styron's mind as he works out the immense gothic labyrinth that is the weighty, passionate novel we are reading now.

Sophie's Choice is a courageous, in some ways masterly book, a book very hard to review for the simple reason that the plot—even the double entendre in the title—cannot be given away. Certain things can be said without too much harming the novel's considerable effect: The story treats two doomed lovers, Nathan Landau, a brilliant, tragically mad New York Jew, and Sophie Zawistowska, a beautiful Polish survivor of Auschwitz, and their intellectual and emotional entrapment, for better or worse, of the novelist-narrator.

Thematically, the novel treats the familiar (which is not to say trivial) Styron subject, the nature of evil in the individual and in all of humanity. Brooding guilt is everywhere: in the narrator's story of how, when his mother was dying of cancer and could not take care of herself, he once went on a joy ride with a friend, failed to stoke up the fire in his mother's room and, when he returned, found her half-frozen, teeth chattering, shortly after which catastrophe—whether or not as a result of it—she died; in the narrator's awareness that the money he lives on as he writes his first novel comes directly from the sale of sixteen-year-old slave, a boy who, having been falsely accused of accosting a Southern young lady, was sent into a kind of slavery few survive; in the memories of the novel's wonderful complex heroine, Sophie, a Catholic turned atheist and a woman who, for love of her son, made inept attempts at collaborating with the German SS; in the drug addiction and occasional fiendish violence of the gentle, humorous, intelligent and humane—but also mad—Nathan Landau. In the stories of Sophie's Resistance friends; in the stories of the narrator's father and his friends, and so on.

The novel's courage lies partly in this: After all the attacks on Styron, especially after *The Confessions of Nat Turner*, which some blacks and liberals (including myself) found offensive here and there, we get in *Sophie's Choice* the same old Styron, boldly and unmercifully setting down his occasional lapses (or his narrator's) into anti-Semitism, anti-feminism and so forth, baring his chest to whatever knives it may possibly deserve, even begging for it. Those who wish to can easily prove him anti-black, anti-white, anti-Southern, anti-Yankee, anti-Polish, anti-Semitic, anti-Christian, anti-German, anti-American, anti-Irish—the list could go on and on. No bigotry escapes him; the worst that can be said of humanity Styron claims for himself, wringing his hands, tearing his hair, wailing to all the congregation, *Mea Culpa*! (Only in their taste in music are he and his characters faultless.)

Such all-inclusive, self-confessed sinfulness should absolve a man, and in a way, of course, it does; no reader of *Sophie's Choice* can doubt that Styron has put immense energy into trying to understand and deal justly with the evils in American history and the European holocaust, to say nothing of the evil (as well as the good) in his characters. Yet for all the civilized and, in the best sense, Christian decency of Styron's emotions when he's watching himself, the rabid streak is always ready to leap out and take command.

One example must suffice: After the double suicide of Nathan and Sophie at the end of the novel, the narrator, trying to get to their bodies, finds himself blocked by a police cordon. Styron's observation is that "everywhere stood clots of thuggish policemen chewing gum and negligently swatting their thick behinds." He adds: "I argued with one of these cops—a choleric ugly Irishman—asserting my right to enter. . ." The scene is crowded with these piggish policemen, also "a cluster of wormy-looking police reporters"; not one of them is portrayed as timidly decent; none of them can be seen as, merely, confused children in grown-up bodies. Styron is far more just in his treatment of the Southern racial bigot Senator Bilbo, or Sophie's viciously anti-Semitic, woman-enslaving father, Professor Zbigniew Bieganski, or even the master of Auschwitz, Rudolph Hess.

My point—and I labor it because it seems to me important—is this: Styron's justice and compassion, the desperate struggle to get to the bottom of even the most terrible, most baffling evils—the holocaust, above all—and to come back a just and loving man are impressive, almost awesome, precisely because we know by his slips that they are not natural to him but earned. When he forgets the ideal he sets for himself, as he does with the cops, with a Unitarian minister we meet later, with the McGraw-Hill organization men we meet in the first chapter, and as he does in numerous other places, he shows us how serious this novel is as not merely a story of other people's troubles, but a piece of anguished Protestant soul-searching, an attempt to seize all the evil in the world—in his own heart first—crush it, and create a planet fit for God and man.

In a moving passage near the end of the novel, Styron admits that he has not succeeded, quite, in doing what he set out to do. He writes (recalling his earlier dream): "*Someday I will understand Auschwitz.* This was a brave statement, but innocently absurd. No one will ever understand Auschwitz. What I might have set down with more accuracy would have been: *Someday I will write about Sophie's life and death, and thereby help demonstrate how absolute evil is never extinguished from the world.*" Though no one will deny that writing about the holocaust and its aftermath in personal terms—"Sophie's life and death"—may be the best thing one can do to wring at least some fragmentary sense out of these numbing times, I wonder if Styron's scaled-down goal is not as innocently absurd as the earlier goal. "Absolute evil." What a chaos of medieval phantoms nestles in those words! Like absolute good, a concept abandoned in Styron's vision as in much of modern Christianity, absolute evil is the stuff of which witch cults, country sermons and gothic tales are made.

As I said at the outset, Styron is very conscious of being one of the last to work a dying literary tradition—in effect, the Southern Gothic, the vein mined by, among many others, Walker Percy, Robert Penn Warren and, possibly, William Faulkner. (In my opinion, Faulkner has too much humor, even joy, to belong.) Styron makes a point, in *Sophie's Choice*, of naming his influences—Thomas Wolfe, Faulkner, Robert Penn Warren, etc.—and claims, in Nathan Landau's voice, that he has surmounted them. In *Sophie's Choice* he does far more than that: He transfers, down to the last detail, the conventions and implicit metaphysic of the Southern Gothic—especially as it was handled by Robert Penn Warren—to the world at large. It is no longer just the South that is grandly decayed, morally tortured, ridden with madmen, idiots and weaklings, socially enfeebled by incest and other perversions; it is the world.

The requisite madman is Nathan Landau; the requisite webs of guilt reach out toward the present from Auschwitz and the American North and South. For slavery and the necessary racial-taint theme, Styron chooses (besides America) Poland, occupied for centuries first by one cruel master, then another, pitifully devoted to both German culture and Nazi-style anti-Semitism, and genetically so mixed that blond Polish children can be saved from the death camps by being slipped into the Aryan Lebensborn, or New Youth Program. The Southern Gothic must have vaguely symbolic weather—if possible, murderously hot and muggy (Brooklyn in the summer will do fine)—and some crazy old house—Styron chooses Yetta Zimmerman's huge old apartment house, entirely painted, from end to end, in Army-surplus pink. Doom must hang over everything, ominously, mysteriously forewarned throughout the novel; and of course there are special requirements of style and plot.

Styron is, of course, a master stylist; but notice the precisely gothic quality of the following passage, which I've chosen by opening at random. Note the intricacy of the sentences, the ironic use of jarring images, sly biblical hints (the Professor's hiss), the inclination to choose objects that are old, "authentic" and likely to spell doom; note the fondness for suspense and rhythms that seem to pant. Sophie's father, the Professor, I ought to explain, having long ago written a Polish tract arguing that Jews should be exterminated, is now trying to get an audience with some—any—bureaucrat among the occupying German forces, hoping to curry favor. Styron writes:

> Loathing her father now, loathing his lackey—her husband—almost as much, Sophie would slip by their murmuring shapes in the house hallway as the Professor, suavely tailored in his frock coat, his glamorous graying locks beautifully barbered and fragrant of *Kölnischwasser*, prepared to sally forth on his morning supplicatory rounds. But he must not have washed his scalp. She recalled the dandruff on his splendid shoulders. His murmurings combined fretfulness and hope. His voice had an odd hiss. Surely today, even though the Governor General had refused to see him the day before—surely today (especially with his exquisite command of German) he would be greeted cordially by the head of the *Einsatzgruppe der Sicherheitzpolizei*, with whom he had an entree in the form of a letter from a mutual friend in Erfurt (a sociologist, a leading Nazi theoretician on the Jewish problem), and who could not fail to be further impressed by these credentials, these honorary degrees (on authentic parchment) from Heidelberg and Leipzig, this bound volume of collected essays published in Mainz, *Die Polnische Judenfrage*, etc. and so on. Surely today. . . [The ellipsis is Styron's.]

The hothouse quality of the style—the scent of overripe black orchids—seems to be thoroughly appropriate, as suited to rotting Europe as to the decaying Old South. The only question I would raise is Heisenberg's: Does the instrument of vision—in this case, the transferred Southern Gothic form—seriously alter the thing seen?

But even more than style and setting, the glory of the Southern Gothic is plot. We must get surprise after surprise, revelation after revelation, each more shocking and astonishing than the last. (Unavoidably, but nonetheless to my great annoyance, I have already given away one surprise: We do not know till near the end of the novel that our beloved Nathan Landau is a maniac.) Insofar as plot is concerned, *Sophie's Choice* is a thriller of the highest order, all the more thrilling for the fact that the dark, gloomy secrets we are unearthing one by one—sorting through lies and terrible misunderstandings like a hand groping for a golden nugget in a rattlesnake's nest—are not just the secrets of some crazy Southern family but may be authentic secrets of history and our own human nature: why people did what they did at Auschwitz—people on every side—why often the Polish underground hated the Jewish underground, on which their lives sometimes depended; how the Catholic, Protestant and Jewish souls intertangle in love and hate, and can, under just the right conditions, kill.

Sophie's Choice, as I hope I have already made clear, is a splendidly written, thrilling book, a philosophical novel on the most important subject of the twentieth century. If it is not, for me, a hands-down literary masterpiece, the reason is that, in transferring the form of the Southern Gothic to this vastly larger subject, Styron has been unable to get rid of or even noticeably tone down those qualities—some superficial, some deep—in the Southern Gothic that have always made Yankees squirm.

Judging at least by its literary tradition, the South has always been an intensely emotional and, in a queer way, idealistic place—emotional and idealistic in ways not very common in, say, Vermont or New York State or, anyway, upstate. I would never claim that Yankees are more just and reasonable than Southerners; I would say we hide our evil in a different style. Though we may secretly cry our hearts out at a poem like, say, James Dickey's "Celebration," we wince at novels in which characters are always groaning, always listening in a painful joy to classical music, always talking poetry—much of it having to do with terminal disease. And we blush at passages like the following:

> I don't recall precisely when, during Sophie's description of those happenings [I] began to hear [myself] whisper, "Oh God, oh my God." But I did seem to be aware, during the

time of the telling of her story. . . that those words which had commenced in pious Presbyterian entreaty became finally meaningless. By which I mean that the "Oh God" or "Oh my God" or even "Jesus Christ" that were whispered again and again were as empty as any idiot's dream of God, or the idea that there could be such a Thing.

Which is not to deny that the story that follows this gothic introduction is not terribly moving and shocking.

In short, though I am profoundly moved by *Sophie's Choice* and consider the novel an immensely important work, I am not persuaded by it. Styron's vision may have humor in it—he tells us about Nathan's hilarious jokes, none of which turn out to be funny on the page—but if so, not an ounce of that humor is in the novel. Perhaps it may be argued that, in a book about American guilt and the holocaust, humor would be out of place. But it seems to me that humor is central to our humanity, even our decency. It cannot be replaced, as it is in *Sophie's Choice*, by great classical music or (a major concern in the novel) sex. If anything, classical music leads in exactly the wrong direction: It points to that ideal Edenic world that those master musicians, the Poles and the Germans, thought in their insanity they might create here on earth by getting rid of a few million "defectives." I'm not, God knows, against Bach or Beethoven; but they need to be taken with a grain of salt, expressing, as they do, a set of standards unobtainable (except in music) for poor silly, grotesque humanity; they point our hearts toward an inevitable failure that may lead us to murder, suicide or the helpless groaning and self-flagellation of the Southern Gothic novel.

A Writer's View
of Contemporary
American Fiction

AT LEAST FOR WESTERN CIVILIZATION, OR at least for the American part of it, the heart of good fiction is always religious. In general it seems that we are all in need of a credible version of what is for human beings—or at least Judeo-Christian or Judeo-Christian-Muslim human beings—the only emotionally satisfying story, a story that convinces us, at least for the moment, that, as Reynolds Price puts it, "history is the will of a just god that knows me." I would not insist that the religious impulse of art requires God as its foundation. We are living in something called "the post-Christian era." I hope that phrase is not supposed to mean that we have seen through Christianity and have returned to everything pagan except the happiness. I hope it means instead that we are now in a position to do, if we will, what the very best Jews, Christians, and Muslims have always done, but do it without nervously consulting God at every turn. I hope it means we can accept God's statement—made gleefully, we are told in the Talmud—"My sons have defeated me! My sons have defeated me!" In other words, I hope it means that the central values of our religiously grounded civilization no longer need depend on subtle arguments on whether or not God exists and has reddish-blond hair.

The central tenet of all our great religions—Zeus-worship, Yahweh worship, Jesus worship, and so on—is, as the Taoists say, "so simple that a Fool, if he were to hear it, would laugh aloud." That central tenet is this: we believe that some things are physically and spiritually healthy for human beings, as individuals and as groups, and other things are not. The rest is ritual and fine distinction. Ritual is the business of organized religion, and as artists and critics we can take it or leave it. Fine distinctions in what is good or bad for us are, I will argue, the business of art. Religion and philosophy are of course notorious for trying to get into the artist's act—the act of finding and dramatically enforcing (or re-enforcing) values—but both are notoriously bad at it. Religions make up codes, which have a way of sounding fine until religion A meets religion B. Philosophy makes up, among other fictions, theories of behavior that sound fine until someone like Raskolnikov—or Melville's tragically misguided Captain Vere—tries to act on them.

It is possible to formulate some useful generalizations, categories which may help us put the jumble and confusion of modern American fiction in some order. But most people would agree, I think, with Anthony Hecht's observation that critical categories never really work, they are merely helpful for the moment, because each literary work offers a unique experience—a flow of sensations, expectations raised and satisfied or denied, a slice of the mind's life that cannot be equated with any other slice. The good reader never knows in advance what he wants from literature. We approach a work as we approach someone with whom we may fall in love, with all our sensors aquiver, prepared for surprises, armed against betrayal by the emotional and intellectual touchstones of our past. Nevertheless, categories help in art as in love, if only because, in seeing our neat, ordered boundaries break down, we learn new facts about the jungle they meant to make orderly. Let us try to find, then, some more or less useful categories.

What I take to be the mainline opinion of critics, the opinion of, for instance, Ihab Hassan, holds that contemporary American fiction has two broad movements, counting, of course, only "serious" writers. We have the "innovative" or "experimental" or "post-modern" writers, people like John Barth, Donald Barthelme, Robert Coover, Thomas Pynchon, Mark Helprin, William Gaddis, John Hawkes, and, say, William Gass, and a second group identified with modernism and the American liberal tradition, mainly Jewish writers like Saul Bellow, Arthur Miller, Bernard Malamud, and Norman Mailer, but also liberals with other axes to grind, among them American blacks, feminists, and spokesmen for kindness to animals, like Peter S. Beagle.

Another mainline opinion, one loosely connected with the one I have just mentioned, holds that, with some exceptions, the non-liberal tradition includes writers of two kinds, those who whine because they feel themselves the victims of an absurd universe, and those who whine because not only is the universe absurd, they are pretty weird themselves. Both, as might be expected, tend to write what is called innovative fiction. Having no faith in or love for "reality," including what they take to be the real tradition of fiction, they mock or abandon fiction's old forms, play tricks on the reader, who, after all, must be seen as part of the hostile universe or as one more irrational, unloving creep, like the writer.

Needless to say, both of these mainline opinions have a good deal of truth in them. A great many American writers—though perhaps none I would invite to a party—do consider themselves pitiful victims, if not personally horrible, then surrounded by horrible people in a horrible universe. Think of William Gaddis—a brilliant technician, perhaps the best now at work in America—who has virtually no good to say of anyone or anything except young JR, his "hero," who in the process of *JR* is utterly destroyed. Think of Thomas Pynchon, perhaps the dullest writer now living though he might have been Jonathan Swift if he'd had to write in longhand. Yet the rubrics "victimism," "experimentation," and "liberalism" need overhaul if they are adequately to explain what is going on in American fiction. In *Henderson the Rain King*, Saul Bellow, a liberal, wrote "experimental" fiction. Except in his first two, quite good novels—*The Floating Opera* and *End of the Road*—John Barth is an innovative writer, and yet his novels are filled with exuberant affirmation—all of them, by the way, wrong. Robert Coover, forever mincing or else obscenely chuckling about how nothing can be known, is a closet fascist. He denies the possibility of getting at truth, then rams home his own fierce opinions.

You may already see where I am leading you: to a view of the movements in American fiction as primarily religious manifestations of one kind or another. Let me not move to that directly, however, but first dispense with what I take to be nonsense categories: "innovative," "experimental," and "post-modern." Everything we write is an experiment. Only if the experiment fails do we call the work experimental. We do not call Proust's enormous novel experimental, or Joyce's *Ulysses*, or Homer's *Iliad* and *Odyssey*, though all these were brand-new forms in their days. As for "innovation," it seems to me that most so-called innovative fiction is simply a turning away from America's dominant mode in the early twentieth century, a mode Edgar Poe despised, realism—a sudden new interest, on the part of American writers in the late forties and fifties—just after the Second World War—in Japanese and European fiction and in the fiction of earlier periods, from Homer and the ancient Jews forward.

Almost to a man, those who claim they write "innovative," "experimental," or "post-modern" fiction are desperately attempting to emulate the voice of Old Europeans—who, as far as I can make out, are doing everything in their power to imitate the silly Americans. (The most popular novel in France this last year—Racine's France! Baudelaire's France!—was a soap-opera saga about a family in New Orleans.) We are not post-modern, if post-modernism means, as Ihab Hassan thinks, "indifferent to the truth," and modernism means "concerned about finding and communicating truth." We are all of us zealots, both the realists among us and the fabulists, but our essential fervor expresses itself in a variety of ways, and those ways are what I will call the movements in contemporary American fiction, that is—let us say it plainly, simply—the movements in our modern American fiction.

Though most of the writers I plan to mention would dislike my calling them religious, American writers now at work fall into five main groups: (1) religious liberals and liberal agnostics (often indistinguishable); (2) orthodox or troubled-orthodox Christians; (3) Christians who have lost their faith and cannot stand it; (4) diabolists; (5) heretics.

Let me sketch in just enough detail to show you the usefulness of the system. First a few more historical reminders: America was settled, in the first move of settlement, by people in flight from religious persecution, people who quickly turned persecutors themselves, driving the Quakers to a separate state, burning witches, and so forth. In later waves Catholics came, and Jews. Except as cheap labor, they were not exactly met with open arms. For those Americans who wanted no religion at all, nearly the only live option was to head out West—hence the odd phenomenon of the Bible Belt (largely hard-shell Baptist) and beyond it, except for the Mormons, nothing—a passel of freethinking, atheist, or agnostic cowboys and a few odd trappers, here and there a Jesuit or Methodist preacher. (For all their distortions, our cowboy pictures still reflect this phenomenon.) Meanwhile back East, the more liberal religions were spawning another breed of free-thinkers—Transcendentalists and Unitarians of a certain queer sort: people like Emerson, Thoreau, Walter Whitman (as he preferred to be called), and mad Jones Very. From Emerson to Saul Bellow the line runs straight. The Reform Jew is only barely a Jew, as the Transcendentalist is only barely a Christian. He believes in ethics and civilization, tradition and clear communication. When he writes he uses plot, character, and setting, and he's fairly true to all of them, to prove—in case anyone should doubt—that he's serious. He does not believe, if you press him, in art. He believes in using art to facilitate thought about important issues. Though a kind of realist, he abandons realism the moment his character has something to say that he would not, in real life, say, or the minute his action's inevitable development begins to push him away from his philosophical, sociological, or political subject. He makes use of the I narrator, to give himself room to say everything he pleases, and sometimes he abandons the realist pretense entirely, as Bellow does in *Henderson* (thought to be shockingly new work when it appeared), or as Stanley Elkin does in all his books, especially *Searches and Seizures*, *A Bad Man*, and *The Franchiser*. Mostly the liberal writer's urge to communicate keeps him fairly realistic, even journalistic, as Norman Mailer is in his best work—*The Naked and the Dead*, a novel, and *Armies of the Night*, a journalistic work. When he shifts to the advance-guard style, as Mailer did feebly and clumsily in *An American Dream* and more successfully in *Why Are We in Vietnam?*, he loses credibility with serious-minded readers. Except for Walt Whitman, the liberal tradition has produced no great writers, certainly no great recent writers, though Malamud frequently comes close. To a man, they make lumpy, misshapen fictions, fictions soon dated, fictions that drone like the lectures Unitarians substitute for sermons, fictions which, in two words, are insufficiently alert. Bad writers in this crowd show the fault most clearly, E. L. Doctorow, for instance, who in *Ragtime* suddenly abandons probability so that a character—a young man totally in control of his penis—may come lurching from a closet to spray a lady with his semen, which falls over her, Doctorow says, like "ticker-tape and bullets." To take a cheap shot at capitalism ("ticker-tape and bullets" turning women into objects), Doctorow abandons whatever insight an honest following of action might have led him to. Bellow will do the same at the drop of, for instance, the name Eisenhower. Let them stumble into their favorite crank area, and they twitch and go into their tirade like Tolstoy in his fierce, final days. In Malamud—especially the tight, early work of Malamud—we almost never see this, but the fact remains that for all those writers, or almost all, message is far more important than form; they tend not to care about Coleridge's dictum that "Nothing can permanently please that does not contain in itself the reason why it is as it is and not otherwise." If we admire the liberals, we admire them more for their goodness than for their art; and too often, as in Doctorow, even the goodness is partly illusory. Saul Bellow is patently and annoyingly a male chauvinist pig. Doctorow lies about history to make his ethically liberal points.

Traditionally in America, orthodox Christians are of two kinds—those who believe the Christian message on salvation and damnation and believe mankind can eventually reach heaven, and those who believe Christianity is right but are convinced, as Hawthorne and Melville were, that the world, in its refusal to follow the rules, is doomed. Hawthorne was of course somewhat more hopeful than was Melville, especially in Melville's last books.

It is Christianity—hellfire Protestant Christianity—not the terrible state of the world, that makes the idea of apocalypse so important in modern American fiction; and it is Christianity of a gentler sort that gives such importance to the idea of resurrection, physical or spiritual. Hawthorne, Poe, and Twain were all resurrection men. (Twain, after the death of his daughter, turned black-hearted and sorrowful and thus became fountainhead of another movement in our fiction.) And we still have, of course, our resurrection men. (*The Resurrection* was the title of my own first published novel, which I intended as a debate with Mr. Tolstoy. I was young then, and inclined toward the persuasion that entropy is all.) Ellison belongs with this camp, as does, most notably and most recently, John Cheever. All of his novels end in resurrection, but in the last two this idea—and also the overt Christianity of the idea—are impossible to miss.

In *Bullet Park* Nailles saves his son from death by crucifixion, helped by a miracle; in *Falconer*, Cheever's newest novel as of this writing, the central character, Farragut, escapes from prison by becoming, for all practical purposes, a corpse. An even more thrilling resurrection comes at the end of Charles Johnson's brilliant first novel, *Faith and the Good Thing*. A beautiful black girl, Faith, after a tragic life which leaves her a ghastly physical monster, burned and blinded but tragically wise, becomes a "Swamp Woman" or witch, and the horrible old creature who formerly had that job turns into an innocent and beautiful young girl. Or there is the resurrection of Jethro Furber at the end of William Gass's most impressive work so far, *Omensetter's Luck*.

As I have said, not all our contemporary American orthodox Christians are as optimistic as John Cheever, Charles Johnson, and William Gass. Most are in Melville's end of the tent, writing of evil as William Gaddis does in *JR*, writing traditional satires against mankind (but in odd, modern form), and preaching apocalypse as Thomas Pynchon does in *Gravity's Rainbow*, or slyly revealing through murky symbolism, uncertain, half-lit characters and situations, and splendidly blurred syntax, that the Devil has arrived (as in *The Confidence-Man*) and we'd better wake up and pay attention, the main subject in John Hawkes. Think of the mysterious evils lurking in Hawkes's *The Cannibal*, *The Beetle-Leg*, or *The Lime Twig*, *Blood Oranges*, and so forth. Hawkes, I might mention, is as experimental a writer as you are likely to find; but the origins of his experiment, as of Melville's, are clear: among other things, Christian nightmares, those grotesque and gloomy medieval plays, *Pilgrim's Progress*, gothic fiction, Charles Williams, and scary bad movies about gangsters and murderers. He is, like his imitator William Palmer, a realist whose base of actuality is the nightmares we have in sleep.

Robert Coover would of course be extremely annoyed at my calling him a Christian, and I certainly won't call him a good Christian, but it is a fact, I think, that like that benighted, rant-filled hater-of-Baptists-and-almost-everybody-else Harry Crews, Coover at his worst works exactly like the meanest fundamentalist Baptist. (There are, of course, good and subtle Baptists.) Coover distrusts reason and makes a point of the fact—tiresome and wrongheaded as any bigoted deacon; he insists that you take his side, love what he loves, hate what he hates, and he is certain that the modern world is in for it. Some of his fiction is more or less straightforward—*The Universal Baseball Association* and his *Origin of the Brunists* (a superb book, the basis of his high reputation). Most is his work is "experimental"—as is *Pricksongs and Descants*. But in either mode, he is the American fundamentalist Christian gone wrong. He has all the old emotions, but he no longer believes the text, and that annoys him. In his plays he makes sneering fun, goes out of his way to talk dirty, like a schoolboy or an anally fixated adult, and reveals—as these writers so often do—an almost obsessive fascination with the character of Jesus. In the stories and novels he is forever dickering with form (neatness is another part of anal fixation), as if imagining that maybe if he is clever enough, God will like him. Occasionally, as in *The Origin of the Brunists*—a brilliant book in spite of everything I've said—he achieves the power of a great country sermon.

Other American writers popular just now are more successfully ex-Christian. If one feels that Coover may one day give up the struggle and join his church brethren, one does not feel that about Donald Barthelme, John Barth, or—after *Omensetter's Luck*—William Gass. All of these writers have, in common with Coover, the ex-Christian's love of bathroom humor and fifth-grader irreverence. Jewish-American writers treat sex and the elimination of bodily wastes in a way entirely different from both practicing (or more-or-less-practicing) Christians and lapsed Christians. We get, on one hand, the straightforward statements of Malamud and Bellow, or on the other hand, the comic and traditional wailing exaggerations of Philip Roth and Stanley Elkin. For Barth and Gass and, to a lesser extent, Barthelme, such things are dirty and wonderfully exciting—sin! Like American Catholic girls at drive-ins, they get themselves breathless but are terrified when begged to produce. They do produce, of course, these American writers, because frankness about sex and elimination seems to them a proof of maturity, as we see it in New York, which is to say, Europe.

A more important characteristic of the apostate Christians is their whining, whimpering, or bravely smiling misery. Barth, though by nature a cheerful man, talks endlessly, even in his earlier novels, about the meaninglessness of life. No one believes for a moment that he profoundly believes what he says, it's merely fashionable French existentialist bullshit; nevertheless, on he prattles about suicide and how it makes no difference one way or the other. A pagan Greek would stare in bafflement. "Who cares if life has meaning?" he would say. "Stop nattering and play your flute." Barthelme's fictions are all one sad confusion, often very funny, sometimes touching, frequently tiresome because we suspect as we read that we've heard all this better said before, by Samuel Beckett. If we read on, it is because Barthelme turns phrases nicely; but no one reads on through many stories. Enough is enough. The trouble, of course, is that the apostate Christians—all of them "innovative," as they like to say themselves—have a boring worldview. Like Melville's Captain Ahab they think only of themselves and their obsession, the rumor of God's death. Their endless frittering around with style—for example Barth's elephantine imitation of eighteenth-century writing in *The Sot-Weed Factor*—is self-indulgence, that is, as Longinus would say, "frigidity," a greater concern with showing themselves off than with their subject matter. Self-regarding style—the writer's intrusive, winking and leering personality—is more important to these writers than fictional character or thought. Indeed, they often abandon the concept of character, as Gass does philosophically in *Fiction and the Figures of Life* and practically in such works as *Willie Masters' Lonesome Wife*, where the narrator, that is the wife, is Language. These writers may also, as Gass does (or claims he does), abandon the idea that fiction is a way of thinking.

But let me turn now from the apostate Christian to my last two categories, diabolists and heretics.

Of these, I mean to say almost nothing. By diabolists I mean writers who claim to love death and evil—a claim that, outside the Marquis de Sade, always turns out to be false, as it is for William Burroughs, whose attacks on order turn out to be a plea for freedoms denied by a tight-sphinctered Christian and capitalist society. In *The Ticket That Exploded*—my favorite of Burroughs's books, a novel about how human civilization is all a ghastly accident—we discover that by understanding the accident, knowing its principles, we can perhaps redeem it, or at the very least can transform it within our own personalities just as Blake transforms the world in his splendid idea, "I gaze on the dark, Satanic mills; I shake my head; they vanish"—an idea that helped trigger my own short novel *Grendel*.

And by heretics—my last category—I mean such writers as John Updike, religious men whose ideas of religion I dislike. Updike's message, again and again, is a twisted version of the message of his church, neo-orthodox Presbyterianism: Christ has saved us; nothing is wrong; so come to bed with me. At the end of Updike's *A Month of Sundays*, the central character fornicates with God him(her)self.

Such are the real and significant movements, it seems to me, in contemporary American fiction. One can always slice the pie in some other way, and the system I offer is not intended to be neat. One might put Coover with the flat-out apostates—he would probably prefer it— and so would William Gaddis and Thomas Pynchon. Let them go where they please—the boundaries are, God knows, vague enough. Yet the central principle behind this way of looking at our modern American writers seems to me correct: even in their self-assertive agnosticism or atheism, American writers are influenced by religion in a way only a few Englishmen still are, and only a very few educated Frenchmen. Politicians in America prate on endlessly about Democracy and God, and the voters seem to like it: if they didn't, the politicians would stop. In America religion is still, I think, the chief intellectual and emotional influence on writers, because we openly believe it in all its archaic oddity, or because it serves as our substitute for class, or because we believe the religious claim and need it, or because we've lost our ability to believe it and are secretly or openly mad as hell. Like Mark Twain toward the end.

So-called experimental fiction has thus its special though not exclusive popularity among writers of two kinds: on the one hand, the whole spectrum of writers I have called Christian apostates; on the other, what I have called Christian orthodox writers, or in some cases troubled Christian orthodox writers, like John Hawkes and, say, myself. The two groups of writers, Christian and apostate, are often lumped together by critics and reviewers, much to the advantage of the orthodox, who could otherwise be scorned, in educated circles—especially in New York and, I suspect, most of Europe—as superstitious medieval barbarians, which we probably are.

The perspicacious eye can make out a world of difference, needless to say, between the experimental fictions of a Christian apostate and the work of a plain old-fashioned Christian, whether a troubled Christian, like George Herbert or John Donne, or a Christian full of blind confidence, like John Milton. The two kinds of writers—and still other kinds, such as hurt Jewish liberals like Philip Roth—use their methods for different ends, and even when they use the same devices—as (to borrow an image from William Gass) we may use a carrot either for food or as the nose for our snowman—they use those identical devices in dissimilar ways.

I would like to look now at the meaning of it all in somewhat closer detail—first, the meaning of the rise of American experimental fiction, then the meaning of certain experimental devices in various writers' work, focusing on just a few fictions, thus offering some touchstones for dealing with those devices and with other devices you will find to be similar. From this discussion I will move to brief and general remarks on why some of the experiments are more successful than others, what virtue or utility we may claim for the better and worse writers, and what value we may place, tentatively at least, on the American experimental movement as a whole. Let me admit in advance that I speak from, more or less, inside the movement. Thus, when I attack the "new" fiction, I attack selectively—perhaps sometimes without knowing I do so—not with the intention of tearing out the weed but only with the intention of pruning it a little.

One thing that is likely to strike the reader of the "new fiction" is what I would call its "spectacular technique." I mean the phrase as a term of approval: in much contemporary American fiction virtuosity is one of the things that keep us reading. But I also mean the phrase literally, as a description of technique that catches and may even distract the reader's eye, in other words, rightly or wrongly obtrusive technique. The obtrusion may show itself in various forms, for instance the blatancy of the fiction's "irreality," to use Borges's word, as in the stories and novels of Nabokov, Kosinski, Hawkes, Pynchon, Barthelme, or, sometimes, Gardner; in Albee's plays, or Stoppard's; and in Coover's plays and stories, for example "A Pedestrian Accident," of which I will be speaking a little later. The obtrusiveness may show itself in the form of so-called metafictional devices insisting on the reader's awareness of the page as physical object—the book as book. For instance, John Barth, in *Chimera*, has a genie who in the end turns into the book the reader is reading, and in *Giles Goat-Boy* has a librarian who, at a splendid crucial moment, is reading a book which tells of the event in which she is participating, which is the reason she can save the day. Other writers draw attention to the work as object in other ways, for example the use of cut-outs, questions and answers for the reader, or odd typography, as in Gass's brilliant though annoying *Willie Masters' Lonesome Wife* or, say, Molinaro's even more annoying "Chiaroscuro: A Treatment of Light and Shade." Again, writers have returned to the use of illustration—a notable feature in all my work (a feature suppressed in England and in most translations), in Kurt Vonnegut's *Breakfast of Champions*, and in some of the stories of John Updike, for example "Under the Microscope." The most obvious of all obtrusive devices, of course, are those involving point of view or "voice." To these last I will return in a moment.

But first let me remind you of a fact not always borne in mind by critics: though the various experimental writers I have mentioned have a great deal in common, may even be said to share a common theory, or possibly two or three rival theories (not that such theories need to be conscious), so that we may describe American new writers as a "school" or as a "group of schools," it is for the most part not true that they got their ideas from each other. I don't mean that there was no exchange of influence. They published together in the same little magazines and later, in some cases, with the same New York editors, the only ones who would take them. But what they had most in common was their cultural and educational background in the forties and fifties. I myself have spent the past twenty years teaching and writing books about medieval literature. What could be more natural for a child of Walt Disney and the Saturday cartoons? When I began to insist that my novels be illustrated, I had no idea that other writers could do the same. When I turned to myth (*Grendel*) and to the interpenetration of reality and dream (*The Sunlight Dialogues*), I was thinking not of John Hawkes but of what *Pinocchio* had led me to, of *Beowulf* and the work of Chaucer, Malory, and Dante. And when I began to use what I like to call lexicographical blisters—archaic words, words made up from Latin or Greek, and so on—I was thinking of the quirky textures of old paintings, the cranky vocabulary of later Middle English verse; I had no idea that Ken Kesey would do the same. At the Iowa Writers' Workshop, where, like Flannery O'Connor and everybody else, I'd gone to study my trade, I'd arrived too late and so encountered not the great white company of earlier days but Freudian novelist Marguerite Young, sodbuster Robert O'Bowen, and wooden allegorists like Calvin Kentfield, writers of the sort who, to set us yawning, divide their books about life in the Navy into sections entitled Earth, Air, Fire, and Water, then arrange the plot to fit traditional platitudes about the titles. I quit the writers' workshop and went up the hill to take classes in Italian, Greek, and Latin, to John McGalliard's Old English class, where people still cared about stories, still found books exciting, though what they talked of in class was endings and conjunctions, optatives and bilabial *f*s, and language as cultural and epistemological frame. It was that that I studied, not contemporary literary theory. The point is, I worked out my theory on my own, choosing on my own among the influences I'd accept, and I'm convinced most other writers in this so-called movement did the same. An odd bit of evidence in support of that opinion is the following: because I was sick to death of realism, I wrote, shortly after graduate school, a book called *The Forms of Fiction*—working in collaboration with a friend in the college where I taught, Lennis Dunlap. *The Forms of Fiction* was an anthology, but a new kind of anthology. Instead of collecting realistic stories, as in those days everybody else did, we collected and defined the various older prose forms—yarn, sketch, fable, tale, and, barely nodding to convention, short stories and novellas. *The Forms of Fiction*, we were sure, would be a revolutionary book. But almost the same month it was published, a young writer of fiction named George P. Elliot, whose fabulist short story "Among the Dangs" is one of the few great achievements among the early so-called innovative fiction, George P. Elliot, whom I did not know then and who did not know me (though he once sent my magazine a play which, knowing nothing about contemporary theater, I rejected), George P. Elliot published a book called *The Types of Fiction*. We had written, for all practical purposes, the same book. Both, I might mention, were widely adopted. George Elliot also, by the way, became editor of an experimental little magazine at about the same time my magazine, *MSS*, was discovering William Gass, Joyce Carol Oates, and numerous others.

Experimental fiction was, in the middle and late fifties (if not earlier), an idea whose time had come. It may have come out of the world situation, the disorientation of modern life, the American sense of reality misplaced, the alleged "absurdity of daily life" of which we hear so much from European-oriented New York City intellectuals, inclined to pay especially close attention to New York City writers with a similar orientation, or to midwestern Jewish writers like Herb Gold, Philip Roth, and Al Lebowitz, not to mention Saul Bellow, for whom the European holocaust had far more tragic immediacy than anything that happened in their lifetimes in Cleveland, St. Louis, or Chicago. It is true, we may say in defense of the critical commonplace on disorientation, absurdity, etc., that some of the new writers, such as Hawkes and Vonnegut, when not yet in their twenties, had seen war and its aftermath, and before that had seen the Great Depression, and that a few of the older innovators—Howard Nemerov, Andrew Lytle, and, I would have to add, since he has one foot solidly in the innovative camp, Saul Bellow—a few of those older innovators may indeed be described as distressed if not shattered idealists, brokenhearted or indignant liberals who abandoned conventional fiction for the same reasons as did Beckett and Calvino. But such writers were clearly the exception in America. World War II and all it signified produced a flood of realistic or realistic-symbolic novelists, people too intent upon bearing strong angry witness to the horrors they'd seen to take time messing around with form or aesthetic epistemology. *The Naked and the Dead* is a wartime sodbuster through and through, new in its emotion and reported experience, but as technically old-hat as a dimestore card for Mother's Day. And so it is with the rest—James Jones, Joe Heller, Edward Lewis Wallant, Mordecai Richler, William Eastlake, Gore Vidal, Vance Bourjaily, James Gould Cozzens, Herman Wouk— the list goes on and on, and not another Saul Bellow, Howard Nemerov, or Andrew Lytle in the pack. Later Mailer would turn fabulist, when a new generation had shown him how. Later Philip Roth, John Updike, and John Cheever would abandon their crisp, *New Yorker* style, their symbol-laden verisimilitude.

But then, right then—while the writers in New York were witnessing with almost journalistic directness—far off in the plains of Illinois, Iowa, and Missouri—homes, respectively, of *Accent* magazine, *Western Review*, and *Perspective*—and also down in the agrarian Christian South, rich in magazines like *Sewanee Review*, and also over in the pastures of Ohio, where the Southerner John Crowe Ransom had his *Kenyon Review*—in those country outposts the bomb was being constructed that would blow up the realist conventions. The South—Edgar Allan Poe's South—was the center of the literary revolution: one might call it Lee's revenge. After the political debacle at Louisiana State University, Austin Warren fled to Iowa, where he taught and shared an office with the Utah ex-Mormon cowboy Jarvis Thurston, who became founder of *Perspective* and the St. Louis Renaissance: Ray B. West was in Iowa, founder of the *Western Review*; the appallingly well-read René Wellek was in and out; also there was the medievalist John McGalliard, another Southerner, rebel and breakaway from the Cleanth Brooks and Robert Penn Warren New Critical team that had popularized the close reading of fiction like Jean Stafford's and, in *Understanding Fiction*—a vastly influential textbook—held up Poe's "The Fall of the House of Usher" as an example of how not to write.

These were not agonized or angry Jewish liberals, but philosophers, aestheticians, political conservatives and moderates, people who looked out at World War II from the safety of the American Heartland, looked out thoughtfully, with deep concern but little panic, deplored Nietzsche's thought not like people who have lost families to the ovens but only as good Christian gentlemen and concerned observers. They imported for their magazines—and in their books wrote about—European fiction, and like Faulkner, when they thought about the demise of European civilization, they thought, at the same time, about the crumbling traditions of the South. If they wrote with passion, they wrote at comfortable old desks, making available the thoughts of war-torn Europe, but thinking of disaster—as does Faulkner in all his Snopes stories, or Robert Penn Warren in *All the King's Men*—in terms of hanky-panky and family disruption or, in Flem Snopes's case, sexual impotence. As Alfred Kazin has remarked, they could see Flem Snopes making it to the Mansion; they didn't think about the White House.

Enter the next generation, the generation alleged to be concerned with "the American Nightmare." What happened in the war was not too fully reported in the *Batavia Daily News*. As far as I could tell, by way of Lowell Thomas, we'd won splendidly, as was right. I was personally miserable—my girlfriend lived a thousand miles away and I had pimples. My father was always grumbling about Joseph McCarthy, but it was true that the Unions were ruining the country; thank God we had a man we could trust in the White House, Eisenhower; and despite the best efforts of the Democrats, the farm was making money. I went to college and thus evaded the Korean war. There, for the first time, I heard in detail about the holocaust, which made me read with passionate interest—though to some extent the passion was Christian charitable affectation and maybe curiosity—the novels of Malraux, Gide, Proust, and Camus, the philosophy of Nietzsche, Kierkegaard, and Sartre. It was very exciting. Also, I was now only two hundred miles from where my girlfriend lived, and since the farm was doing well, I had a motorcycle. Someone pointed out, to my wonderment and joy, that there was "meaning" in Edgar Allan Poe. I encountered

Moravia, Kafka, and late Tolstoy. I saw European movies where some-times, for a second or two, they would let you see the girl's naked breasts. I sent stories to the *Saturday Evening Post*; they were rejected. I kept being beaten there by Salinger and Vonnegut, but I was too young, too innocent to understand. Like young writers all over America, though I didn't know it, I began to drift toward queer writing, like that of Flannery O'Connor and Eudora Welty or William Faulkner at his wildest, or like that, of course, of the Europeans. All through the heartland young writers were doing likewise, many of them guided by the Southern intellectuals and the little magazines I've mentioned. While I was copying out pages by hand, for typographic oddity, Bill Gass was cutting holes in his pages and Bob Coover, who is always the crazy one, was cutting, editing, and shuffling in the style of a film-editor. (Burroughs was doing the same, but Coover didn't know it.) Something was in the air, a common dissatisfaction—both among younger and among older American writers—with what was called conventional fiction. Some as yet undiscovered new theory of fiction's methods and purposes was struggling to be born. We fooled around, tried things, chopped, pasted, drew pictures, read fairy tales. Hunting.

Now that the fumbling search is more or less over, at least for some of us, now that we can look around and notice, partly in delight, partly in embarrassment, that all over America writers like ourselves were doing the same thing—we can begin to articulate what we were doing.

I hope it's clear that I am saying all this for a reason. Experimental fiction, as we may call it for convenience, was not an intellectual movement but a phenomenon: its theory was not worked out in ad-vance, programmatically, or if it was, was worked out independently by a raft of people, some wiser, some less wise. And so the common devices of the experimenters must be considered as solutions to basic aesthetic questions and impulses—or else, perhaps, as symptoms of a widespread disease.

I think we can see this if we consider one such solution or symptom, obtrusive technique, or rather one form of obtrusive technique, namely, the new writer's fondness for tricks with point of view and voice.

As Philip Stevick and others have pointed out, one distinguishing feature of the new fiction, if we contrast it with the old—that is, with the fiction of such typical writers as Jean Stafford or Carson McCullers a quarter of a century ago—is the new writer's rejection of the realist's idea that as a writer he ought to efface himself, "sit like God in the corner of the universe paring his nails," as Joyce said (an opinion he himself soon abandoned). The new writers, at least most of the time, will have none of it. They are forever calling noisy attention to themselves, clambering all over you, bawling for affection like Spanish Harlem ghetto kids being given a nice healthy summer in the terrifying stillness of New Hampshire or Vermont. I'm aware that you know already what I mean, but let me give you some examples.

John Barth in "Life-Story," about a writer trying to write, writes:

> Another story about a writer writing a story! Another regressus in infinitum! Who doesn't prefer art that at least overtly imitates something other than its own processes? That doesn't continually proclaim "Don't forget I'm an artifice!"? That takes for granted its mimetic nature instead of asserting it in order (not so slyly after all) to deny it, or vice-versa? Though his critics sympathetic and otherwise described his own work as avant-garde, in his heart of hearts he disliked literature of an experimental, self-despising, or overtly metaphysical character, like Samuel Beckett's, Marian Cutler's, Jorge Borges's. The logical fantasies of Lewis Carroll pleased him less than straightforward tales of adventure, subtly sentimental romances, even densely circumstantial realism like Tolstoy's. His favorite contemporary authors were John Updike, Georges Simenon, Nicole Riboud. He had no use for the theater of absurdity, for "black humor," for allegory in any form, for apocalyptic preachments meretriciously tricked out in dramatic garb.

Later in the same story, Barth writes:

> The reader! You, dogged, uninsultable, print-oriented bastard, it's you I'm addressing, who else, from inside this monstrous fiction. You've read me this far, then? Even this far? For what discreditable motive?

In many of his fictions—*Chimera*, for example—Barth includes himself as a character. Ron Sukenick does the same. In all Sukenick's novels, *Up, Out,* and *98.6,* the central character is himself or self-confessed projections of himself, as it is in his superb short story, "What's Your Story?" In this last, the narrative shoots straight from the writer's consciousness-at-the moment to the page he is writing—or anyway that's the fictional pretense. The story opens with a description which turns out to be not of the actual scene, in the usual sense, but of two paintings the narrator is looking at; then he looks at a mirror (I think), then at what can be seen from his window, all of these presented as indivisible reality, the domain of the narrator's playing consciousness. The narrator, that is, Sukenick, looks at his writing desk, remembers a conversation, thinks about writing, hears what might be a gunshot outside, imagines being visited by an assassin. Pictures, real world, memory, fantasy—all have the same immediacy. His story closes:

> The droplets rain from the eaves. The shadow of a cloud dims the snow dazzle. George Washington crosses the Delaware on the walls. I sit at my desk, making this up, and keep an eye on the road, waiting for a car to come cruising around the curve, a shiny black Cadillac, an enormous four-door sedan. A gunshot echoes through the distance. They'll be back. Against that day prepare.
>
> You sit at your desk, you look down at the slum. You begin to understand how it works. Or you drown in it. People are on your side or they're not. You make contacts, compare notes. It helps you to breathe. Let's not suffocate in your own experience.
>
> They'll be back, are already here, always with me. A gunshot echoes through the distance. The gypsy wakes, if he's still alive, faces the lion, and picks up his lute.
>
> Start with immediate situation. One scene after another, disparate, opaque, absolutely concrete. Later, a fable, a gloss, begins to develop, abstractions appear. End with illuminating formulation. Simple direct utterance.
>
> A gunshot echoes through the distance.
>
> They'll be back, are already here, always with us.
>
> "The communication of our experience to others is the elemental act of civilization."
>
> They're coming for you.
>
> What's your story?

In my own fiction I have on various occasions played with tricks of point of view and voice much like those in the passages just quoted. *The King's Indian* collection contains a true-life story, "John Napper Sailing Through the Universe," in which the central character is or was John Gardner, and in the "The King's Indian" itself, that is, the featured novella, one can find numerous allusions to—or, rather, straight-across revelations of—the narrator (myself) behind the fictional narrators (myself in two projections), and one will of course also find a good deal of talk—I hope more interesting than John Barth's—about the writer writing, a device I believed (at the time) that I'd gotten from Homer, Apollonius, and Chaucer. I also at one time included myself among the cast in another book of mine, the mock-realistic novel *Nickel Mountain*. But during the time I worked on that novel—between the ages of nineteen and forty—the device became too common (it was also inherently arch) so I suppressed it. The device is also central in an epic-length poem I wrote, *Jason and Medeia*, begun in 1963, published ten years later. There I used, or maybe misused, the traditional epic narrator in some rather odd ways. Beginning as a passive observer of the story, or dream-vision, he occasionally finds himself roughly hauled into it for real, as here:

> In horror I felt myself/ falling to the mud, my spectacles dangling, precariously hooked/ by one ear. I squealed like a rat incinerated,/ my mind all terror, my left hand clutching at my spectacles, right hand/ stretching to snatch some hold on the back of the sweatwashed giant/ in front of me. I fell, sank deep in the mud; the maniacal/ crowd came on, stepping on my legs, battering my ribs./ On the back of my left hand, blurry as a cloud, fell a scarlet drop of blood. "Dear goddess!" I whimpered. I'd surely gone mad! It was/ no dream, surely, this fangling pain! A foot sank, blind/ on the four fingers of my thin right hand and buried them;/ thick yellow water swirled where they'd been, then reddened with blood./ My mind grew befuddled. My vision was awash./ Then hands seized me, painfully jerked me upward, at the same time/ heaving back at the crowd. I gave myself up to the stranger,/ clinging still to my spectacles. My rescuer shouted,/ struck at the crowd with his one free arm like a

wounded gorilla./ We came to a wall, a doorway; he dragged me inside... (From Book XVII)

Why, we ask, are those obtrusive narrators so popular with the new writers? I will suggest three main reasons, none of them the first that springs to mind, egomania. First, I would argue that, consciously or not, the new writer feels—or rather some new writers feel—that this obtrusive technique aligns him with classical, not romantic tradition, the romantic being a tradition he dislikes, or anyway feels himself obliged to shun even when (as Barth says he does in one of the passages I've quoted) he likes it better than the kind of thing he's doing. Second, point-of-view or voice obtrusiveness provides him with instant access to a central concern in nearly all modern fiction, aesthetic epistemology, the asking of the question "How does the artist know what he thinks he knows?" And third, when the writer has abandoned authenticating realism, or verisimilitude, the self-effacing narrator becomes not only useless baggage but a noisome encumbrance, like hydrofoils in a country of levitators.

Begin with the impulse toward the classical. Leslie Fiedler has claimed—and most critics agree with him—that the development of fiction since the eighteenth century shows an increasing concern with "inwardness," an increasing fascination with the "minute-by-minute content of consciousness," and reflects, in its broad evolution of technique, "the transition from the objective, social, and public orientation of the classical world to the subjective, individualist, and private orientation of the life and literature of the last two hundred years" (*Love and Death in the American Novel*, Cleveland and New York, 1962, p. 176). Joe David Bellamy glosses Fiedler's idea as follows:

> To put it another way, in traditional fiction, we meet "characters" who are looking out—at society, manners, plots; in the early twentieth-century novel of consciousness or modernist short fiction, we are inside a character (or characters) looking out. In the world of the contemporary superfictionist, we are most frequently inside a character (or characters) looking out. In *or* these inner phantasms are projected outward, and in a sometimes frightening sometimes comic reversal, the outside "reality" begins to look more and more like a mirror of the inner landscape—there is so little difference between the two.

The general thesis on the development of the novel down to modern times is no doubt right; but when we come to the new fiction several facts should give us pause. It is again and again to ancient and more recent classical models that the new writers turn. Barth has for years been studying the Indian *Ocean of Story*, not to mention the *Thousand and One Nights* from which he draws *Chimera*. His first notably "innovative" novel, *The Sot-Weed Factor*, is written in imitation of eighteenth-century style, with eighteenth-century satirical humor (humor assuming a societal standard of taste, the basis of satire), and his tone—there and everywhere—even more important, his theme in each work—is invariably one appropriate to an old-fashioned Enlightenment rationalist, though he is not quite that, as we will see. In *Giles Goat-Boy* he treats innocence and education, for the most part public education, though the Barth hero—any Barth hero—must first discover his identity, in this case by the social act of fathering a child, before he can save his community. (Most eighteenth-century philosophers would agree.) In *Chimera* he speaks mainly of the right and proper relationship between the sexes, not simply what relationship he hopes to find with Sally Rosenberg, now his wife, but the relationship that ought to obtain between male and female human beings in an ordered society. Ordered society is for that reason made the secondary theme: social disorder must be corrected for the winning of the Medusa; Bellerophon must learn that romantic heroism, "individualism," is impossible. He does all the things done by heroes in books and becomes, only, the perfect imitation of a hero. The genie of the tale, the writer of the story, now becomes the book, the reader's instrument of instruction. The book's fall in Maryland, Barth's birthplace and the location of his present university post, Johns Hopkins, is one last affirmation of the writer's proper function, not romantic individualist and howler, but servant of his proper community. This is a far cry from Gide's use of myth in *Thesée*, an existential perversion of the Theseus story, where all that matters in the end—or all that really matters, despite Icarus's lofty, unintelligible babblings and Oedipus's woe—is Theseus's affirmation, "*J'ai vécu!*"

At first glance Ronald Sukenick's technique in "What's Your Story?" may seem a further step in the withdrawal inward. But the fascination in this fiction with "the minute-by-minute content of consciousness" has an explicit social and moral purpose. Sukenick dramatizes—that is, delineates through presented events—the significance of thinking and writing, and ends, like the teacher and neo-rationalist he is (as are many of these writers), with a "gloss," as he says, an "illuminating formulation," namely, "the communication of our experience to others is the elemental act of civilization." We may grant the ironic under-cutting in the polysyllabics—"illuminating formulation." But the irony is part one of a one-two punch. All but the faintest trace of irony vanishes when he throws punch two in his final lines: "They're com-ing for you. What's your story?"

I can't easily tell you how my own obtrusive narrator works in *Jason and Medeia*, a poem of several thousand lines, but obviously in retell-ing a classical myth, thus joining the company of Barth, Hawkes, Updike (in his best book, *The Centaur*), and all those others, one of my interests was in trying to understand—imaginatively, from inside—our civilization's archetypal and probably oldest myth of male and female, darkness and sunlight, reason and intuition—not to impose by wit and raw power my own romantic vision on a grumpy universe but to understand those mysteries centuries of my relatives have found, or imagined they've found, in the visions and revisions of Apollonius and Euripides.

This is not to say that we who write the so-called new fiction are truly rationalists, that we have found the long-sought formula for turn-ing back time and can stand before you as complete eighteenth-century men, innocent of nineteenth- and early twentieth-century individualist affirmations and disillusionments. Once you've discovered atoms, dis-covered that the universe has more holes in it than motes, you can never again lean on an innocent wall. But whereas fiction in the forties and fifties was overloaded with worries about such things, most fiction today takes the healthy view—though a view that can easily be carried too far—that wringing one's fingers and exclaiming "What is real?" is a tiresome thing to do; better to get on with our civilized and civilizing business, merely registering our knowledge that our knowledge may be faulty by parody of the old uneasiness. Dream becomes reality, reality becomes dream. The endlessly repeated business, even when shrugged off, can still have interest, even moral implications. Our poems may change our lives, dent our hats, smash our fingers, and our lives may change—for better or worse—our poems. John Napper, the wise old artist of my story "John Napper Sailing Through the Universe," knows and teaches one important truth out of this: nothing exists for sure, until we make it; don't sit staring at the abyss, then. Make!

It's what my character Mad Queen Louisa understands in another way: strike out for good, bring the witch to repentance, at least insofar as you understand what's good—bearing carefully in mind, as I wrote in one of the Louisa stories, that "she [Queen Louisa] was insane and could never know anything for sure, and perhaps the whole story was taking place in a hotel in Philadelphia."

But obtrusive point of view or voice is of course not always, in new fiction, a means of acknowledging the "reality" problem and then dismissing it. If in some moods we wish simply to shrug off the question "What is the artist's authority for this story?"—the question that put Joseph Conrad, Stephen Crane, and William Faulkner, Andrei Biely and Vladimir Nabokov through those elaborate experiments in point of view, retreats from the lying authorial omniscience to such "strategies" as the unreliable narrator, the communal voice, narration through successive centers of consciousness (as in *The Sound and the Fury*), and edited and re-edited narrative (as in *Ada*)—if in some moods we're inclined to shrug off all that, in others we still find the question interesting, though few these days think it alarming. Writers do feel the age-old desire of artists to tell "the truth." Whereas the self-effacing narrator was truthful by definition and convention, to be accepted pretty much as we accept the rules of whist, the obtrusive narrator is somebody (or something), therefore non-omniscient and available for questioning. His plump and all too noticeable existence raises questions at once, like a stranger in the bedroom, and if the questions are not at once shrugged off they become inescapably part of the fiction.

The new fiction abounds in studies of aesthetic epistemology—the relation of art and its subject, art and morality, even art and religious faithfulness (as in Cynthia Ozick's *Bloodshed*). As we might expect of a professional philosopher, William Gass has addressed these matters repeatedly. In his superb novella "The Pedersen Kid," a nightmare search for a murderer is pursued because of a story, impelled past the point of no return by boasts and myths, and crowned by the narrator's simultaneous moral and aesthetic affirmation/observation that whatever it may mean, he has played his part, fulfilled, if you like, his *beot*—his boast or word. In Gass's *Omensetter's Luck*, a man who lives by thought and language, Jethro Furber—a man out of touch with what we call "real life"—comes into conflict with a man, Omensetter, who has not yet risen out of life into reflection. Through Omensetter, Furber reaches the connection he needs, reaches in fact salvation, though Omensetter is not so lucky. In these works the narration is not exactly obtrusive, though the writing is so brilliantly, earthily poetic that it tends in that direction. I can see, in fact, only a degree of difference between Gass's style here and the self-regarding style of Barth's *Sot-Weed Factor*, where we are mercilessly chained to the pace of eighteenth-century prose. *Willie Masters' Lonesome Wife*, narrated by Language itself, is quite another matter. Here Gass attacks the problem of language and knowledge most directly, teasing many of the same questions he teases in his essays, especially those in the first and fourth sections of his *Fiction and the Figures of Life*. I think no one will deny that philosophically at least, *Willie Masters'* is a minor masterpiece. It may even be a masterpiece by a certain set of aesthetic criteria—intelligence, orderly arrangement, and so forth. But for me, at least, the answer to the question in the title—"Will he Master?"—is "who cares?" or perhaps, more emphatically, "No—not without real characters and hopefully a little love interest to give oomph to all those academic metaphors of sex and post-coital depression." But I digress.

The obtrusive narrator, when used as a springboard to serious or even mock-serious discussion of knowledge and art, works one way when kept inside the story's drama, as in Sukenick's story or the passage I've quoted from *Jason and Medeia*, another way when set in opposition to the fiction's dramatic elements, as in Barth's "Life-Story," where the writer's academic asides to the reader, and so on, contrast with his dramatized relationship with his family, or again in Barth's famous story "Lost in the Funhouse," where authorial asides on fictional technique interrupt a beautifully and imaginatively rendered story of three people going to a Funhouse, a pair of lovers and the girl's younger brother. In one case, of course, the philosophical questions rise out of drama. In the other, they are meant to be a part of the drama, playing the role of discourse in a debate or would-be dramatic struggle between discourse and storytelling. In "Lost in the Funhouse" the method no doubt works, at least for readers willing to put up with it. The two lovers enjoy the Funhouse and each other, being fond in both the new and old sense—not very bright. The younger brother, much more intelligent but scornful of what he has never experienced, wanders back into where the control-levers are—the things that make the Funhouse work—and begins to play with them. He enjoys the machinery, and never emerges. So it can be, Barth is saying, with knowledge and experience, art and life. Neither the lovers, mired in sensation, nor the boy, clever but disdainful, has the truth, though the boy, pulling levers, can give the lovers amusement, even heighten their pleasure in each other. So the artist, thinking about fiction's techniques, can make wonderful fictions, may even be of use in the world; but if technique supplants love, he is "lost." The message—or discovery—is one to which Barth comes repeatedly: true art is loving, community-oriented, social. Or to put it another way, art's road to knowledge is through the heart. Technique is useful—indispensable, perhaps, though many of the rules for writing fiction in Barth's asides are rules his story has disobeyed—but technique for its own sake, or for the sake of the artist's personal amusement and self-expression, is empty nattering.

Barth's opinion in this matter is not one held universally by American writers of new fiction, though I, for one, agree with it. Some would say, as does Gass in America or Raymond Queneau in France, that technique is the only reality we have, that is, that language shapes the reality we see: to change the language is to change the world. In *Fiction and the Figures of Life* Gass gives some examples, showing how by altering the grammar and syntax of a description we change our experience. This is of course a familiar fact to professional philologists like Queneau: when we think in German we see the world differently than when we think in French, or Greek, or Chinese. To know this, Gass would say, is to know that we have no sure knowledge to communicate, hence fiction lies if it claims it has usefulness or relevance in the world. A fictional work is simply one more object, exactly as valuable as a bird or tree. We can enjoy it, but we cannot live by it. The familiar answer to Gass's argument is that if I make a bomb according to an expert's directions I can trust it to explode. In certain respects that answer evades the issue, since nitroglycerine, black powder, and copper wire, etc., are verbal signifiers of a very simple order; but let us not worry that matter here. What is interesting in Gass's notion, even though finally we may agree it's inadequate, is that it puts us into a relationship with words that the self-effacing realist narrator never thought of or, if he thought of it, would be hard put to make use of.

Whereas the self-effacing narrator quietly, unobtrusively puts the wine on the table, seats the guests, and starts the conversation, confidently describing the world fact by fact, telling lies without knowing it, the man who thinks of language as a shaper of realities is like the "pure" mathematician who works difficult equations on the twenty-fifth dimension, a dimension which, so far as we know, does not exist. The linguistic shaper neither lies nor tells the truth, he merely makes structures never before known and of possible interest, even perhaps beauty, like an elegant mathematical proof which has no application. There are, of course, writers who actually do this, though their readership, understandably, is not wide. William Gass himself seems to have done it in *On Being Blue*, a book I am unable to get into. William Burroughs does it—but also other things as well—in the various *Nova Express* books. If some writers find such things interesting to do, and readers after them find them interesting to look at, we can have, as generous people, no serious objection; the world now contains a few more toys.

But the idea that language shapes new realities is of course more interesting than I admit in what I've so far said. Some mathematical investigations do have applications, helping us to figure out how tall flagpoles are, or how many apples we can get for fifty cents. Among nearly all people, blindness has been thought a curse. To the ancient Greeks it was often thought a blessing: like the probably apocryphal blind Homer, the sightless learn to see with their tongues. New uses of language and of what we may as well call the metalanguage of fiction's conventions may, like algebra's, lead us to insight into how things are or, at very least, how they are not.

Fiction grounded on verisimilitude argues the reader into believing what he's told by loading him down with facts he can't get out of. It names Detroit's streets and important and unimportant landmarks, it speaks of blacks and of Catholic Polish girls named Wanda, whose fathers and older brothers work at "Ford's," it mentions off-hand that Windsor, Ontario, lies to the south. The narrator of all this keeps his dignity, like one of those English bankers who wears black so we'll know he's dependable; and he narrates in American standard English, or in some third- or first-person variant instantly recognizable as sincere; he puts setting, character, and action first and avoids purple prose. But for the narrator of the tale, fable, or yarn, on the other hand, forms which depend not on verisimilitude but on the willing suspension of disbelief for the moment, or on the reader's indifference to the fiction's truth—no such restrictions apply: nothing matters except that the narrator be, in somebody's judgment, interesting.

Everyone loves make-believe, some world he can get involved in—the distant planet worlds of science fiction, the infernal yet ominously sunlit dream-worlds of John Hawkes, nightmare worlds of ambiguous emotion and elusive meaning, like the world in Rudolph Wurlitzer's story "Quake," fairy-tale worlds, also the familiar familial South of realist-symbolic fiction. The metafictionist's idea of language as an instrument for shaping reality, a fictional reality we may compare with what actually seems to happen in our lives—a fictional construct which therefore may prove a source of knowledge, like hyperbolic geometry, without which we could never have reached Mars with our probe—the metafictionist's idea of language as instrument of discovery is the old traditional idea of language. And yet there is something patently wrong with some part of the metafictionist's program. A metafiction works if it is of interest to somebody—anybody. The problem is the somebody.

At a conservative estimate, 90 percent of the so-called new fiction is soporific. Ron Sukenick's novels are published by small presses, not the New York Establishment, because—brilliant as they may be at certain moments—they're boring. They have no plots, no real characters, no theme, nothing to follow but the play of Sukenick's imagination, one damn thing after another. In his full-length novels, though they do have plot, John Barth is equally dull. In his two longer novels, Pynchon works like laughing gas—a little fascinating weirdness, a few guffaws, then Morpheus. Gass's *Omensetter's Luck* has plot, characters, and a fine thematic profluence, but in the central section—the one that makes it innovative—a section in which Jethro Furber babbles, playing with language and metalanguage, dramatizing for us his lack of connection with "real life," our response is mainly, after a while, a snore. In all these cases what turns us off is the character of the writer: his self-indulgence—the same thing that turns us off in the somewhat less innovative Bellow (*Humboldt's Gift* and *Herzog*) when he drops his fiction and lets his central character lecture us as the Devil is said to lecture—for all eternity—in Hell. We snore for the same reason when Updike begins on fornication or the joys of the blow job. Somebody may be interested, but the somebody, we have to assent, is a damn fool. He likes what ought not to be liked, stern old Tolstoy would say—and did say, speaking of Maupassant.

It's the same mistake, but a different form of it, that ruins the fiction of Bob Coover. In "A Pedestrian Accident" the central character has been run over by a truck and lies in the street, paralyzed and dying. The trucker is self-defensive and indifferent to the lot of the dying man, Paul. An old slut who once rented him a room appears, along with a gawking, callous crowd, and finding that Paul cannot speak to contradict her, tells an outrageous story of her sexual pleasures with him. Three authority figures—a policeman, a physician, and a priest— who turns out to be a bum waiting for Paul to die so that he can steal Paul's clothes—add to his misery, playing familiar slapstick movie roles, none of them in this case funny, not even "black-comic," like the humor of Beckett, but merely cruel and outrageous, stirring the reader to anger. Eventually the crowd leaves, rain falls on our miserable victim, a dog takes a bite of him and runs away. Paul, an ex-Christian, knows it all means nothing, and since Paul's voice is the only one treated with sympathy and respect in the story, we are invited to agree. Indeed, a godless, ugly universe is a given in the story, an absolute, somehow revealed premise we are expected to share, since to doubt it would be stupidity. The story ends:

> For an instant the earth upended again, and Paul found himself hung on the street, a target for the millions of raindrops somebody out in the night was throwing at him. There's nobody out there, he reminded himself, and that set the earth right again. The beggar spat. Paul shielded his eyes from the rain with his lids. He thought he heard other dogs. How much longer must this go on? he wondered. How much longer?

Note that the upending of the earth, so that "Paul found himself hung on the street," sets up a crucifixion image—here a mocking one. Note the angry irony in the phrase "that set the world right again." Note the emotion-charged, intellectual confusion in the equation of the beggar's spit and the rain, since the latter has been said to come from "nobody." Read the story and you will see that in its verbose development—for instance its endless repetitions of the slapstick movie cliché "Now stop that," a comic device drawn from Jack Benny and

Bud Abbott, here applied to the spluttering policeman who cannot stop the old slut's ugly story—Coover's story is tiresome. Read the story and you will see also—here as so often in Gass's fiction—the bedroom and bathroom materials (I refuse to call them "humor") function not like the farts cut by medieval devils in a mystery or the scatology in Jonathan Swift but only as puerile impudence or anal fixation. Somebody may be amused, somebody may think all this fashionable bullshit to be highly intelligent, but if so, somebody, we must assert, is badly mistaken.

We are in need, obviously, of some sort of more or less effective criteria for what is authentically interesting, and what is not. In this regard, let me simply give suggestions: good fiction, traditional or experimental, is fiction the experienced, intellectually and emotionally mature reader recognizes, immediately or eventually, as intelligent and tasteful. It does not bully the reader, as Coover's fiction so often does, though it may playfully pretend to bully him, as Barth does in "Life-Story." In realistic fiction we call this bullying "sentimentality," the practice of demanding emotional effect without providing sufficient dramatic cause. Stanley Elkin regularly offends in this way, for instance in the faked, moralistic conclusions of the pharmacist's tale in *The Dick Gibson Show* or "The Bail Bondsman" in *Searches and Seizures*. William Gass sometimes slips into the same error in "The Pedersen Kid" and "In the Heart of the Heart of the Country." Good fiction, traditional or experimental, is emotionally honest. That is a point too often lost sight of by critics who imagine they must look at the new fiction in a wholly new way, as if Barthelme's having run an art gallery and having picked up, for fiction, some of the concerns of the younger visual artists (parody, the incorporation of trash culture, and the fracturing or upending of conventional ways of seeing and representing), or as if Barth's use of discourse in the development of his fictions, made emotional honesty obsolete. Coleridge's claim has not ceased to hold, that "Nothing can permanently please that does not contain in itself the reason why it is as it is and not otherwise." It is of course true that new art of any kind requires some measures of sophistication and open-mindedness, perhaps even, initially, a short stint in the English Department of some graduate school; and it is of course also true that in the capitalist world—or in anti-capitalist societies bent on proving they can do anything the capitalists do—true innovation must forever compete with what Anthony Hecht has called, complaining of an all-too-common tendency in contemporary poetry, "fraudulent and adventitious novelty." In fact, frequently—as in the work of John Barth and William Gass—the real thing and the shoddy imitation appear together. But for all the tedious writing it has produced, for all the intellectual and emotional cheating it has sheltered and even celebrated, for all its availability as a tool to people whose highest allegiance is to fashion, for all its vulnerability to misconstruction by well-meaning, serious-minded critics, it seems to me that the so-called new fiction has opened a door that has been left closed too long. In America, no real masters have stepped through it since Poe and Melville. The new fiction means no harm to the genteel tradition. It offers an alternative to the endlessly repetitive, wearisomely sensitive well-dressed cousin to the sodbuster—or, rather, given its willingness to try anything, it offers—in potential, at least—a thousand alternatives, all of which must stand or fall, finally, on the grounds that they do or do not do the real work of art.

————————

American experimental fiction after World War II came not out of the horrors of the war, at least not directly, as an expression of disorientation and the collapse of values, those terrible recognitions that produced the great wave of witnessing, transplanted sodbusters like *The Naked and the Dead*. It came, instead, as the end-product of an attempt, largely by Southern American intellectuals and their students in the American heartland, to understand those horrors, and their American implications, while keeping them at arm's length. Experimental fiction originally came, that is, not from radical but from conservative thought and feeling. Putting the matter oversimply but not altogether falsely, we might say that, flinching from Auschwitz photographs, diaries, and depopulated shoes, suits, and spectacles, Southern American intellectuals turned their eyes to European philosophy books and to European fiction—the works of Kafka, Gide, Proust, Vittorini, and many more—fictions that had presaged the collapse of what we'd thought to be Europe's values, and saw in such books— those Southern intellectuals—parallels between Europe's situation and that of the American South. For Jew, they said in effect, read Negro; for industrial Germany, read ambitious, unprincipled Flem Snopes and the Yankee North. What passion this movement had came from authentic concern about the moral issues and about the survival of Southern aristocratic attitudes. Southern intellectuals did make a serious effort to see their culture honestly, and many were successful in this effort, though that fact was not always obvious to Northerners. They were, and had been since the American Civil War, a defeated culture and the victims of enormous cultural prejudice. William Faulkner, John Crowe Ransom, Allen Tate, even Flannery O'Connor, Carson McCullers, Caroline Gordon, Katherine Anne Porter, and Eudora Welty, however courageous their self-examination, were scrutinized for slips into bigotry and unreconstructed rebelliousness, and every slip, real or imagined (if many were real, far more were imagined), was pounced upon by liberal Northerners eager to place blame. Southern fiction became more gothic and more Christian-allegorical than it had ever been before, which is to say, Southern writers increasingly emphasized, in terms of comic-book or Southwestern yarn hyperbole, the hypocrisy, even madness of Southern life—a real element, but by no means the only real element, in their experience. Southern thinkers and critics—old-fashioned essayists in modern dress—became increasingly abstract, aesthetic, and metaphysical, except for those like Russell Kirk, who in violent reaction took increasingly outrageous positions, especially on race. Both as a means of asserting their intelligence and cultivation, and as a means of ending hostile criticism, Southern writers became increasingly subtle and arcane, while Southern criticism—mainly at this time the fully evolved New Criticism—became increasingly formalistic and morally evasive, regularly arguing, in Northrop Frye's words, that "no work is better than another by virtue of what it says." Hence the difficult, experimental style in the books of William Faulkner, and his famous ambivalence, as in Quentin Compson's cry "I don't hate the South." As I've said, it was this moral concern, this recognition of the European parallel, and this vulnerability to hostile criticism that led to the little-magazine fascination with the translation and publication of Europe's newer, odder writers and to the willingness of Christian Southern intellectuals to entertain the opinions of existentialists, even nihilists. The Southern intellectual climate, which soon spread north and west, favored sophistication and a muting of emotion, especially the emotion of religious conviction—favored a fiction of grotesques, like that of Eudora Welty or Flannery O'Connor, whose "good" people, such as "the Misfit" in "A Good Man Is Hard to Find," seem at first glance to be the worst people; and the same climate favored myth, dream, or "fabulation," as Robert Scholes calls it—fiction like that of Andrew Lytle or, if one may draw the obvious parallel, that of Jorge Borges, writing in fascist Argentina though his favorite poet, he says, is Walt Whitman. Hypothetical realities—dream worlds, mythic worlds—can be used to give cover to the writer's morality. They can also, of course, allow the storyteller to keep talking when he has nothing to say, nothing he believes in.

As I have suggested above, a good way to look at contemporary American fiction is to study it in terms of the various religious, or non-, or anti-religious emotions it expresses. We are perhaps now in a position to understand that suggestion a little more clearly. First we have the liberal tradition. It may be either Jewish or Christian, racially white or black (or, of course, anything else). In general it produces realistic or "conventional" fiction, for the simple reason that it has important information to communicate and wants the largest possible audience. Hence the realism of post–World War II novels—Mailer, Jones, Cozzens, Wouk, and so forth—and the realism of Vietnam novels like the early works of Tim O'Brien. When this strain in our fiction uses innovative methods, as does Ellison in *Invisible Man* or Bellow in *Henderson* and *Humboldt's Gift* (also in other books to a lesser extent), the innovation is never so extreme as to scare away the audience: it flavors the message, enriching and deepening it or, as in *Humboldt's Gift*, cartooning it a little; it never in any way obscures it.

Second, we have what I called orthodox or troubled-orthodox Christian fiction; I would have added, except that it would have muddied the waters, that we might also include here those Jewish writers, like I. B. Singer, whose main subject is the comforting and explanatory value of their religion. Let us now include them—Philip Roth when he was young as in *Goodbye, Columbus*; Cynthia Ozick; Sol Yurick; and many others. These writers, speaking to a narrower audience, an audience of the converted, may write either "conventional" or "experimental" fiction. It's the subject, and not the form, that's important. John Hawkes writes obscure books—mysterious landscapes, shape-shifting characters, plots strangely twisted, like the plots of our nightmares; we feel lost in an absurd, mad universe except that sometimes we are pulled up short, given hints of direction, by some traditional

Christian image or idea—the slain lamb in the story "The Traveller," the equation of will and a tiny crack in a dam in *The Beetle-Leg*. Nothing could show more clearly the religiously secure writer's freedom to write as he pleases, knowing his position in advance, than Mark Helprin's *A Dove of the East*, in which old-fashioned non-realistic tales, realistic nineteenth-century fictions, and modern realism sit comfortably side by side.

We have, third, apostate Christians—that is, Christians who have turned against their religion—and we may as well add apostate Jews and liberals—for example Philip Roth in his more recent work. Whether we call Robert Coover an apostate who protests too much, hence a closet hell-fire preacher, or a flat-out apostate mysteriously full of hatred for the Father he claims does not exist, he belongs in this current in our fiction, or else swims along close by. Sometimes, of course, as in "The Elevator," he simply avoids all meaning, as does, he thinks, the universe.

And finally we have diabolists and heretics. We have no full-time diabolists, though both Burroughs and Nabokov play at it. In *Ada*, Nabokov claims—through a character but with a note of authority, that all of America's great charitable institutions—hospitals for epileptics, and so on—were originally founded as whorehouses. Mocking things he knows to be decent and even effectively good, and praising things not good, is a Nabokov specialty, though at the core his fiction is always moral. If his shocking gangsterism in trifling matters is sometimes of value, deflating false piety, the diabolical impulse is nonetheless a tiresome one; I cannot imagine why anyone would choose it except as exhibitionism.

The only significant heretic in America, I've said, is John Updike.

I've summarized and slightly expanded these things in order to prepare the way for my point on moral fiction. My purpose is to argue that, except for fictions which work strictly as toys—if such things are really possible—and except for fictions we value for their power as expressions of honest though neurotic emotion and wrongheaded opinion, good fiction is moral. It reinforces our best impulses and undermines our temptation toward that which is unhealthy for individuals and society. It may be either conventional or experimental, and it may come from a person who, in his private life, claims to be Christian, Muslim, Jewish, agnostic, atheist, or anything else. It holds up visions of the possible, helps us to evaluate our acts, conserves—fair-mindedly and compassionately—all that is good in our culture, and seeks to expunge what is bad. It may do all this comically, tragically, or in any other way; but to be truly moral, it must do what it does fairly well.

How can fiction be moral? I do not mean that it must be designed to preach some doctrine. To my modern Protestant soul, fair-minded, charitable, and empathetic debate is moral, strenuously just reasoning; compulsion, even that of a compelling hell-fire sermon, is not. It may be the case that certain of the Biblical stories are literally true (I doubt it), and that our belief in or cowering submission to the stories has something to do with narrative technique, namely with direct and unvarnished presentation of what the speaker knows to be so, since, like John beside the lake the day Jesus appeared, resurrected, he has personally experienced it. This is a good argument for brevity in sodbuster fiction about the horrors of war or the glory of family land, and good advice for people wishing to communicate real or imagined experiences like those of Castaneda in Mexico; but it seems to me to have nothing to do with reaching or expressing what really is true, not just credible.

It seems to me that long fiction is by nature descriptive and analytical, not evangelical, though good description and analysis may incline us toward conversion. Short forms can, conceivably, convert, if their energy is sufficient. I can conceive of being turned into a Buddhist by a series of immensely intelligent and moving poems or fables, or possibly by a play. But the end of *Anna Karenina*, though it gives me a sense of what it might be like to be a devout Christian—as do the works of Lloyd C. Douglas, *The Green Light*, *The Robe*, and so on—not even Tolstoy's book successfully turns me to religion except insofar as I'm a convert in need of reinforcement.

Though fiction often, if not invariably, rises from some form of religious emotion—the urge to celebrate, ritualize, justify, or judge, or else (as in Coover) the urge to cry out when one finds oneself in the wilderness—good fiction has, essentially, nothing to do with evangelism. It has to do with living well in this world, both alone and in society, a condition which may or may not include God. It describes conflicts and effects of human attitudes, compulsions, modes of thought and action—in a word, values. It may be conventional or experimental, depending upon the nature of the values studied and the artist's technical predispositions: one speaks of the decline of a family in one way, the tyranny of literary conventions over moral behavior in another. It gives us tentative as opposed to obligatory myths.

Let me spell out what I mean:

The effect of the best art is to humanize by offering descriptions of just behavior, positive models. A moral fiction, then, should present useful examples, models of creative process. This sort of fiction communicates its moral meaning, its willingness, through a process which is in total—and in specific ways—an honest and rigorous mode of thought, an investigation in concrete rather than abstract philosophy, but one which, at the same time—and here is the essential qualification—offers a culture the positive rather than the negative exemplar. This, of course, expunges, anathematizes, if you will, works which present stereotypic, easy, and sentimental modes which confirm unconsidered prejudices and false righteousness. Such works may be moralistic but not necessarily moral, in the sense that these works may be so doctrinally patterned that the argument scrupulously controls off discovery and the possibility of change.

A work of moral fiction is always vital, "open," in that it probes and examines rather than conforms and proves. The distinction is, precisely, between stylized, even lovely, propaganda and aesthetic integrity, and the difference lies in method. The former is not a process, but a confirmation of system; the latter is a system through an affirmation of process.

The "creative" aspect, then, is not merely the province of the writer during the act of fictionalization, "closed" when the text is completed to the author's satisfaction, but, in a broader and real way, a participatory right of the reader in the act of discovery.

A fiction which is moral depends upon this multiple-dialogue between author, text, and reader. A fiction which is not moral, in the sense that I am using the term, definitely and purposely does not.

Real art creates myths a society can live instead of die by, and clearly all modern society is in need of such myths. What I claim is that such myths are not mere hopeful fairy tales but the product of careful and disciplined thought. They are not built of rant and melodrama, the stock-in-trade of the sodbusters or the apocalyptic bawlers, such as William Gaddis and Thomas Pynchon; not built of moaning, whining, sniggering, leering, or the playing of sophisticated games, either the verbal games of William Gass or the icy symbolic games of Updike, the posturing pastoring whereby the sheep look up and are not fed. What I claim is that moral myth burns away all that is desiccated, clears polluted streams, casts nets toward the future; that working at art is a moral act; that a work of art is a moral example; and that false art can be known for what it is if one remembers the rules. The black abyss stirs a certain fascination, or we would not pay so many writers so much money to keep staring at it. But the black abyss is merely life as it is or as it soon may become, and staring at it does nothing but confirm that it is there. It seems to me time that artists start taking that fact as pretty thoroughly established.

Bellefleur

Bellefleur IS THE MOST AMBITIOUS BOOK TO come so far from that alarming phenomenon Joyce Carol Oates. However one may carp, the novel is proof, if any seems needed, that she is one of the great writers of our time. *Bellefleur* is the symbolic summation of all this novelist has been doing for twenty-some years, a magnificent piece of daring, a tour de force of imagination and intellect.

In *Bellefleur* Miss Oates makes a heroic attempt to transmute the almost inherently goofy tradition of the gothic (ghosts, shape-shifters, vampires and all that) into serious art. If any writer can bring it off (some will claim it's already been done), Joyce Carol Oates seems the writer to do it. One thinks of the astonishing, utterly convincing scene in her novel *The Assassins* where Stephen Petrie, a child sitting at his desk in school, has his terrifying out-of-the ody experience, and the scenes in which Hugh, his artist brother, has his brushes with the Angel of Death; one thinks of the psychic business in *Childwold*, the ominous rappings of tyrannical spirit in *Wonderland*, the horror-ridden, love-redeemed world of William James and his circle in *Nightside*; above all one thinks of *Son of the Morning*, Miss Oates's magnificently convincing study of a snake-handler and miracle-worker, Nathan Vickery.

What we learn, reading *Bellefleur*, is that Joyce Carol Oates is essentially a realist. She can write persuasively of out-of-the-body experiences because she believes in them. But she does not really believe in a brutal half-wit boy who can turn into a dog, a man who is really a bear, vampires or mountain gnomes. (In one scene members of the Bellefleur family come across some gnomes escaped from Washington Irving, thunderously bowling on a mountain meadow. One of the gnomes gets captured and, though his whole race is inexplicably mean, turns into a devoted servant of the novel's heroine, Leah. Why? Who knows? The world is mysterious.)

Miss Oates believes in these legendary characters only as symbols; and the problem is that they are not symbols of the same class as those she has been using for years, the symbols provided by the world as it is viewed when it is viewed (as Miss Oates always views it) as a Christian Platonist's "vast array of emblems." The only really frightening scenes in *Bellefleur* deal with real-world atrocities—a boy's stoning of another boy, for instance, or the murder of a family by a bunch of drunken thugs—and these scenes in fact come nowhere near the horror of scenes in earlier novels by Miss Oates, such as the murder of Yvonne in *The Assassins*. What drives Miss Oates's fiction is her phobias: that is, her fear that normal life may suddenly turn monstrous. Abandoning verisimilitude for a different mode (the willing suspension of disbelief), she loses her ability to startle us with sudden nightmare. Still, the tale is sometimes thrilling. The opening chapter (strongly recalling that wonderful collection of ghost stories, *Nightside*) has prowling spirits, a weird storm, a glorious scary castle in the Adirondacks, all presented in an absolutely masterly, chilling style; but the chapter's crowning moment comes when a frightening, vicious, rat-like thing, which none of the frightened occupants can identify, is allowed out of the rain (screaming) into the house and, when seen in the morning, turns out to be a mysteriously beautiful cat. The transformation startles us, catches us completely by surprise (classic Oates), fills us with awe and vague dread, prompting the question we so often ask when reading her: *What in heaven's name is the universe up to now?*

I cannot summarize the plot of *Bellefleur*; for one thing, it's too complex—an awesome construction, in itself a work of genius—and for another, plot surprises are part of the novel's glory. Suffice it to say that this is the saga of the weird, sometimes immensely rich Bellefleur family over several generations, a story focused mainly on Gideon Bellefleur and his power-mad, somewhat psychic, very beautiful wife Leah, their three children (one of them extremely psychic) and the servants and relatives, living and dead, who inhabit the castle and its environs. It's a story of the world's changeableness, of time and eternity, space and soul, pride and physicality versus love.

Much as one admires the ambition of *Bellefleur*, the novel is slightly marred by it: It too noticeably labors after greatness. The book has most of the familiar Oates weaknesses: the panting, melodramatic style she too often allows herself; the heavy, heavy symbolism; and occasional aesthetic miscalculations that perhaps come from thinking too subtly, forgetting that first of all a story must be a completely persuasive lie. In *Bellefleur*, the artifice undermines emotional power, makes the book cartoonish.

I will give just one example to show what I mean. At the end of *Bellefleur*, Gideon, the focal character—now so wasted that people call him "Old Skin and Bones"—crashes his plane and destroys himself and his family estate. He does this in company with a personage known only as "the Rasche woman." We have no idea why she willingly goes along, knowing his intent—a hard thing to believe. Miss Oates, who can create a totally convincing character in half a page, makes a point of not characterizing the Rasche woman at all; no one, not even her lover Gideon, knows her first name. I think that Miss Oates expects her most devoted readers to know that the name has appeared before (for instance, in *The Assassins* there is a Marxist called Rasche, or sometimes Raschke, an equally shadowy figure). As Melville once said, "Something further may allow of this Masquerade." It's an interesting business, another reminder that sometimes the fabric of reality rips and strange beings crawl through; but a catastrophe scene at the end of a novel is a bad place to sacrifice convincingness for the sake of larger meaning.

I have mentioned already that the novel's construction is complex. I must add that the construction sometimes forces the author into what will seem to some readers unfortunate corners. In the first few chapters Miss Oates mentions numerous small details (various queer artifacts, including a drum made of human skin, and numerous odd characters, such as an aunt who never comes out by daylight, a mad, saintly hermit and so on). Each of these details will later get its fully developed story, and some of the details set up in the beginning will lead to stories (motifs) to which the novel will return repeatedly.

Unhappily, some of these motifs or plot strands—whose recurrence is unavoidable once the machinery gets rolling—are somewhat boring. For example there is the child Raphael, whose chief—in fact only—interest in life is, well, this stupid pond. He stares into it, every few chapters, and sees there a framed sample of teeming, ever-changing total reality. (Miss Oates's descriptions of nature in *Bellefleur* are astonishingly good, but after a while a pond is a pond). Or again, there is Jedediah Bellefleur, one of the recurring types in Miss Oates's fiction, the saintly man who, like Stephen in *The Assassins* or Nathan in *Son of the Morning*, loses his hold on God.

Jedediah is interesting, up to a point, and he's both dramatically and symbolically crucial to the story; but I at least am sorry when, every few chapters, we have to return to Jedediah and watch him staring at something improbably called Mount Blanc or struggling with his not very interesting demons. ("He's nuts, that's all," we say, and slog on.) In the end Jedediah proves worth it all. He loses his sense of holy mission, thus becoming an appropriate focus of the blind and raging life force Miss Oates writes about in all her work. Jedediah cares nothing about the world, nothing about God, but after his family's near-extinction by massacre, he is persuaded to leave his mountain and found the new Bellefleur line. The point is, of course, one made in *Son of the Morning* and elsewhere. Loving God completely, one cares nothing about the world, not even about people, whom one sees, rightly, as mere instances; but on the other hand, completely loving oneself or the world, one loses one's soul and becomes (as does Gideon in the end) a figure of death.

Whatever its faults, *Bellefleur* is simply brilliant. What do we ask of a book except that it be wonderful to read? An interesting story with profound implications? The whole religious-philosophical view of Joyce Carol Oates is here cleanly and dramatically stated. She has been saying for years, in book after book (stories, poems, a play and literary criticism), that the world is Platonic. We are the expression of one life force, but once individuated we no longer know it, so that we recoil in horror from the expression of the same force in other living beings. "Don't *touch* me," Gideon Bellefleur keeps saying, as Yvonne Petrie said in *The Assassins*, Laney said in *Childwold* and a host of other characters said elsewhere. Blinded to our oneness, we all become assassins, vampires, ghosts. We are all unreflectable nonimages in mirrors, creatures of time, and time is an illusion; we are all sexual maniacs, lovers engaged in a violent struggle to become totally one with those we love (copulation and murder are all but indistinguishable); we are all crazily in love with the past—first our own Edenic childhood, second the whole past of the world. So Leah, in *Bellefleur*, strives to reconquer the whole immense original Bellefleur estate—and ends up dead, not even buried, burnt up with the house after the plane crash.

Bellefleur is a medieval allegory of *caritas versus cupiditas*, love and selfishness versus pride and selfishness. The central symbol of the novel is change, baffling complexity, mystery. One character makes "crazy quilts" in which only she can see the pattern. Another has been trying all his life to map the Bellefleur holdings, but everything keeps changing—rivers change their courses, mountains shrink. Time is crazy. In fact what is known in Shakespeare criticism as "sliding time" becomes a calculated madness in *Bellefleur*. Chapters leap backward and forward through the years—and that's the least of it. Our main dramatic focus, though she's a minor character, is the psychic child Germaine Bellefleur, whom we follow from birth to the age of four. But *in the same time* her father passes through twenty or thirty years, and the setting passes through something like a thousand years, with hints of a time-span even greater. People regularly get taller or shorter, depending on. . . whatever. The holy mountain in the Adirondacks to which Jedediah goes to find God is at first 10,000 feet high but by the end of the novel only 3,000 feet high.

Joyce Carol Oates has always been, for those who look closely, a religious novelist, but this is the most openly religious of her books—not that she argues any one sectarian point of view. Here as in several of her earlier works the Angel of Death is an important figure, but here for the first time the Angel of Life (not simply resignation) is the winner. In the novel's final chapters Gideon Bellefleur turns his back on all he has been since birth, a sensualist; starves himself until we see him as a death figure; finally becomes his family's Angel of Death.

But there's one further chapter, set far in the past, entitled "The Angel." Whereas Gideon's flight and kamikaze self-destruction as he crashes his plane into his ancestral home are presented in mystical metaphors (the rise into spiritual air, and so on), the final chapter is utterly physical. An Indian boy, a friend of the family, comes to Jedediah on his mountain and tells him to return to the world. With no belief in God and no interest in the worldly, Jedediah returns to the woman he once loved and becomes the father of those who will figure in this novel, becomes the instrument of the blind life force that, accidentally, indifferently, makes everything of value, makes everything beautiful by the simple virtue of its momentary existence. Thanks to Jedediah, God goes on senselessly humming, discovering Himself. That is, in Miss Oates's vision, the reason we have to live and the reason life, however dangerous, can be a joy, once we understand our situation: We are God's body.

Joyce Carol Oates is a "popular" novelist because her stories are suspenseful (and the suspense is never fake: the horror will really come, as well as, sometimes, the triumph), because her sex scenes are steamy and because when she describes a place you think you're there. pseudo-intellectuals seem to hate that popularity and complain, besides, that she "writes too much." (For pseudo-intellectuals there are always too many books.) To real intellectuals Miss Oates's work tends to be appealing partly because her vision is huge, well-informed and sound, and partly because they too like suspense, brilliant descriptions and sex. Though *Bellefleur* is not her best book, in my opinion it's a wonderful book all the same. By one two-page thunderstorm she makes the rest of us novelists wonder why we left the farm. How strange the play of light and shadow in her graveyards! How splendid the Bellefleurs' decaying mansion! How convincing and individual the characters are—and so many of them! In one psychic moment, when the not-yet-two-year-old Germaine cries "Bird—bird—bird!" and points at the window before a bird crashes into it, breaking its neck, we're forced to ask how anyone can possibly write such books, such absolutely convincing scenes, rousing in us, again and again, the familiar Oates effect, the point of all her art: joyful terror gradually ebbing toward wonder.

Italian Folktales

ITALO CALVINO'S *FIABE ITALIANE—ITALIAN Folktales*—was published in Italy twenty-four years ago, to the delight of all Italians, and has now at last been translated into English. I cannot say how good the translation is, since I haven't been able to compare the two versions, but I am told by literary Italian friends that it's excellent. Stylistically, the English is everything we would expect in a good translation of such a master as Calvino: colloquial but never corny, plain-spoken, economical, wry and flexible, and sometimes—like the best authentic folk-speech everywhere—stunningly lyrical, capable of turning (as at the end of the first tale, "Dauntless Little John") unexpectedly somber, moving. Even if this impression of the translation's probable accuracy should prove wrong, the book is, I think, impossible to recommend too highly. Every school and public library ought to own it; so should every parent, and so should every reader who loves stories.

Calvino is possibly Italy's most brilliant living writer. Few European books to be found in American drugstores, airports and college bookshops have been able to match the appeal of such works as Calvino's *The Baron in the Trees, Cosmicomics, t zero* or *The Nonexistent Knight and The Cloven Viscount.* His less popular books, *Invisible Cities* (prose poems), *The Watcher and Other Stories* and *The Castle of Crossed Destinies,* are equally masterful in their ways. His vivid, delightful, offhandedly learned fantasies have made him even more popular in Italy and throughout Europe, especially France, where he now lives, serving on the editorial staff of the publishing firm Giulio Einaudi Editore.

It is in part Calvino's happy combination of talents—master storyteller, experienced editor as well as scholar, critic and sometime university lecturer—that makes *Italian Folktales* the superb book it is; and partly, of course, the praise must go to generations of unlettered old Italian women from every district (the origin of each tale is given), the traditional transmitters and sly revisors of the tales.

Calvino's long introduction is both an explanation of his method in collecting and editing the *fiabe* and a classic statement of the nature and meaning of folktales or, in the broadest sense, fairy tales. For two years, he tells us, he read and sorted numerous collections, old and new, bad and good, of Italian tales, searching out the best, hoping to bring together (as he has done) an assortment representative of all parts of Italy, from Sicily to Tuscany, Venice and somewhat beyond, and representative, too, of all of the folklorists' standard "types."

The difficulties were numerous; I can take time to mention only one of them here. For sundry reasons, Italy never went through the kind of romantic folk revival most of Europe went through in the nineteenth century—Germany at the time of the Grimm brothers, for instance. While the Germans and after them the French, Swedes and British were diligently hunting down tales and variants, searching, as Wilhelm Grimm put it, for the broken jewels of the Old Religion scattered "beneath the Christian grass and flowers"—in other words, while much of Europe was turning to the folktale in search of cultural roots, both linguistic and, loosely, magical—sunny Catholic Italy treated her tales as simply tales, changing them, localizing them, combining and recombining them more freely than did cultures more soberly concerned about their heritage. One result is that many of the published tales Calvino had as sources were highly conscious, sometimes silly literary elevations of folk material, while others were authentic-sounding folktales directly traceable not to Boccaccio's folk sources but to the *Decameron* itself.

Calvino's job was to "feel out," through a painstaking comparison of variants and through the power of his own imagination, the scattered, broken jewels not of the supposed Old Religion but of the authentic folk voice and method. He becomes, in effect, the most recent voice in the history of each tale's transmission. This is not to say that he treats the tales cavalierly, making them simply the springboard for original works. He adds, deletes or alters with wonderful reserve, and in his notes to the tales he lets us know what he has done and what happens in the more important variants.

A major consideration, for any such editor, must be folktale theory: In retelling old stories should one bend one's spectacles in the Germanic way, toward "ancient religion" and national consciousness? Or in the way of the "Indianists," concerned to find allegories about the sun and moon, the foundations for religious and civil evolution? Or in the way of anthropologists, inclined to find representations of bloody initiation rites? Or in the way of the Finnish school, interested in migrations and therefore ever watchful for types and motifs? Or should one read and revise in the way or ways of the Freudians?

Calvino's answer, for the Italian tales at least, is that though some of these approaches may be useful, the folktale is essentially something much more basic, more universal and profound.

"Folktales are real," he says.

> Taken all together, they offer, in their oft-repeated and constantly varying examinations of human vicissitudes, a general explanation of life preserved in the slow ripening of rustic consciences; these folk stories are the catalog of the potential destinies of men and women, especially for that stage in life when destiny is formed, i.e., youth, beginning with birth, which itself often foreshadows the future; then the departure from home, and, finally, through the trials of growing up, the attainment of maturity and the proof of one's humanity. . . . There must be fidelity to a goal and purity of heart, values fundamental to salvation and triumph. There must also be beauty, a sign of grace that can be masked by the humble, ugly guise of a frog; and above all, there must be present the infinite possibilities of mutation, the unifying element in everything: men, beasts, plants, things.

Though the Italian tales are all of the standard fifty-some types and have the standard motifs (only one, according to the late Stith

Thompson, is unique), they have a personality—or several related but distinct regional personalities—all their own. As a group they contrast most sharply, to my mind, with the German and Austrian tales, which are among the most powerful to be found in all folklore but are often marred by gratuitous cruelty. All folktale traditions contain, of course, some cruelty and even, like nature, a fair amount of casual injustice—unsatisfactory brides offhandedly killed by the ensorcelled prince and never atoned for (here in "Serpent King" and "King Crin," for instance) or the child whose head the father cuts off and takes home so that enemies will not know the family's identity (as in "The Man Who Robbed the Robbers").

But there is relatively little of this in the Italian tales. They mention life's cruelty, then hurry on. There is very little here, to put it another way, of that malicious pleasure in the misfortunes of others which to Nietzsche seemed a standard component of human character. The Italian tales do not needlessly frighten children into dutiful citizenship. They mention axes but do not dwell on them; they do not gleefully slam the woodbox cover and chop off the innocent child's head.

The Italian tales differ from the German in various other ways as well—in their democratic attitudes (on which more later), in their cultural details (princesses make lasagne), but above all in their earthiness and realism or, more precisely, their delight in the interplay of the fabulous and the particularized real. Tales are often set in real towns; witches live in actual houses on actual streets. As for the earthiness, though all folk traditions have some of that in them, we hardly hear, in the German tales, anything like the following:

The wise fool Giufà and his mother are in a tree, below which bandits are dividing their spoils. "In a few minutes, Giufà whispered, 'Mamma, I have to make water.' 'What!' 'I have to.' 'Wait.' 'I can't wait another minute.' 'Yes, you can.' 'No, I can't, Mamma.' 'Go on and do it, then.' And Giufà did it. When the bandits heard water coming down, they said, 'How about that, it's starting to rain!'" German earthiness is in general less simple and direct, more self-consciously naughty.

What the Italian tales do have in common with the best of the German tales—and with the best tales from Russia, China and so forth—is superb design. Often, like the Russian tales, they are extraordinarily rich in characterization—partly an effect of the considerable length and episodic complexity of many of the tales (the structure gives character room) and partly an effect of the tellers' special interest in the way people are.

Often the brilliant characterization shows up in odd places—in the Italian special handling of the wise-fool tradition in the tales of Giufà and his Mamma, in the strange, sad tale of the merman Nick Fish, in the glorious Italian version of the crafty animal who makes her pauper friend the richest man in the kingdom ("Giovannuzza the Fox") and in the magnificent, solemn final tale in Calvino's collection, the tale about acceptance of old age and death, "Jump into My Sack."

On the whole, the world of the Italian tale is gentle; its favorite theme is love (both boy-girl love and family love). Often the love theme is developed in a style one can only call operatic. In "The Canary Prince," a maiden locked in a tower finds means of drawing a yellow-clad prince to her room as a canary. Her stepmother puts pins on the cushion on the windowsill so that one day, when the canary lands, he's horribly stabbed and, when back in human form, lies at death's door. The maiden climbs down from her tower on knotted sheets and, in disguise, cures him, then returns to her tower. Lovesick dummy that he is, the prince returns as a canary to her room, turns back into a man, and pitifully complains of her cruelty. After much of this, the maiden explains and all is well.

Or take the wonderful tale called "The Parrot." A certain merchant's daughter "of marriageable age"—a phrase almost as common as "once upon a time" in other traditions—is left by her father, who goes on a business trip. A bad king lusts after her and sends agents to knock at her door. With girlish curiosity and vitality she would gladly answer, but she has a clever parrot who's good at stories, like Scheherazade. (The forgotten Muslim influence on the Italian folktale—as on the Spanish—is everywhere evident.) Again and again, as the maiden turns her ear to the knock, the following transpires: " 'It's a fine story,' said the merchant's daughter. 'Now that it's over, I can receive that woman who claims to be my aunt.' 'But it's not quite over,' said the parrot. 'There's still some more to come. Just listen to this!' " She listens and listens, and finally her father comes home and the parrot turns into a handsome prince, who has all this time been chastely, discreetly in love with her.

The Italian tale never touches—or wants—the metaphoric brilliance of the African tales (from the Masai, speaking of a woman to whom a lover has just proposed: "She was as still as when a great tree falls in the jungle") and knows nothing of African mind-breaking paradox. The Italian folktale has no trace of the other-worldly softness of British and, especially, Irish folktales—no skimmering of fairies, "lighter than noonday light."

Though girls may be transformed into apples or pears, and though a roomful of gossamer weaving may flow out of a walnut, the Italian tales are too fond of peasant wit, too fond of real-world cunning (in the Calabrian tales), too fond of the real sky, land and water of Italy to be anything but heartily realistic. When hungry people go out into a cabbage field and pull a very large cabbage whose roothole is a tunnel to Hell, the marvelous happens almost incidentally: It's the convincing hunger, the people, the field of cabbages that stand out in our minds. The Devil himself, in another tale, is as common as dirt, except that his nose is silver.

The Italian tales have none of the splendid enamelwork of the Chinese and Japanese, and also lack the standard expectation of in-human patience found in Middle Eastern and Oriental tales. It is true that in one tale a maiden cannot win her love until she's worn out seven pairs of iron shoes, seven iron mantles and seven iron hats, but she manages it all rather quickly. The tale is "King Crin," the tragi-comic saga of a king's son whose misfortune is that he's a pig. The local baker's daughter redeems him after the pig has killed her two sisters—redeems him partly because of her cleverness, partly because, strange to say, she loves him. (Presumably she loves him even more when he becomes a handsome prince.) The weird realism of "King Crin" is typical. Possibly only a child who has raised and loved pigs will understand the fondness with which the baker's third daughter rubs the bristles of her dear husband's back.

Two further features of Italian tales require comment. One is their essential democracy (especially in the Tuscan tales); the other is their high regard for clever, energetic—or occasionally clever, fat and lazy—women.

Just as the Italian storytellers are in general unclear about the fine distinctions between witches and dragons, giants and ogres—features borrowed from folktales elsewhere—the tale-tellers of Tuscany are un-clear about what, exactly, kings might be. (Florence was, you will remember, the birthplace of Italian democracy and the Renaissance.)

In Tuscan tales kings look out their windows into the windows of neighbor kings. In the *fiabe*, as in other European folktales, kings marry peasants; but only in Italy does it seem not worth remark. In most traditions the marriage makes a point: A peasant may be morally worthy of a king. In Italy, marriage itself, not the fact that the marriage is to a king, is the triumph. The only real advantage to being a king is that when you're in trouble you can yell "Counselors! Counselors!" and somebody will come. (An Italian folk-king can hardly lift a finger without his counselors.)

In the Sicilian tales—and elsewhere—the tale-tellers often show special interest in, as Calvino puts it, "feminine characters who are active, enterprising, and courageous, in contrast to the traditional concept of the Sicilian woman as a passive and withdrawn creature." This is especially evident in the tales of one tale-teller, "an illiterate old woman, Agatuzza Messia," a "seventy-year-old seamstress of winter quilts" in Palermo, whose tales were written down by the amateur folklorist Giuseppe Pitrè (1841–1916). She creates, or passes on to us, superbly individualized, clever young women in such tales as "The Wife Who Lived on Wind" and "The King of Spain and the English Milord." But perhaps the most delightfully clever and yet, in the end, mature and touching of the folk heroines are the emperor's daughter in "Serpent King" (from Calabria) and the girl animal of astonishing subtlety, in the end betrayed for all her pains, "Giovannuzza the Fox" (from Catania, Sicily).

I have only been able to suggest the riches in this large collection, and I've necessarily left a good deal unmentioned—the tales of saints and miracles come to mind—but I have perhaps said enough to establish my main point. Calvino's collection stands with the best folktale collections anywhere.

Fiction in *MSS*

ALL OF THE FICTION IN THIS FIRST VOLUME of the new *MSS* is by relatively unknown writers, some of them previously unpublished, some just beginning to be noticed. My chief concern as fiction editor is to print, not the work of the already famous—they have outlets enough—but the work of writers who, in my opinion, promise to be the beloved and admired writers of the next generation. If sometime in the future I publish fiction by someone with an instantly recognizable name, I will do it with reluctance, only because I like the story so much I cannot stand not to publish it even though doing so means robbing space from some little-known writer who needs and deserves it. For a magazine there are of course advantages and disadvantages in a policy like mine. Including famous writers helps to sell magazines; but then, it's not absolutely necessary that *MSS* sell like crazy. We're not under pressure from advertisers or, to tell the truth, anyone else. The only strong pressure I feel as fiction editor is the pressure of an ideal: to find and print the kind of fiction I, as a reader, would be pleased to come across.

My taste is of course not everyone's, and in what follows I would not want to be understood as trying to bully some reader into liking what I like. I suspect that what I like is pretty generally liked, though I may be wrong; in any case, it includes a pretty wide range of fiction and excludes nothing *on principle*, though of course it is true that some kinds of fiction tend, in general, not to interest me much. My object here is to describe the kinds of fiction I would like to stumble onto in some dentist's office or library or on a friend's coffeetable—the kinds of fiction I therefore choose for *MSS*—so that you, reading these stories, can understand more clearly how it is that I do such a brilliant job, or (you may decide) make such stupid mistakes.

When I was a child—I mean between, say, eight and fifteen—my favorite magazine in the world, and possibly the only magazine I knew of, was the *Saturday Evening Post*. (There is still a magazine by that name, but in my opinion it shouldn't be confused with the *Saturday Evening Post*.) What was wonderful about the *Post* was that it really had stories. Plots. Characters. Interesting places and occupations. Some of the stories were perhaps a little low-class, like the ones about Tugboat Annie, for instance; but some of them were by people like William Faulkner, J. D. Salinger, and Kurt Vonnegut. All of them, low-class or not, had one dependable quality: they were stories. People in them set out after things, encountered difficulties, and either won in the end or lost. I don't say that's the only kind of fiction I like, but for me it's the main continent of fiction, and everything else gets its bearings and directions from that vast solidity.

In this kind of fiction—real "story" fiction—what basically happens, I think, is this: the writer sets off in the reader's mind a vivid and continuous dream, a dream as alive and convincing as any nightmare or sex-dream or dream that makes the dreamer laugh aloud in his sleep. The fictional dream is *vivid* in the sense that the writer has provided enough concrete detail to allow the reader to imagine people, places, and events with great clarity. The writer knows and is able to tell exactly how a tired lawyer tosses his glasses onto his desk, or an elegant old madwoman licks jelly off her napkin at a party. In really first-rate storytelling fiction, we see things more vividly than we see in the room around us when we look up from the book. And the fictional dream is *continuous* in the sense that the writer never distracts us from the scene we're imagining by some grammatical mistake, or obvious mistake of characterization (for instance making a congressman shoot an ice-cream man when everything we know about life tells us he wouldn't really do it), or some mistake of mannerism (some cute trick of writing that makes us pay more attention to the writer than to the fictional

l5lsss

dream), and so on. In storytelling fiction we see things happening and we understand instantly, usually without being told, why they happen as they do. In the fictional dream, as in our dreams as we sleep, there is some urgent concern—something that needs to be achieved and cannot be achieved easily, something worth achieving in the first place, though possibly crazy. (Much of the greatest fiction we know is about people who've set out to do crazy things which for some reason we approve of—Ahab's whale hunt, Raskolnikov's attempt to beat the law, Achilles' outrageous demand that the universe be fair.)

As a writer I think nothing is harder than this kind of story—the necessity of making everything believable, slipping in all the necessary details without ever being caught at it, and, worst of all, finding a story worth telling in the first place, a story that's not old-hat or cheaply predictable or so original it strikes the reader as goofy. To be worth telling, a story has to mean, and mean interestingly, either because it takes us mentally where we never were before—to some startling new idea or understanding of things—or because it surprises us with the unexpected familiar. All so-called "experimental fiction" is child's play beside this—which is not to deny that experimental fiction can be interesting. The story may be about ordinary people and familiar emotions, as is Joanna Higgins's "The Courtship of Widow Sobcek," or it may be utterly strange, as are several stories in this issue—Roberta Gupta's "The Cafe de Paris," Ron Hansen's "Playland," Greg Michaelson's "The Dream Stealer," and Sigrid Nunez's "The Bird That Ate the Stars"—but whatever its mode it must reward our fundamental childlike wish for suspense and, in the end, satisfaction.

Not every story in future issues of *MSS* will be of this kind: but those that are not will in every case be fictions that directly play off this—so to speak—norm. In normal storytelling, highly self-conscious style can be distracting; but what is a defect in normal storytelling can be turned into a virtue in another kind of fiction: in normal storytelling, outrageous improbability is a defect, but in another kind of fiction it can be a delight: and in normal storytelling, a stupid theme is the death of fiction, but in another kind of story, moronic values pursued by moronic characters (I think of Laurel and Hardy) can be a joy.

All this doesn't say much, I realize, since it's mainly abstract. The test will be the stories we print. But I hope I've made at least this much clear: though my chief concern is the publication of new writers, that is not my only concern. Another, just about equal with the first, is the publication of stories that are, in one way or another—even if they're tragic—a joy to read. That is the goal of all editors, no doubt. If magazines differ, it's because the personalities of editors differ, some taking pleasure in one thing, some in another. I hope my choices are the ones you would have made.

What
Writers Do

E VERYONE KNOWS AT LEAST IN A GENERAL
way what writers—that is, writers of fiction—do. They write fiction.
But even for writers themselves it's not easy to say just what that
means. We listen to the sentence "They write fiction" and nod impa-
tiently, as if the thing were too obvious to need saying, which in a
way it is, because we all agree, as speakers of English, on what "they"
means, and "write" and "fiction." But maybe we nodded too hastily.
What *do* we mean, to start with the easiest question, by "they"—that
is, "writers"?

Most of us are snobs and would be inclined to say at once that
we need not concern ourselves with the obvious fact that writers are
of various sorts ranging from, say, John Jakes (of the Bicentennial series)
to Kurt Vonnegut, to Herman Melville. As warthogs, IRS agents, and
zebras are all animals, these dissimilar beings—Jakes, Vonnegut, and
Melville—are all writers; but though the problem here might amuse
a chimpanzee or a positivist, it does not seem, to us snobs, worth attention. The word *writers*, and the pronoun we substitute for it, has
various meanings, but the only one we really care about is the one
which refers to the class represented by Melville. The trouble with
this hasty, respectable judgment lies of course in the fact that every
individual writer, even a stern-minded person like Melville, is different

people at different times. In one mood, or in one crowd, the serious writer writes fairy tales; in another he writes ponderous novels; in still another, dirty limericks. A great writer is not great because he never writes dirty limericks but because, if he does write one, he tries to write a very good one.

Any writer who's worked in various forms can tell you from experience that it all feels like writing. Some people may feel that they're "really" writing when they work on their novels and just fooling around when they write bedtime stories for their children; but that can mean only one of two things, I think: either that the writer has a talent for writing novels and not much talent for writing children's stories, or else that the writer is a self-important donzel who writes both miserable novels and miserable children's stories. I would say that even in a given work a writer is many different people. Just at the moment when his novel is most serious—most strenuously laboring to capture some profound idea through meticulous analysis of characters in action—the Melvillean heavyweight suddenly notices (as John Jakes would do) that the serving-girl in the corner has lowered her bodice a little, trying to catch the central character's eye. I don't mean that our serious writer's mind has wandered; I mean that another side of him, after vigorous signaling, has gotten his attention. Or to put it another way, wanting to write like Tolstoy at his solemnest, he has suddenly discovered in himself an urge to write like, say, Henry Fielding. If he gives in to the impulse, as he may or may not, and pursues the romance the lowered bodice has invited, he may suddenly, at the height of idealistic love, or the depth of debauchery, find himself feeling a little cynical somehow, or puritanically pious; or he may find himself distracted by the ferns outside the window, which lure him to delicate appositions and fluttering rhythms, lyricism for its own sake.

What's happening here, of course, is not that several writers inside one writer's head are clubbing each other for control of the typewriter keys. The true writer's mind is not a jungle but a noble democracy, in which all parties have their say, even the crazy ones, even the most violently passionate, because otherwise justice, balance, sanity are impossible. Wanting to write like Tolstoy at his solemnest, the writer finds a part of himself rising to object to a hint of pompous braying, agrarian bigotry, righteousness unredeemed by humor. Swinging toward Fielding, the writer finds a part of himself complaining about the absence of highmindedness. Scanning possibilities like a chess-playing computer, weighing the votes of his innumerable selves, following now this leading voice, now that, the writer-multitude finds out, page by page and draft by draft, the sane and passionate whole which is his novel.

Every fine writer has within him a John Jakes, a Marquis de Sade, a James Michener, a William Gass, a Melville. If his multitude of selves is rich but anarchic, uncontrollable, so that his work bulges here with pornography, there with dry philosophy, he is likely to be a "serious" writer but not a very good one. If for one reason or another his selection of selves is limited, he is likely to be a lesser writer. Some writers are limited because they are, simply, not very rich personalities: they contain in them no Melville, no Marquis de Sade. Other writers are limited because, though rich in selves, they voluntarily disenfranchise large segments of their inner population to satisfy the whim of some market: they avoid ideas, or sex, or—as in the stock "*New Yorker* story"—unfashionable emotion.

Writers whose stock of selves is limited by simplicity of personality we dismiss—uncharitably but not unjustly—as stupid. Writers limited by concern about market we dismiss as commercial. How do we distinguish these lesser kinds of writers from the serious, even sublime writer who limits himself by the choice of some relatively simple form—Shakespeare in the sonnets, Hawthorne in his stories for children? And how, we may as well ask in the same breath, does the simplicity of a sonnet or children's story differ from the simplicity of a porno or mystery thriller?

If you accept my metaphor of the writer as democracy, the answer to both questions seems obvious. The whole community cannot get together on a porno or the usual emotionally simpleminded thriller, at least so long as the porno or thriller remain recognizable themselves, conscious and intentional distortions of human experience. (Ross McDonald is the superior mystery writer he is precisely because he refuses to abide by the usual rules of his form, consistently writing, so to speak, better than necessary.) On the other hand, the sonnet and children's story—or the parable, tale, yarn, sketch, and so on—do not of necessity oversimplify or distort. When the whole community argues about war, pollution, or energy, it argues in one way; when it argues about building swing sets on the playgrounds, it argues in another. I think no part of a writer need be suppressed to write

Charlotte's Web or the juveniles of Joan Aiken. It is true, of course, that the children's story, like the traditional gothic tale, tends to use a very special language; but it is not a language into which large parts of our common experience cannot be translated.

One might put it this way: important thought is important only insofar as it communicates with those at whom it is aimed; no sensible human being goes on talking when all of his audience has walked away. Great children's literature talks about the complexity of human experience in a way interesting and meaningful to children; bad children's literature talks about what some mistaken person imagines children care about. The bad children's writer writes as he does either because, being of limited personality, he thinks children care about no more than he does, or because, being commercial, he wants to satisfy formulas made up by fools and statisticians.

Great children's writers, like great writers of any other kind, are complex, multitudinous of self. To speak only of living American writers, think of the children's fiction of Nancy Willard, Hilma Wolitzer, or Susan Shreve. All of these writers, as it happens—not by chance—are also respectable writers of adult fiction or poetry. For contrast think of Maxine Kumin or Roald Dahl, occasionally unsatisfying writers both for children and for adults because, in each case, one side of the writer's personality—the angrily righteous—overwhelms the democratic balance with pious despotism.

So much for the "they" in the truism about writers, "They write fiction." Let me turn to "write."

Writing is an action, a different action from talking. The only conceivable reason for engaging in writing is to make something relatively permanent which one might otherwise forget. That would seem to imply that one thinks there is some value in the thing not to be forgotten—either some value already achieved, as in the case of a good recipe for scalloped potatoes, or some potential value, as in the case of a love poem which stinks at the moment but has the right spirit and might get better under revision. Writers of the Melvillean class, that is, "serious" writers, write only in the second sense: they write works that with luck and devotion may be improved by revision—or, in the end, works that *have* been so improved, so that we may class them with other human treasures, such as good recipes for scalloped potatoes. If one looks at the first drafts of even the greatest writers, like Tolstoy and Dostoyevsky, one sees that literary art does not come flying like Athena, fully formed, from Zeus's head. Indeed, the first-draft stupidity of great writers is a shocking and comforting thing to see. What one learns from studying successive drafts is that the writer did not know what he meant to say until he said it. A typo of "murder" for "mirror" can change the whole plot of a novel.

To put all this another way, what oral storytellers seem to do is figure out certain parts of the world by telling stories about these parts. The Greeks, as you know, made much of this. Whereas most civilizations feared and hated blindness, the Greeks elevated it, at least as a symbol: the blind man was the man who had to see with his tongue, understanding the world by telling of it. What writers do is somewhat different. They figure out the world by talking about it, then looking at what they've said and changing it. I don't mean, of course, that oral storytellers don't polish and repolish; I only mean to say that there's a great difference between the power and precision of the two instruments—a difference as great as that between, say, a reading glass and a microscope. Think again of Homer. A fair pile of prehomeric poetry survives, all of it fairly good, most of it battle poetry, all the battle pieces relatively short, at least in comparison with the *Iliad*. The standard heroic poem before Homer's time probably ran to about the length of one or two books of the *Iliad*. It may be true, as tradition says, that Homer was a blind oral poet, like Demodokos, his character in the *Odyssey*; but it does not seem likely. Homer appeared at the very moment when writing was reintroduced in ancient Greece, and the complexity of his poems—repeated, cunningly varied references to bows, looms, Odysseus's bed and the great phallic pillar which supports it—images we're forced to describe, finally, as richly and ingeniously symbolic—can only be accounted for in one of two ways: either by a theory that Homer was vastly more intelligent than any other human being who ever lived, or by a theory that Homer wrote things down, studied them patiently and stubbornly, like Beethoven, and, like Beethoven, endlessly, brilliantly revised.

Or think of the sudden, astonishing rise of serious "popular" literature in the late Middle Ages and early Renaissance; I mean the use, in writers like Boccaccio, Chaucer, and Shakespeare, of salacious stories and folktales as the base of psychologically and philosophically serious literature. Before Boccaccio's time, as has recently been pointed out, writers used parchment. To make a Bible you had to kill three hundred cows. Books cost a lot, in money and cattle-blood. One used parchment only for things of the greatest importance—religious writings, cathedral plans, the shopping lists of kings. Then in Boccaccio's time paper was introduced, so that suddenly it was possible for Boccaccio to write down a dirty joke he'd heard, fool around with it a little— change the farmer's daughter to a nun, for instance, or introduce comically disparate high-class symbolism—and produce the *Decameron*. Chaucer did the same only better. We have two drafts—by no means all that once existed—of Chaucer's story borrowed from Boccaccio, *Troilus and Criseyde*. For artists, writing has always meant, in effect, the art of endless revising.

Now let me turn to the third term in the formula "They write fiction." What oral storytellers tell and retell we call legends, a tricky word that, if we derive it from Latin, means "that which is read," and if we take it (by false etymology, a once common one) from Anglo-Saxon, means—as a result of the softening of *g* to *y—lying*. Even in the beginning no one knew what to do with that. The primary meaning of *legend* in the Middle Ages was "a saint's life." In any case, *fiction* was from the beginning something else; it can only come from the Latin and means "something shaped, molded, or devised." As everyone knows, the origins of words don't prove much; but it seems true that we still use *fiction* in the original sense, not to describe some noble old lie which can be told, with no great loss, in a variety of ways, but to describe a specific kind of made-up story, a story we think valuable precisely because of the way it's shaped. You can tell the legend or fairy tale of *Jack and the Beanstalk* pretty much any way you please, as long as you don't throw out Jack, the giant, the colored beans, or the beanstalk. Jack can make three trips, or two, or one; he can trade in the cow (or something) for the colored beans either on the way into town or at the fair; and so on. To tell Faulkner's *As I Lay Dying*, Joyce's "The Dead," or William Gass's "In the Heart of the Heart of the Country," one has to use the writer's exact words or all is lost. The essential difference between what we think of as "fiction" and what we think of as "legend" is that, relatively at least, the shaping in fiction counts more heavily.

In the broadest and perhaps most important sense, fiction can go wrong in two ways: it fails as basic legend or it fails in its artifice.

Most of the fiction one reads—I mean contemporary fiction, but the same may be said of fiction done in Dickens's day, most of it by now ground to dust by time's selectivity—is trash. It makes no real attempt at original and interesting style, and the story it tells is boring. This is simply to say, of course, that if fiction moves too far from its model, legend, and abandons story, it fails to satisfy our age-old expectations; if it does not move far enough, telling its story without concern for style, it fails to satisfy other, newer expectations. What writers do, if they haven't been misled by false canons of taste or some character defect, is try to make up an interesting story and tell it in an authentically interesting way—that is, some way that, however often we may read it, does not turn out to be boring.

The odds against a writer's achieving a real work of art are astronomical. Most obviously the "they" of our "They write fiction" formula—in other words, the writer's personality—may go wrong. Every good writer is many things—a symbolist, a careful student of character, a person of strong opinions, a lover of pure tale or adventure. In a bad or just ordinary novel, the writer's various selves war with one another. We feel, as we read, not one commanding voice but a series of jarringly different voices, even voices in sharp and confusing disagreement.

The war of the writer's selves can result in great fiction only in the case of an extraordinarily great writer, which is to say, an almost supernaturally wise man—one who has the rare gift of being able to see through his own soul's trickery. Very few people of the kind who make good writers—rather childlike people, as psychologists have often pointed out—are wise in life. They become wise, if they do, by revision—by looking over what they've written down again and again, a hundred times, two hundred, each time in a slightly different mood, with a different model ringing in their ears: one day the writer looks over what he's written just after spending a few hours reading Tolstoy; another day he rereads his own work just after seeing a play by Samuel Beckett, or some simpleminded but good-hearted movie like *The Sound of Music*, or just after returning from his mother's funeral. That process, endless revision and rereading—in different moods, with different models in mind—is the writer's chief hope.

Or anyway it is his chief hope if he has known all along what fiction is and has been trying to write real fiction. I have said that true fiction is, in effect, oral storytelling written down and fixed, perfected by revision. Let me refine that a little now. What is it that the writer is trying to achieve—or ought to be—as he endlessly fiddles with rough drafts?

A true work of fiction is a wonderfully simple thing—so simple that most so-called serious writers avoid trying it, feeling they ought to do something more important and ingenious, never guessing how incredibly difficult it is. A true work of fiction does all of the following things, and does them elegantly, efficiently: it creates a vivid and continuous dream in the reader's mind; it is implicitly philosophical; it fulfills or at least deals with all of the expectations it sets up; and it strikes us, in the end, not simply as a thing done but as a shining performance.

I will not elaborate that description in much detail. Some if it I've mentioned before, here and there; some of it seems to me to need no elaboration. I've said, first, that fiction creates a vivid and continuous dream in the reader's mind. Any reader knows at a glance that that is true, and that if a given work does not bring a vivid and continuous dream to the reader—almost instantly, after five or six words—the fiction is either bad or, what may be the same thing, a so-called metafiction. One can derive all the principles of effective fiction from the idea that the writer must make his dream vivid and continuous. The dream is not vivid, of course, if too many words are abstract, not concrete, if too many verbs are passive, too many metaphors familiar or dull, and so on; and the dream is not continuous if some element in the writing distracts the reader from the story to thoughts about the stupidity of the writer—his inability to use proper grammar, his excessive loquacity, his deviation into sentimentality, mannerism, or frigidity, and so on. If the student writer can get rid of every one of those common errors which regularly undermine vividness and continuousness, a finite list not difficult to spell out, then that student can consistently avoid writing bad fiction. Whether or not he can write *great* fiction is of course another matter, one of genius or the lack of it. When the writer is finally writing true fiction, the best he is capable of, he may well discover that he'd better start making some carefully calculated mistakes, disguise his insipidity.

It's the law of the vivid and continuous dream—for it is, I think, something close to an aesthetic law for fiction—that makes writing fiction what I've described as a "wonderfully simple thing." All the writer has to do is see with absolute clarity and vividness, and describe without mistake exactly what he's seen. That was Faulkner's genius—to see very clearly. No one forgets his image of the falling lantern and the fire starting in "Shingles for the Lord," or his image of a Negro shanty's dirt yard, "smooth as an old, worn nickel." What offends in Faulkner, as has often been remarked, is his failure to value that clarity of vision, again and again mucking it up—especially toward the end—with outrageously mannered prose, that is, prose calculated to obscure the vision and call attention to the writer. Joyce did the same. At the end of his life, clear-headedly looking back, he thought "The Dead" the finest thing he'd ever done, and Tolstoy's "How Much Land Does a Man Need?" the finest work of fiction ever written. It had been Joyce himself, of course, who made the claim that the writer should be inconspicuous in his work, like God off in the corner of the universe paring his nails. In *Dubliners* and *Portrait* he'd been true to that ideal; from that point on—however great the books in certain ways—Joyce went for mannerism, and the sad truth is he carried most of twentieth-century fiction with him.

To do the wonderfully simple thing real writers do at their best, one needs only to look clearly and levelly at one's character and his situation. If the writer sees his character clearly, and if the character is, as all human beings in fact are, unique in certain respects, that character will inevitably behave in ways no one else would behave in that precise situation. It will prove impossible to write a story which could be equally well played in a film version by Robert Redford, Dustin Hoffman, Alan Arkin, Richard Dreyfuss, or Frank Sinatra. If the writer sees each and every one of his characters clearly—even the most minor walk-ons—he can never for a moment slip into cliché. Following actions and reactions second by second through a significant chain of events, keeping a sharp eye out to catch every wince or grin or twitch, always checking his imagination against experience (how do misers really behave in the world?), the writer almost cannot help coming up with a dream worth following—not a passive dream, of course, but one the reader struggles with, judges, tries to second-guess, a dream of reality more vivid and powerful than all but the rarest, keenest moments of reality itself.

Of course part of what makes this dream so vivid and powerful is that, like our best nightmares, the dream is thematic, or, as I put it earlier, it is implicitly philosophical. I would say that, at their best, both fiction and philosophy do the same thing, only fiction does it better—though slower. Philosophy by essence is abstract, a sequence of general argument controlled in its profluence by either logic (in old-fashioned systematic philosophy) or emotional coherence (in the intuitive philosophies of, say, Nietzsche and Kierkegaard). We read the argument and it seems to flow along okay, make sense, but what we ask is, "Is this true of my mailman?" or "Do I really follow the Golden Rule because, unlike Prussian officers, I am a coward? Do I *know* any good Prussian officers?" Fiction comes at questions from the other end. It traces or explores some general argument by examining a particular case in which the universal case seems implied; and in place of logic or emotional coherence—the philosopher's stepping stones—fictional argument is controlled by mimesis: we are persuaded that the characters would indeed do exactly what we are told they do and say, whether the characters are lifelike human beings or a congress of insects given human traits. If the mimesis convinces us, then the question we ask is opposite to that we ask of philosophical argument; that is, we ask, "Is this true *in general?*" Convinced by Captain Ahab, we want to know if in some way his story, the story of a madman, applies to all human beings, mad or sane. In great fiction the writer, inching along from particular to particular, builds into his work arrows or vectors pointing us toward the general. He does this, we know, in numerous ways—by relating his particulars to some symbolic system recalling a familiar set of questions of values, by playing his plot off against some old and familiar plot, as Joyce does in *Ulysses*, by old-fashioned allegory, by explicit authorial comment, by arranging that his characters discuss the important issues within the story (the method of Tolstoy and Dostoyevsky), or by some other means.

What happens in great fiction is that, while we are occupied with the vividness and convincingness of detail—admiring, for instance, the fact that Captain Ahab's personal crew is made up of Chinese never before seen on the ship until now, with the first lowering of the longboats—we are also occupied with the neatness and power of the philosophical argument. When reading great fiction, one never feels that the writer has wandered from the subject. The true writer sets up for us some important question, in dramatic form, and explores it clear-mindedly, relentlessly. We read of Raskolnikov's initial indecision about whether or not he has the right to commit murder, and we instantly recognize the universal significance of the question and lean forward tensely, waiting to see what will happen. We delight in the particulars—the fact that he is very nearly caught on the stairs—and we delight simultaneously in seeing the implied universals. It's in this sense that true fiction is implicitly philosophical.

I need say nothing about the next standard I've mentioned, that fiction at its best satisfies our expectations. At the end of a mystery, we want all the questions answered, red herrings explained away, false clues justified, and so on. In a more serious kind of novel, we want all important issues dealt with, no character left hiding forever behind the tree where the author put him and forgot him. It may be that, finishing the novel, we at first imagine that some thread was left un-tied—for instance, some symbolic idea. Two different characters may have been subtly identified as Eden serpents, and as we finish the novel we at first can't see how the double identification was resolved. Care-fully rereading, we discover that the seeming contradiction was indeed resolved, and the belated satisfaction of our expectation gives pleasure. But whether the satisfaction is immediate or purposely delayed, it must sooner or later come.

Finally, I've said that in the best fiction we get not just a piece of work—efficient energy that moves something—but a "shining perfor-mance." We say not just "What a true and good book!" but "What magnificent writing!" To win our applause, it cannot have the fake magnificence of mannerism—flights of purple prose, avant-garde trickery, artifice aimed solely at calling attention to the artificer. It must have the true magnificence of beautiful (some would prefer to say "interesting") technique: adequate and "inspired"—that is, revised, rerevised, polished to near perfection. We recognize this at once, I think, in acting. Some actors do a perfectly good job—we are never distracted to the actor behind the character played—while other actors do a brilliant job: we *do* think of the actor, not as a human being at war with the part being played, but as an artist whose skills come singing through the part, making the character more interesting and "real" than we could have hoped or dreamed from a reading of the script.

What the writers I care most about do is take fiction as the single most important thing in life after life itself—life itself being both their raw material and the object of their celebration. They do it not for ego but simply to make something singularly beautiful. Fiction is their religion and comfort: when they are depressed, they go not to church or psychoanalysis but to Salinger or Joyce, early Malamud, parts of Faulkner, Tolstoy, or the Bible as book. They write, themselves, to make things equally worthy of trust—not stories of creeps and cynics but stories of people capable of a measure of heroism, capable of strong and honest feeling at least some of the time, capable of love and sacrifice—capable of all this, and available as models for imitation. Everything true writers do, I think, from laborious plotting on butcher paper or three-by-five cards to laborious revision, draft after draft, they do to create *characters*—the center and heart of all true fiction—characters who will serve till Messiah comes, characters whose powerful existence in our minds makes a real-life messiah unnecessary. Imperfect, even childish human beings, writers raise themselves up by the techniques of fiction to something much better than even the best of writers are in everyday life: ordinary mortals transmuted for the moment into apostles.

Cartoons

TRYING TO FIGURE OUT THE CHIEF INFLU-
ences on my work as a writer turns out to be mainly a problem of
deciding what not to include. I grew up in a family where literary
influence was everywhere, including under the bridge on our dirt road,
where I kept my comic books. My father is a memorizer of poetry
and scripture, a magnificent performer in the old reciter tradition. (I
once did a reading in Rochester, N.Y., near Batavia, where I grew up.
After I'd finished several people remarked that I was a wonderful
reader—"though not quite up to your father, of course.") He did readings of everything from Edgar Guest to Shakespeare and The Book
of Job at the monthly Grange meetings, in schools, churches, hospitals.
While he milked the cows, my mother (who'd once been his high school
English teacher) would read Shakespeare's plays aloud to him from
her three-legged stool behind the gutter, and he would take, yelling
from the cow's flank, whatever part he'd decided on that night—
Macbeth, King Lear, Hamlet and so on.

My mother was a well-known performer too, except that she mainly
sang. She had one of those honey-sweet Welsh soprano voices and sang
everything from anthems to the spirituals she'd learned from an old
black woman who took care of her during her childhood in Missouri.
Often my mother performed in blackface, with a red bandana, a

practice that may sound distasteful unless you understand that she wasn't kidding; she was authentic, flatting, quarter-toning, belting it out: She was amazing. They frequently worked together, my mother and father, and were known all over western New York. Sometimes they were in plays—my mother often directed—and wherever we went, riding around in the beat-up farm truck or just sitting in the kitchen, they sang, always in harmony, like crazy people.

The house was full of books, very few of them books that would now be thought fashionable aside from the Shakespeare and Dickens. My parents read aloud a lot—the narrative poems of Scott, miles of Longfellow, spooky stories by Edgar Allan Poe, the poems of Tennyson and Browning, also rather goofy religious writers (I loved them; what did I know?) like Lloyd C. Douglas and some woman whose name escapes me now, who wrote Jesus-filled love stories with titles like *A Patch of Blue*. My grandmother, who was bedridden through much of my childhood, was especially fond of this religious lady, and one of my more pleasant chores was to read her these tender little novels. The climax was always the moment the boy shyly touched the girl's hand. I've never found anything more sexually arousing than that Jesus-filled, long-delayed touch. I mean it was smut, it nearly made me a pervert, and not a court in the land could nail her.

My favorite authors, at least when I was between the ages of eight and eighteen, were in what might be described as the nonrealistic tradition: God, Dickens and Disney. One of my less pleasant chores when I was young was to read the Bible from one end to the other. Reading the Bible straight through is at least 70 percent discipline, like learning Latin. But the good parts are, of course, simply amazing. God is an extremely uneven writer, but when He's good, nobody can touch him. I learned to find the good parts easily (some very sexy stuff here too), and both the poetry and the storytelling had a powerful effect on what I think good fiction ought to be!

Dickens I ran into when I was in my early teens, when I began to find the Hardy boys tiresome and unconvincing. I never liked realism much, but the irrealism of the two boys having long conversations while riding on motorcycles (I was big on motorcycles myself) was more than I could put up with. Running across Dickens was like finding a secret door. I read book after book, and when I'd finished the last one I remember feeling a kind of horror, as if suddenly the color had gone out of the world; then luckily I discovered that when you went back to one of the ones you had read first, you couldn't remember half of it, you could read it again and find it even better, so life wasn't quite as disappointing as for a moment I'd thought.

For me at that time Disney and Dickens were practically indistinguishable. Both created wonderful cartoon images, told stories as direct as fairy tales, knew the value of broad comedy spiced up with a little weeping. I have since learned that Dickens is occasionally profound, as Disney never deigns to be; but that was never why I valued Dickens or have, now, a bust of him in my study to keep me honest. Unconsciously—without ever hearing the term, in fact—I learned about symbolism from Dickens and Disney, with the result that I would never learn to appreciate, as I suppose one should, those realistic writers who give you life data without resonance, things merely as they are. Dickens's symbolism may never be very deep—the disguised witches and fairy princesses, Uriah Heep and his mother flapping around like buzzards, or all the self-conscious folderol of *A Tale of Two Cities*— but in my experience, anyway, it spoils you forever for books that never go *oo-boom*.

There were other important influences during this period of my life, probably the most important of which was opera. The Eastman School of Music presented operas fairly often (and of course played host to traveling opera companies, including the Met). From Dickens and Disney (not to mention God) it took no adjustment to become opera-addicted. The plots of most operas (not all, heaven knows) are gloriously simple-minded or, to put it more favorably, elemental; the stage is nothing if it is not a grand cartoon (Wagner's mountainscapes and gnomes, Mozart's crazies, Humperdinck's angels, the weirdness and clowning that show up everywhere from "La Bohème" to "The Tales of Hoffmann"). I was by this time playing French horn, and of course I'd always been around singing. So I got hooked at once— hence my special fondness now for writing librettos.

By the time I reached college my taste was, I'm afraid, hopelessly set. Predictably I was ravished by Melville—all those splendid cartoon images, for instance Ahab and the Chinese coolies he's kept hidden until the first time he needs to lower away after whale—and of course by Milton, who must be considered one of the all-time great cartoonists, as when Satan

Puts on swift wings, and toward the Gates of Hell
Explores his solitary flight; sometimes
He scours the right hand coast, sometimes the left,
Now shaves with level wing the Deep, then soares
Up to the fiery concave touring high.

(It's true, Milton's a little boring now and then, and Milton teachers often don't value the cartoonist in him and want to know things about *Paradise Lost* that only some kind of crazy could get seriously interested in; but never mind.) I'm afraid the embarrassing truth is that the whole literary tradition opened out, for me, from Disney and his kind. I got caught up in the mighty cartoons of Homer and Dante (much later Virgil and Apollonius), the less realistic eighteenth- and nineteenth-century novelists (Fielding, Smollett, Collins and the rest), the glorious mad Russians (Tolstoy, Dostoyevsky, Biely), and those kinds of poets who fill one's head with strange, intense visions, like Blake, Coleridge and Keats.

For me the whole world of literature was at this time one of grand cartoons. I thought of myself mainly as a chemistry major and took courses in English just for fun. I guess I thought literature was unserious, like going to the movies or playing in a dance band, even an orchestra. It did not seem to me that one ought to spend one's life on mere pleasure, like a butterfly or cricket. Beethoven, Shakespeare, Richard Strauss, Conan Doyle might be a delight, but to fritter away one's life in the arts seemed, well, not quite honest. Then I came across the New Criticism.

At the first college I went to (for two years) I'd read nearly all of the Modern Library, partly for fun, partly because I felt ignorant around my fellow students, people who could talk with seeming wisdom about Camus and Proust, Nietzsche and Plato—I soon discovered they hadn't really read what they claimed to have read, they'd just come from the right part of town—but I'd never in any serious sense "studied" literature. (I took a couple of courses where one was examined on what Carlyle and Cardinal Newman said, without much emphasis on why or to whom.) But when I moved to Washington University in St. Louis I got a whole new vision of what literature was for—that is, the vision of the New Criticism. Like the fanatic I've always been, I fell to analyzing fiction, digging out symbols and structural subtleties, learning about "levels" and so on.

I don't say this was a foolish activity—in fact I think the New Critics were basically right: It's much more interesting to talk about how literature "works" than to read biographies of the writer, which is mainly what the New Criticism replaced. Working with the famous books by Cleanth Brooks and Robert Penn Warren, I began to love things in fiction and poetry that I'd never before noticed, things like meaning and design, and, like all my generation, I made the great discovery that literature is worthwhile, not a thing to be scorned by serious puritans but a thing to be embraced and turned cunningly to advantage. I learned that literature is Good for you, and that writers who are not deeply philosophical should be scorned. I began to read realists—two of whom, Jane Austen and James Joyce, I actually liked—and I began to write "serious" fiction; that is, instead of writing pleasant jingles or stories I desperately hoped would be published in the *Saturday Evening Post* or maybe *Manhunt*, I began shyly eyeing the *Kenyon Review*. With a sigh of relief (though I'd enjoyed them in a way) I quit math and science and signed up, instead, for courses in philosophy and sociology and psychology, which I knew would make me a better person and perhaps a famous writer so brilliant and difficult that to get through my books you would need a teacher.

This period lasted longer than I care to admit. On the basis of my earnestness and a more or less astonishing misreading of Nietzsche (I was convinced that he was saying that only fiction can be truly philosophical) I won a Woodrow Wilson fellowship to the University of Iowa, where I meant to study in the famous Writers' Workshop but soon ended up taking medieval languages and literature, the literature God had been nudging me toward all along: *Beowulf, The Divine Comedy*, the Gawain poet and Chaucer. The scales fell from my eyes. My New Critical compulsion to figure out exactly how everything works, how every nuance plays against every other, had suddenly an immense field to plow. I continued to read and think about other literature—I went through a Thomas Mann phase, a Henry James phase and so on—but I found myself spending more and more time trying to figure out medieval works.

It seems to me that when I began working on medieval literature, in the late '50s and early '60s, scholars knew little about even the greatest works in that literature. No one had really figured out the structure of the works of the Gawain poet, not to mention *Beowulf* or the poetry of Chaucer. People were still arguing about whether or not *Beowulf* is a Christian poem; people were still trying to shuffle around *The Canterbury Tales.* The usual New Critical method, which is to stare and stare at the work until it comes clear, was useless on this material, because again and again you found yourself staring at something that felt like a symbol or an allusion, or felt that maybe it ought to be some kind of joke but you couldn't see the humor. To figure out the poem you had to figure out the world it came from—read the books the poets knew, try to understand aesthetic principles abandoned and forgotten centuries ago. One had no choice but to become a sort of scholar.

Literary detective work is always fun, for a certain kind of mind at least, but the work I did on medieval literature, then on later classical literature, was for me the most exciting detective work I've ever done or heard of. The thing was, not only did you solve interesting puzzles, but when you got them solved you found you'd restored something magnificent, a work of art—in the case of *Beowulf* or *The Canterbury Tales*—supremely beautiful and noble. One unearthed tricks of the craft that nobody'd known or used for a long, long time—tricks one could turn on one's own work, making it different from anybody else's and yet not crazy, not merely novel.

I think every writer wants to sound like him- or herself; that's the main reason one sees so many experimental novels. And of course the risk in the pursuit of newness is that, in refusing to do what the so-called tradition does, one ends up doing exactly the same thing everybody else trying to get outside the tradition does. For better or worse (I'm no longer much concerned about whether it's better or worse), I joined up with an alternative tradition, one with which I felt almost eerily comfortable. My church-filled childhood delighted in discovering a Christianity distant enough—in fact, for all practical purposes, dead enough—to satisfy nostalgia without stirring embarrassment and annoyance, as modern Christianity does. For instance, when one reads about "ensoulment" in a medieval book—that is, when one reads arguments on precisely when the soul enters the fetus, and the argument comes from someone of the thirteenth century—one can read with interest; but when one hears a living Christian hotly debating ensoulment, hoping to be able to support abortion without feelings of guilt, one shrinks away, tries to get lost in the crowd.

I found in medieval culture and art, in other words, exactly what I needed as an instrument for looking at my own time and place. I of course never became for a moment a medieval Christian believer, but medieval ideas and attitudes gave me a means of triangulating, a place to stand. And, needless to say, medieval literature had built into it everything I'd liked best from the beginning, back in the days of God, Dickens and Disney, of grotesques (cartoon people and places), noble feeling, humor (God was perhaps a little short on humor) and real storytelling.

I said earlier that I'm no longer much concerned about whether the work I've done and am doing is for better or worse. That is not quite as true as I might wish. Egoistic ambition is the kind of weed that grows out of dragon's blood: The more you chop it away the more it flourishes. But it's true that at a certain point in one's career one begins to face up to one's limitations, and the way to stay sane at such a moment is to soften one's standards a little—find good reasons for approving lumpy but well-intentioned work, one's own and everybody else's.

To put all this another way, when I think back now over the influences which have helped to shape the way I write, I notice with a touch of dismay that they were as much bad influences as good ones. I won't criticize God (anyway, He's almost certainly been misquoted), but clearly the influence of Dickens and Disney was not all to the good. Both of them incline one toward stylized gestures. Instead of looking very closely at the world and writing it down, the way James Joyce does, brilliantly getting down, say, the way an old man moves his tongue over his gums, or the way a beautiful woman plays with her bracelets, a writer like me, seduced by cartoon vision, tends to go again and again for the same gestural gimmicks, a consistent pattern of caricature (compare the way doors in Dostoyevsky are forever flying open or slamming).

I look over my fiction of twenty years and see it as one long frenzy of tics—endlessly repeated words like *merely* and *grotesque*, a disproportionate number of people with wooden fingers and a dreary penchant for frowning thoughtfully or darting their eyes around like maniacs. I seem incapable of writing a story in which people do not babble philosophically, not really because they're saying things I want to get said but because earnest babbling is one of the ways I habitually give vitality to my short-legged, overweight, twitching cartoon creations. And needless to say, from artists like Dickens and Disney I get my morbid habit of trying to make the reader fall into tender weeping.

The whole New Critical period I went through, and the scholarly period that followed it, betrayed me, I think, into an excessive concern with significance. It's probably the case that novels and stories are more interesting if, in some sense or another, they mean something. But it has begun to dawn on me that—in fiction, as in all the arts—a little meaning goes a long way. I think what chiefly made me notice this is the work of my creative writing students. Until about five years ago, I never taught creative writing, only medieval literature and now and then a little Greek. When I began to look hard and often at student writing, I soon discovered that one of the main mistakes in their writing is that students think (probably because they've taken too many English literature courses) that fiction is supposed to tell us things—instruct us, improve us, show us.

In a sense of course they're right, but only in a subtle and mysterious sense. When one has analyzed every symbolically neat detail in a story like "Death in Venice" or "Disorder and Early Sorrow"—when one has accounted for every verbal repetition, every pattern and relationship, and set down in alphabetical order every thought to be lifted from the story—one discovers that, when you come right down to it, Mann has told us nothing we didn't know already. More by my writing students' early bad examples (they later get better) than by all the good literary examples I ever read, I've come to see that fiction simply dramatizes. It gives importance to ideas, it seems to me, pretty much in the way the string on which a handful of pearls have been strung gives a kind of importance to the pearls. When I read my earliest, most ingeniously constructed fictions (*The Resurrection* and *Grendel*) I find I can no longer figure the damn things out—would that I'd kept all my charts! Insofar as such books are interesting, for me at least, they're interesting because I like the characters and hope, as I reread, that life (the rest of the book) won't treat them too badly.

I don't mean, of course, that I intend never again to use symbols or design my stories so that the reader has the kind of experience William James described with such delight: "There goes the same thing I saw before again." What I do mean is that when I was three or four, or twelve or thirteen, I understood fiction more profoundly than I understood it through most of my writing years. I understood that a story, like a painting, or like a symphony, is one of the most wonderful, one of the most useless, things in the world. The magnificence of a work of art lies precisely in the fact that nobody made the artist make it, he just did, and—except when one's in school—nobody makes the receiver read it, or look at it, or listen to it: He just does. The influence of my writing students has been to lead me to understand (or imagine I understand) that art's value is not that it expresses life's meaning (though presumably it does, as do butterflies and crickets) but that it is, simply, splendidly, *there.*

I think of the performances my mother and father would sometimes do at, for instance, the monthly meetings of the Grange. The way the night would go is this: First everybody would crowd into one immense room with trestle-tables and white-paper tablecloths, the tables all loaded down with food, all the red-faced farmers and their plump wives and children finding folding chairs near friends, and somebody would tap a water glass with the side of his spoon and would say a quick, self-conscious prayer, and then everybody would eat.

It was a wonderfully pleasant social time, lots of jokes and stories and abundant country food; but it wasn't a time they chose solely for its pleasantness: If you wanted to get farmers to come from all over the county late at night, after chores, you had to feed them. Then they'd all go into another room and have their business meeting— how much or how little they should organize, how to keep the feed-mills, the truckers and the United States Congress in line. Nobody much cared for the business meeting, though sometimes somebody would "get off a good one," as they used to say.

Then, when the work was done my mother and father would stand there in the middle of the big, bright room and say poems or sing. How strange it seemed to me that all these serious, hardworking people should sit there grinning for an hour or more, listening, for instance, to my father telling them an endless, pointless story of a ghost in armor, or a ship rescued by pigeons, or somebody called Dangerous Dan McGrew. It was absurd. I wasn't just imagining it. The whole thing was deeply, weirdly absurd. Clearly if one is to devote a lifetime to doing something as crazy as that, one had better do it well—not necessarily because there is any great virtue in doing it well but only because, if one does it badly, people may wake up and notice that what one's doing is crazy.

Julius Caesar and the Werewolf

---

*"J*ULIUS CAESAR AND THE WEREWOLF" IS
John Gardner's only posthumously published work of short fiction. It ap-
peared in the September 1984 issue of Playboy. *While other uncollected*
stories exist—"The Darkening Green" from a 1972 Iowa Review, *a coyote-*
trickster fable written especially for an anthology, dozens of unpublished
works—only "Julius Caesar and the Werewolf" seemed strong enough to
include in this final collection of his prose.

As to Caesar's health, there seems to me no cause for alarm. The
symptoms you mention are, indeed, visible, though perhaps a little
theatricized by your informant. Caesar has always been a whirlwind
of energy and for that reason subject to nervous attacks, sudden tempers,
funks and so forth. When I was young, I confidently put it down to
excess of blood, a condition complicated (said I) by powerful intermit-
tent ejections of bile; but phlebotomy agitates instead of quieting him,
sad to say (sad for my diagnosis), and his habitual exhilaration, lately
increased, makes the bile hypothesis hogwash. I speak lightly of these
former opinions of mine, but you can hardly imagine what labor I've
put into the study of this man, scribbling, pondering, tabulating, while,
one after another, the chickens rise to confront a new day and my

candles gutter out. All to no avail, but pride's for people with good digestion. I bungle along, putting up with myself the best I can. (You'll forgive a little honest whining.) No man of science was ever presented with a puzzle more perplexing and vexatious than this Caesar, or with richer opportunity for observing the subject of his inquiry. He's interested in my work—in fact, follows it closely. He allows me to sit at his elbow or tag along wherever I please—an amusing spectacle, Caesar striding like a lion down some corridor, white toga flying, his black-robed physician leaping along like a spasm behind him on one good leg, one withered one.

In any event, at the age of 55, his animal spirits have never been more vigorous. He regularly dictates to four scribes at a time—jabber, jabber, jabber, sentences crackling like lightning in a haystack, all of his letters of the greatest importance to the state. Between sentences, to distract his impatience, he reads from a book. Or so he'd have us think, and I'm gullible. It saves time, I find, and in the end makes no big difference. His baldness more annoys him, it seems to me, than all the plots of the senators. For years, as you know, he combed his straggling blond hairs straight forward, and nothing pleased him more than the people's decision to award him the crown of laurel, which he now wears everywhere except, I think, to bed. A feeble ruse and a delight to us all. The reflected light of his bald pate glows like a sun on the senate-chamber ceiling.

His nervous energy is not significantly increased, I think, from the days when I first knew him, many years ago, in Gaul. I was transferred to the legion for some disservice to the state—monumental, I'm sure, but it's been 35 years, and I've told the story so many times, in so many slyly self-congratulating versions, that by now I've forgotten the truth of it. I was glad of the transfer. I was a sea doctor before. I don't mind telling you, water scares the pants off me.

I remember my first days with Caesar clear as crystal. He struck me at once as singular almost to the point of freakishness. He was taller than other men, curiously black-eyed and blond-headed, like two beings in one body. But what struck me most was his speed, both physical and mental. He could outrun a deer, outthink every enemy he met—and he was, besides, very strong. We all knew why he fought so brilliantly. He was guilty of crimes so numerous, back in Rome, from theft to assault to suspicion of treason, that he couldn't afford to return there as a common citizen. (It was true of most of us, but Caesar was the worst.) By glorious victories, he could win public honors and appointments and, thus, stand above the law, or at least above its meanest kick. Whatever his reasons—this I have to give to him— no man in history, so far as it's recorded, ever fought with such effectiveness and passion or won such unshakable, blind-pig devotion from his men. He was not then the strategist he later became, killing a few left-handed and blindfolded, then persuading the rest to surrender and accept Roman citizenship. In those days, he painted the valleys red, weighed down the trees with hanging men, made the rivers run sluggish with corpses. He was always in the thick of it, like a rabid bitch, luring and slaughtering seven at a time. His body, it seems to me, runs by nature at an accelerated tempo: His sword moves much faster than a normal man's. And he's untiring. At the end of a 12-hour day's forced march, when the whole encampment was finally asleep, he used to pace like a half-starved jaguar in his tent or sit with a small fish-oil lamp, writing verse. I wonder if he may not have some unknown substance in common with the violent little flea.

Through all his wars, Caesar fought like a man unhinged, but I give you my word, he's not crazy. He has the falling sickness, as you know. A damned nuisance but, for all the talk, nothing more. All his muscles go violent, breaking free of his will, and he has a sudden, vividly real sense of falling into the deepest abyss, a fall that seems certain never to end, and no matter what servants or friends press around him (he's dimly aware of presences, he says), there's no one, nothing, he can reach out to. From an outward point of view, he's unconscious at these times, flailing, writhing, snapping his teeth, dark eyes bulging and rolling out of sight, exuding a flood of oily tears; but from what he reports, I would say he is not unconscious but in some way transformed, as if seized for the moment by the laws of a different set of gods. (I mean, of course, "forces" or "biological constraints.")

No doubt it adds to the pressure on him that he's a creature full of pangs and contradictions. Once, in Gaul, we were surprised by an ambush. We had moved for days through dangerous, twilit forest and had come, with relief, to an area of endless yellow meadow, where the grass reached only to our knees, so that we thought we were safe. Suddenly, out of the grass all around us leaped an army of women. Caesar cried, "Save yourselves! We're not in Gaul to butcher females!"

In the end, we killed them all. (I, as Caesar's physician, killed no one.) I trace Caesar's melancholy streak to that incident. He became, thereafter, moody and uneasy, praying more than necessary and sometimes pausing abruptly to glance all around him, though not a shadow had stirred. It was not the surprise of the ambush, I think. We'd been surprised before. The enemy was young and naked except for weapons and armor, and they were singularly stubborn. They gave us no choice but to kill them. I watched Caesar himself cut one in half, moving his sword more slowly than usual and staring fixedly at her face.

The melancholy streak has been darkened, in my opinion, by his years in Rome. His workload would rattle a stone Apollo—hundreds of letters to write every day, lines of suppliants stretching half a mile, each with his grievance large or small and his absurd, ancient right to spit softly into Caesar's ear—not to mention the foolish disputes brought in to him for settlement. Some starving scoundrel steals another scoundrel's newly stolen pig, the whole ramshackle slum is up in arms, and for the public good the centurions bring all parties before Caesar. Hours pass, lamps are lit, accuser and denier rant on, banging tables, giving the air fierce kicks by way of warning. Surely a man of ordinary tolerance would go mad—or go to sleep. Not our Caesar. He listens with the look of a man watching elderly people eat, then eventually points to one or the other or both disputants, which means the person's to be dragged away for hanging, and then, with oddly meticulous care, one hand over his eyes, he dictates to a scribe the details of the case and his dispensation, with all his reasonings. "Admit the next," he says, and folds his hands.

And these are mere gnats before the hurricane. He's responsible, as they say when they're giving him some medal, for the orderly operation of the largest, richest, most powerful empire the world has ever known. He must rule the senate, with all its constipated, red-nosed, wheezing factions—every bleary eye out for insult or injury, every liver-spotted hand half closed around a dagger. And he must show at least some semblance of interest in the games, escape for the bloodthirst of the citizenry. He watches the kills, man or lion or whatever, without a sign of emotion, but I'm onto him. He makes me think of my days at sea, that still, perfect weather before a plank buster.

All this work he does without a particle of help, not a single assistant except the four or five scribes who take dictation and the slave who brings him parchment, ink and fresh oil or sandals—unless one counts, as I suppose one must, Mark Antony: a loyal friend and willing drudge but, as all Rome knows, weak as parsley. (He's grown fat here in the city and even less decisive than he was on the battlefield. I've watched him trying to frame letters for Caesar, tugging his jaw over decisions Caesar would make instantly.) In short, the life of a Caesar is donkey work and unquestionably dangerous to health. I've warned and warned him. He listens with the keenest interest, but he makes no changes. His wary glances to left and right become more frequent, more noticeable and odd. He has painful headaches, especially at executions, and now and then he sleepwalks, looking for something under benches and in every low cupboard. I find his heartbeat irregular, sometimes wildly rushing, sometimes all but turning around and walking backward, as if he were both in a frenzy and mortally bored.

Some blame the death of his daughter for all this. I'm dubious, though not beyond persuasion. That Julia was dear to his heart I won't deny. When she was well, he was off with her every afternoon he could steal from Rome's business, teaching her to ride, walking the hills with her, telling her fairy tales of gods disguised as people or people transformed into celestial constellations or, occasionally—the thing she liked best, of course—recounting his adventures. I remember how the girl used to gaze at him such times, elbows on her knees, hands on her cheeks, soft, pale hair cascading over her shoulders and down her long back—it made me think of those beautiful altar-lit statues in houses of prostitution. (I mean no offense. Old men by nature are prone to nastiness.) She was an intelligent girl, always pursing her lips and frowning, preparing to say, "Tut, tut." He taught her knots and beltwork and the nicer of the soldiers' songs, even taught her his special tricks of swordsmanship—because she nagged him to it (you know how daughters are)—and, for all I know, the subtleties of planning a campaign against India and China. I never saw a father more filled with woe than Caesar when the sickness first invaded her. He would rush up and down, far into the night (I never saw him take even a nap through all that period), and he was blistering to even the most bent-backed, senile and dangerous senators, to say nothing of whiny suppliants and his poor silent wife. His poems took an ugly turn—much talk of quicksand and maws and the like—and the bills he proposed before the senate weren't much prettier; and then there was the business with the gladiators. But when Julia died, he kissed her waxy forehead and left the room and, so far as one could see, that was that. After the great funeral so grumbled about in certain quarters, he seemed much the same man he'd seemed before, not just externally but also internally, so far as my science could reach. His blood was very dark but, for him, normal; his stools were ordinary; his seizures no more tedious than usual.

So what can have brought on this change you inquire of and find so disturbing—as do I, of course? (At my age, nothing's as terrible as might have been expected.) I have a guess I might offer, but it's so crackpot I think I'd rather sit on it. I'll narrate the circumstances that prompt it; you can draw your own conclusions.

———————

Some days ago, March first, shortly after nightfall, as I was washing out my underthings and fixing myself for bed, two messengers appeared at my door with the request—polite but very firm—that I at once get back into my clothes and go to Caesar. I naturally—after some per- functory sniveling—obeyed. I found the great man alone in his chamber, staring out the one high window that overlooks the city. It was a fine scene, acted with great dignity, if you favor that sort of thing. He did not turn at our entrance, though only a man very deep in thought could have failed to notice the brightness of the torches as their light set fire to the wide marble floor with its inlay of gold and quartz. We waited. It was obvious that something was afoot. I was on guard. Nothing interests Caesar, I've learned, but Caesar. Full-scale invasion of the Empire's borders would not rouse in him this banked fire of restlessness—fierce playfulness, almost—except insofar as its repulsion might catch him more honor. There was a scent in the room, the smell of an animal, I thought at first, then corrected myself: a blood smell. "Show him," Caesar said quietly, still not turning.

I craned about and saw, even before my guides had inclined their torches in that direction, that on the high marble table at the far end of the room some large, wet, misshapen object had been placed, then blanketed. I knew instantly what it was, to tell the truth, and my eyes widened. They have other doctors; it was the middle of the night! I have bladder infections and prostate trouble; I can hardly move my bowels without a clyster! When the heavy brown cloth was solemnly drawn away, I saw that I'd guessed right. It was, or had once been, a tall, bronze-skinned man, a slave, probably rich and admired in whatever country he'd been dragged from. His knees were drawn up nearly to his pectorals and his head rolled out oddly, almost severed at the neck. One could guess his stature only from the length of his arms and the shiny span exposed, caked with blood, from knee to foot. One ear had been partially chewed away.

"What do you make of it?" Caesar asked. I heard him coming toward me on those dangerous, swift feet, then heard him turn, pivoting on one hissing sandal, moving back quickly toward the window. I could imagine his nervous, impatient gestures, though I did not look: gestures of a man angrily talking to himself, bullying, negotiating—rapidly opening and closing his fists or restlessly flipping his right hand, like a sailor playing out coil after coil of line.

"Dogs—" I began.

"Not dogs," he said sharply, almost before I'd spoken. I felt myself grow smaller, the sensation in my extremities shrinking toward my heart. I put on my mincing, poor-old-man expression and pulled at my beard, then reached out gingerly to move the head, examining more closely the clotted ganglia where the thorax had been torn away. Whatever had killed him had done him a kindness. He was abscessed from the thyroid to the *vena cava superior*. When I looked over at Caesar, he was back at the window, motionless again, the muscles of his arm and shoulder swollen as if clamping in rage. Beyond his head, the night had grown dark. It had been clear, earlier, with a fine, full moon; now it was heavily overcast and oppressive—no stars, no moon, only the lurid glow, here and there, of a torch. In the light of the torches the messengers held, one on each side of me, Caesar's eyes gleamed, intently watching.

"Wolves," I said, with conviction.

He turned, snapped his fingers several times in quick succession—in the high, stone room, it was like the sound of a man clapping—and almost the same instant, a centurion entered, leading a girl. Before she was through the archway, she was down on her knees, scrambling toward Caesar as if to kiss his toes and ankles before he could behead her. Obviously, she did not know his feeling of tenderness, almost piety, toward young women. At her approach Caesar turned his back to the window and raised his hands, as if to ward her off. The centurion, a young man with blue eyes, like a German's, jerked at her wrist and stopped her. Almost gently, the young man put his free hand into her hair and tipped her face up. She was perhaps 16, a thin girl with large, dark, flashing eyes full of fear.

Caesar said, never taking his gaze from her, "This young woman says the wolf was a man."

I considered for a moment, only for politeness. "Not possible," I said. I limped nearer to them, bending for a closer look at the girl. If she was insane, she showed none of the usual signs—depressed temples, coated tongue, anemia, inappropriate smiles and gestures. She was not a slave, like the corpse on the table—nor of his race, either. Because of her foreignness, I couldn't judge what her class was, except that she was a commoner. She rolled her eyes toward me, a plea like a dog's. It was hard to believe that her terror was entirely an effect of her audience with Caesar.

Caesar said, "The Goths have legends, doctor, about men who at certain times turn into wolves."

"Ah," I said, noncommittal.

He shifted his gaze to meet mine, little fires in his pupils. I shrank from him—visibly, no doubt. Nothing is stupider or more dangerous than toying with Caesar's intelligence. But he restrained himself. "'Ah!'" he mimicked with awful scorn and, for an instant, smiled. He looked back at the girl, then away again at once; then he strode over to the corpse and stood with his back to me, staring down at it, or into it, as if hunting for its soul, his fists rigid on his hips to keep his fingers from drumming. "You know a good deal, old friend," he said, apparently addressing myself, not the corpse. "But possibly not everything!" He raised his right arm, making purposely awkward loops in the air with his hand, and rolled his eyes at me, grinning with what might have been malice, except that he's above that. Impersonal rage at a universe too slow for him. He said, "Perhaps, flopping up and down through the world like a great, clumsy bat, trying to spy out the secrets of the gods, you miss a few things? Some little trifle here or there?"

I said nothing, merely pressed my humble palms together. To make perfectly clear my dutiful devotion, I limped over to stand at his side, looking with him, gravely, at the body. Moving the leg—there was as yet no *rigor mortis*—I saw that the body had been partly disemboweled.

The spleen was untouched in the intestinal disarray; the liver was nowhere to be seen. I could feel the girl's eyes on my back. Caesar's smile was gone now, hovering just below the surface. He had his hand on the dead man's foot, touching it as if to see if bones were broken, or as if the man were a friend, a fellow warrior.

He lowered his voice. "This isn't the first," he said. "We've kept the matter quiet, but it's been happening for months." His right hand moved out like a stealthy animal, anticipating his thought. His voice grew poetic. (It was a bad idea, that laurel crown.) "A sudden black shadow, a cry out of the darkness, and in the morning—in some alley or in the middle of a field or huddled against some rotting door in the tanners' district—a corpse ripped and mauled past recognition. The victims aren't children, doctor; they're grown men, sometimes women." He frowned. The next instant, his expression became unreadable, as if he were mentally reaching back, abandoning present time, this present body. Six, maybe seven heartbeats passed; and then, just as suddenly, he was here with us again, leaning toward me, oddly smiling. "And then tonight," he said, "this treasure!" With a gesture wildly theatrical—I saw myself at the far end of the forum, at the great door where the commoners peer in—he swept his arm toward the girl. She looked, cowering, from one to the other of us, then up at the soldier.

Caesar crossed to her; I followed part way. "He was half man, half wolf; is that your story?" He bent over her, pressing his hands to his knees as he asked it. Clearly he meant to seem fatherly, but his body was all iron, the muscles of his shoulders and arms locked and huge.

After a moment, she nodded.

"He wore clothes like a man?"

Again she nodded, this time looking warily at me. She had extraordinary eyes, glistening, dark, bottomless and very large, perhaps the first symptom of a developing exophthalmic goiter.

Caesar straightened up and turned to the centurion. "And what was this young woman doing when you found her?"

"Dragging the body, sir." One side of his mouth moved, the faintest suggestion of a smile. "It appeared to us she was hiding it."

Now Caesar turned to me, his head inclined to one side, like a lawyer in court. "And why would she be doing that?"

At last the girl's terror was explicable.

I admired the girl for not resisting us. She knew, no doubt—all Romans know—that torture can work wonders. Although I've never been an optimist, I like to believe it was not fear of torture that persuaded her but the certain knowledge that whatever sufferings she might put herself through, she would in the end do as we wished. She had a curious elegance for a girl of her station. Although she walked head ducked forward, as all such people do, and although her gait was odd— long strides, feet striking flat, like an Egyptian's—her face showed the composure and fixed resolve one sometimes sees on statues, perhaps some vengeful, endlessly patient Diana flanked by her hounds. Although one of the centurions in our company held the girl's elbow, there seemed no risk that she would try to run away. Caesar, wearing a dark hood and mantle now, kept even with her or sometimes moved a little ahead in his impatience. The three other centurions and I came behind, I in great discomfort, wincing massively at every right-foot lurch but, for all that, watching everything around me, especially the girl, with sharp attention. It grew darker and quieter as we descended into the slums. The sky was still overcast, so heavily blanketed one couldn't even guess in which part of the night the moon hung. Now and then, like some mysterious pain, lightning would bloom and move deep in the clouds, giving them features and shapes for a moment, and we'd hear a low rumble; then blackness would close on us deeper than before. The girl, too, seemed to mind the darkness. Every so often, as we circled downward, I'd see her lift and turn her head, as if she were trying to find her bearings.

No one was about. Nothing moved except now and then a rat researching garbage or scampering along a gutter, or a chicken stirring in its coop as we passed, its spirit troubled by bad dreams. In this part of town, there were no candles, much less torches—and just as well: The whole section was a tinderbox. The buildings were three and four stories high, leaning out drunkenly over the street or against one another like beggars outside a temple, black, rotten wood that went shiny as intestines when the lightning glowed, walls patched with hides and daubs of mud, straw and rotten hay packed in tightly at the crooked foundations. The only water was the water in the streets or in the river invisible in the darkness below us, poisonously inching under bridge after bridge toward the sea. When I looked back up the hill between lightning blooms, I could no longer make out so much as

an arch of Caesar's palace or the firm, white mansions of the rich—
only a smoky luminosity red under the clouds. The street was airless,
heavy with the smell of dead things and urine. Every door and shutter
was unhealthily closed tight.

We progressed more slowly now, barely able to see one another.
I cannot say what we were walking on; it was slippery and gave under-
foot. I was feeling cross at Caesar's refusal to use torches; but he was
the crafty old warrior, not I. Once, with a clatter I mistook for thunder,
some large thing rushed across the street in front of us, out of darkness
and in again—a man, a donkey, some rackety demon—and we all
stopped. No one spoke; then Caesar laughed. We resumed our walk.

Minutes later, the girl stopped without a word. We had arrived.

The man was old. He might have been sitting there, behind his
table in the dark, for centuries. It was not dark now. As soon as the
hide door was tightly closed, Caesar had tipped back his hood, reached
into his cloak past his heavy iron sword and brought out candles, which
he gave to two centurions to light and hold; the room was far too
confined for torches. The other two centurions waited outside; even
so, there was not much room. The man behind the table was bearded,
not like a physician but like a foreigner—a great white-silver beard
that flicked out like fire in all directions. His hair was long, unkempt,
his eyebrows bushy; his blurry eyes peered out as if from deep in a
cave. Purple bruises fell in chevrons from just under his eyes into his
mustache. If he was surprised or alarmed, he showed no sign, merely
sat—stocky, firmly planted—behind his square table, staring straight
ahead, not visibly breathing, like a man waiting in the underworld.
The girl sat on a low stool, her back against the wall, between her
father and the rest of us. She gazed at her knees in silence. Her face
was like that of an actress awaiting her entrance, intensely alive, showing no expression.

The apartment, we saw as the light seeped into it, was a riddle.
Although in the poorest section of the city, it held a clutter of books,
and the furniture, though sparse, was elaborately carved and solid; it
would bring a good price in the markets that specialize in things outlandish. Herbs hung from the rafters, only a few of them known to
me. Clearly it wasn't poverty or common ignorance that had brought
these people here. Something troubled my nostrils, making the hair
on the back of my neck rise—not the herbs or the scent of storm in

the air but something else; the six-week smell of penned animals in the hold of a ship, it came to me at last. That instant, a terrific crack of thunder struck, much nearer than the rest, making all of us, even Caesar, jump—all, that is, but the bearded old man. I heard wind sweep in, catching at the ragged edges of things, moving everything that would move.

The first indication that the old man was aware of us—or, indeed, aware of anything—came when Caesar inclined his head to me and said, "Doctor, it's close in here. Undo the window." The bearded man's mouth opened as if prepared to object—his teeth gleamed yellow— and his daughter's eyes flew wide; then both, I thought, gave way, resigned themselves. The man's beard and mustache became one again, and the flicker of life sank back out of his face. I, too, had certain small reservations. The only window in the room, its shutters now rattling and tugging, was the one behind the bearded man's right shoulder; and though he seemed not ferocious—he behaved like a man under sedation, in fact, his eyelids heavy, eyes filmed over—I did not relish the thought of moving nearer to a man who believed he could change into a wolf. Neither did I much like Caesar's expression. I remembered how once, halting his army, he'd sent three men into a mountain notch to find out whether they drew fire.

I made—cunning old fart that I am—the obvious and inevitable choice. I hobbled to the window, throwing my good leg forward and hauling in the bad one, making a great show of pitiful vulnerability, my face a heart-rending mask of profoundest apology—I unfastened the latches, threw the shutters wide and hooked them, then ran like a child playing sticks in the ring back to Caesar. To my horror, Caesar laughed. Strange to say, the bearded man, gloomier than Saturn until this moment, laughed, too. I swung around like a billy goat to give him a look. Old age, he should know, deserves respect or, at least, mercy—not really, of course; but I try to get one or the other if I can.

"He keep clear...werewolf," the bearded man said. His speech was slurred, his voice like the creakiest hinge in Tuscany. He tapped his fingertips together as if in slowed-down merriment. The night framed in the window behind him was as dense and black as ever but alive now, roaring and banging. Caesar and the two centurions laughed with the old man as if there were nothing strange at all in his admission that, indeed, he was a werewolf. The girl's face was red, whether with anger or shame I couldn't guess. For an instant, I was mad as a hornet, suspecting they'd set up this business as a joke on me; but gradually, my reason regained the upper hand. Take it from an old man who's seen a few things: It's always a mistake to assume that anything has been done for you personally, even evil.

The world flashed white and the loudest crash of thunder yet stopped their laughter and, very nearly, my heart. Now rain came pouring down like a waterfall, silver-gold where the candlelight reached it, a bright sheet blowing away from us, violently hissing. The girl had her hands over her ears. The werewolf smiled, uneasy, as if unsure what was making all the noise.

Now that we were all on such friendly terms, we introduced ourselves. The man's name was Vödfiet—one of those northern names that have no meaning. When he held out his leaden hand to Caesar, Caesar thoughtfully bowed and looked at it but did not touch it. I, too, looked, standing a little behind Caesar and to his left. The man's fingernails were thick yellow and carved with ridges, like old people's toenails, and stranger yet, the lines of the palm—what I could see of them—were like the scribbles of a child who has a vague sense of letters but not of words. It was from him that the animal smell came, almost intolerably rank, up close, even with the breeze from the window. I'd have given my purse to get the palps of my fingers into his cranium, especially the area—as close as I could get—of the *pallium prolectus*. Preferably after he was dead.

"Strange," Caesar said, gently stroking the sides of his mouth, head bowed, shoulders rigid, looking from the werewolf to me, then back. Caesar seemed unnaturally alert, yet completely unafraid or else indifferent—no, not indifferent: on fire, as if for some reason he thought he'd met his match. The fingers of his left hand drummed on the side of his leg. He said, with the terrible coy irony he uses on senators, "You seem not much bothered by these things you do."

The werewolf sighed, made a growl-like noise, then shrugged and tipped his head, quizzical. He ran his tongue over his upper teeth, a gesture we ancients know well. We're authorities on rot. We taste it, insofar as we still taste, with every breath.

"Come, come," Caesar said, suddenly bending forward, smiling, sharp-eyed, and jerked his right hand, fingers tight, toward the werewolf's face. The man no more flinched than an ox would have done, drugged for slaughter. His heavy eyelids blinked once, slowly. Caesar said, again in a voice that seemed ironic, perhaps self-mocking, "Your *daughter* seems bothered enough!"

The werewolf looked around the room until he found her, still there on her stool. She went on staring at her knees. Thunder hit, not as close now, but loud. Her back jerked.

"And yet, you," Caesar said, his voice rising, stern—again there was that hint of self-mockery and something else: lidded violence—"that doesn't trouble you. Your daughter's self-sacrifice, her labor to protect you—"

The man raised his hands from the table, palms out, evidently struggling for concentration, and made a growling noise. Perhaps he said, "Gods." He spread one hand over his chest in the age-old sign of injured innocence, then slowly raised the hand toward the ceiling, or possibly he meant the window behind him, and with an effort splayed out the fingers. "Moon," he said, and looked at us hopefully, then saw that we didn't understand him. "Moon," he said carefully. "Cloud." His face showed frustration and confusion, like a stroke victim's, though, obviously, that wasn't his trouble, I thought; no muscle loss, no discernible differentiation between his left side and his right. "Full moon . . . shine . . . no, but . . ." Although his eyes were still unfocused, he smiled, eager; he'd caught my worried glance at the window. After a moment's hesitation, the werewolf lowered his hands again and folded them.

"The moon," Caesar said, and jabbed a finger at the night. "You mean you blame—"

The man shrugged, his confusion deepening, and opened his hands as if admitting that the excuse was feeble, then rested his dull eye on Caesar, tipped his head like a dog and went on waiting.

Caesar turned from him, rethinking things, and now I saw real fury rising in him at last. "The moon," he said half to himself, and looked hard at the centurion, as if checking his expression. Recklessly, he flew back to the table and slammed the top with the flat of both hands. "Wake up!" he shouted in the werewolf's face, so ferocious that the cords of his neck stood out.

The werewolf slowly blinked.

Caesar stared at him, eyes bulging, then again turned away from him and crossed the room. He clamped his hands to the sides of his face and squeezed his eyes shut—perhaps he had a headache starting up. Thunder banged away, and the rain, still falling hard, was now a steady hiss, a rattle of small rivers on the street. We could hear the two centurions outside the door flap ruefully talking. At last, Caesar half turned back to the werewolf. In the tone men use for commands, he asked, "What does it feel like, coming on?"

The werewolf said nothing for a long moment, then echoed, as if the words made no sense to him, "Feel like." He nodded slowly, as if deeply interested or secretly amused. The girl put her hands over her face.

Caesar said, turning more, raising his hand to stop whatever words might be coming, "Never mind that. What does it feel like afterward?"

Again it seemed that the creature found the question too hard. He concentrated with all his might, then looked over at his daughter for help, his expression wonderfully morose. She lowered her hands by an act of will and stared as before at her knees. After a time, the old man moistened his lips with his tongue, then tipped his head and looked at Caesar, hoping for a hint. A lightning flash behind him momentarily turned his figure dark.

Caesar bowed and shook his head, almost smiling in his impatience and frustration. "Tell me this: How many people have you killed?"

This question the werewolf did seem to grasp. He let the rain hiss and rattle for a while, then asked, "Hundreds?" He tipped his head to the other side, watching Caesar closely, then cautiously ventured a second guess. "Thousands?"

Caesar shook his head. He raised his fist, then stopped himself and changed it to a stiffly cupped hand and brought it to his mouth, sliding the fingertips up and down slowly. A pool was forming on the dirt floor, leaking in. I cleared my throat. The drift of the conversation was not what I call healthy.

The werewolf let out a sort of groan, a vocal sigh, drew back his arm and absently touched his forehead, then his beard. "Creatures," he said. The word seemed to have come to him by lucky accident. He watched hopefully; so did Caesar. At last, the werewolf groaned or sighed more deeply than before and said, "No, but . . ." Perhaps he'd suffered a stroke of some kind unknown to me. *No, but* is common, of course—often, in my experience, the only two words the victim can still command. He searched the walls, the growing pool on the floor, for language. I was sure he was more alert now, and I reached out to touch Caesar's elbow, warning him. "Man," the werewolf said; then, hopelessly, "moon!"

"Men *do* things," Caesar exploded, striking his thigh with his fist. He raised his hand to touch the hilt of his sword, not quite absently, as if grimly making sure he could get at it.

"Ax," the werewolf said. He was working his eyebrows, looking at his palely window-lit palms as if he couldn't remember having seen them before. "*Ax!*" he said. He raised his eyes to the ceiling and strained for a long time before trying again. "No, but . . . No . . . No, but . . ."

Caesar waved, dismissive, as if imagining he'd understood.

Their eyes met. The thunder was distant, the rain coming down as hard as ever.

"Ax," the werewolf said at last, softly, slowly shaking, then bowing his head, resting his forehead on his fingertips, pausing to take a deep, slow, whistling breath through his nostrils. "Ax," he said, then something more.

The girl's voice broke out like flame. She was looking at no one. "He's saying *accident*."

Caesar started, then touched his mouth.

The werewolf breathed deeply again; the same whistling noise. "Green parks—no, but—chill-den—"

Abruptly, the girl said, shooting her burning gaze at Caesar, "He means you. You're strong; you make things safe for children." She shook her hands as if frustrated by words, like the werewolf. "But you're just lucky. Eventually, you'll die."

"The Empire will go on," Caesar broke in, as if he'd known all along what the werewolf was saying and it was not what he'd come here to talk about. "It's not Caesar's 'indomitable will.' We have laws." Suddenly, his eyes darted away, avoiding the girl's.

"*Moon,*" the werewolf wailed.

Caesar's voice slashed at him. "*Stop* that."

It was beginning to get light out. It came to me that the old man was weeping. He laid his head to one side, obsequious. "Thank . . . gods . . . unspeakable . . . no, but . . ." His bulging forehead struggled. The candlelight was doing something queer to his glittering, tear-filled eyes, making them like windows to the underworld. He raised his voice. "No, but. No, *but!*" He gave his head a shake, then another, as if to clear it. Furtively, he brushed one eye, then the other. "Vile!" he cried out. *"No, but..."* His hands were trembling, as were the edges of his mouth. His voice took on pitch and intensity, the words in the extremity of his emotion becoming cloudy, more obscure than before. I had to lean close to watch his lips. I glanced at Caesar to see if he was following, then at the girl.

It was the girl's expression that made me realize my error: She was staring at the window, where the light, I saw at last, was not dawn but a parting of the thick black hood of clouds. There was no sound of rain. Moonlight came pouring through the window, sliding toward us across the room. The girl drew her feet back as if the light were alive.

I cannot say whether it was gradual or instantaneous. His beard and mouth changed; the alertness of his ears became a change in their shape and then bristling, tufted fur, and I saw distinctly that the hand swiping at his nose was a paw. All at once, the man behind the table was a wolf. A violent growl erupted all around us. He was huge, flame-eyed, already leaping, a wild beast tangled in clothes. He was still in mid-air when Caesar's sword thwunked into his head, cleaving it—a mistake, pure instinct, I saw from Caesar's face. Only the werewolf's daughter moved more quickly: She flew like a shadow past Caesar and the rest of us, running on all fours, slipped like ball lightning out the door, and vanished into the night.

It's difficult to put one's finger exactly on the oddity in Caesar's behavior. One cannot call it mania in any usual sense—delusional insanity, dementia, melancholia, and so forth. Nonetheless, he's grown odd. (No real cause for alarm, I think.) You've no doubt heard of the squall of honors recently conferred on him—statues, odes, feasts, gold medals, outlandish titles: Prince of the Moon, Father of Animals, Shepherd of Ethiopia and worse—more of them every day. They're nearly all his own inventions, insinuated into the ears of friendly senators or enemies who dare not cross him. I have it on good authority that those who hate him most are quickest to approve these absurdities, believing such inflations will ultimately make him insufferable to the people—as well they may. Indeed, the man who hungers most after his ruin has suggested that Caesar's horse be proclaimed divine. Caesar seems delighted. It cannot be put down to megalomania. At each new outrage he conceives or hears suggested, he laughs—not cynically but with childlike pleasure, as if astonished by how much foolishness the gods will put up with. (He's always busy with the gods, these days, ignoring necessities, reasoning with priests.)

I did catch him once in an act of what seemed authentic lunacy. He was at the aquarium, looking down at the innumerable, flickering goldfish and carp, whispering something. I crept up on him to hear. He was saying, "Straighten up those ranks, there! Order! Order!" He shook his finger. When he turned and saw me, he looked embarrassed, then smiled, put his arm around my shoulders and walked with me. "I try to keep the Empire neat, doctor," he said. "It's not easy!" And he winked with such friendliness that, testy as I am when people touch me, I was moved. In fact, tears sprang to my eyes, I admit it. Once a man's so old he's started to piss on himself, he might as well let go with everything. Another time, I saw him hunkered down, earnestly reasoning—so it seemed—with a colony of ants. "Just playing, doctor," he said when he saw that I saw.

"Caesar, Caesar!" I moaned. He touched his lips with one finger.

The oddest thing he's come up with, of course, is his proposed war with Persia—himself, needless to say, as general. Persia, for the love of God! Even poor befuddled Mark Antony is dismayed.

"Caesar, you're not as young as you used to be," he says, and throws a woeful look over at me. He sits with interdigitated fists between his big, blocky knees. We're in Caesar's council room, the guards standing stiff as two columns, as usual, outside the door. Mark Antony grows fatter by the day. Not an interesting problem—he eats and sleeps too much. I'd prescribe exercise, raw vegetables and copulation. He has an enlarged subcutaneous cyst on the back of his neck. It must itch, but he pretends not to notice, for dignity's sake. Caesar lies on his couch as if disinterested, but his legs, crossed at the ankles, are rigid, and the pulse through his right inner jugular is visible. It's late, almost midnight. At times, he seems to be listening for something, but there's nothing to be heard. Cicadas; occasional baying of a dog.

It strikes me that, for all his flab, Mark Antony is a handsome man. His once-mighty muscles, now toneless, suggest a potential for heart disease, and there's blue under his too-smooth skin; nonetheless, one can imagine him working himself back to vigor, the dullness gradually departing from his eyes. Anything's possible. Look at me, still upright, thanks mainly to diet, though I'm farther along than he is. I frequently lose feeling in my right hand.

"If you must attack Persia," he says, "why not send me? You're needed here, Caesar!" His eyes squirt tears, which he irritably brushes away. "Two, three years—not even you can win a war with Persia in less time than that. And all that while, Rome and her complicated business in the hands of Mark Antony! It will be ruin, Caesar! Everyone says so!"

Caesar gazes at him. "Are you, my friend, not nobler and more honest than all the other Romans put together?"

Mark Antony looks confused, raises his hands till they're level with his shoulders, then returns them to their place between his knees, which he once more clenches. "You're needed here," he says again. "Everyone says so." For all his friends' warnings, I do not think Mark Antony grasps how thoroughly he's despised by the senate. Caesar's confidant, Caesar's right arm. But besides that—meaning no disrespect—he really would be a booby. Talk about opening the floodgates!

Caesar smiles, snatches a moth out of the air, examines the wings with great curiosity, like a man trying to read Egyptian, then gently lets it go and lies still again. After a moment, he raises his right hand, palm outward, pushing an invisible bark out to sea. "You really would like that," he says. "Away to Persia for murder and mayhem."

Mark Antony looks to me for help. What can I say?

Now suddenly, black eyes flashing, Caesar rears up on one elbow and points at Mark Antony. "*You* are Rome," he says. "*You* are the hope of humanity!"

Later, Mark Antony asks me, "Is he insane?"

"Not by any rules I understand," I say. "At any rate, there's no cause for alarm."

He moves back and forth across the room like a huge, slow mimicry of Caesar, rubbing his hands together like a man preparing to throw dice. His shadow moves, much larger than he is, on the wall. For some reason, it frightens me. Through the window I see the sharp-horned, icy-white half-moon. Most of Mark Antony's fat has gone into his buttocks.

"They'll kill him rather than leave the Empire in my hands," he says. Then, without feeling, his palms pressed together like a priest's: "After that, they'll kill me."

His clarity of vision surprises me. "Cheer up," I say. "I'm his personal physician. They'll kill me, too."

Last night, the sky was alive with omens: stars exploding, falling every which way. "Something's up!" says Caesar, as tickled as if he himself had caused the discord in the heavens. His bald head glows with each star burst, then goes dark. He stood in the garden—the large one created for his daughter's tomb—till nearly sunrise, watching for more fireworks.

Mark Antony's been sent off, plainly a fool's errand, trumped up to get him out of Rome. "Don't come back," says Caesar. "Never come back until I send for you." I don't like this. Not at all, not one damn bit. My life line has changed. My stool this morning was bilious.

All day, Caesar has been receiving urgent visitors, all with one message: "It would be good if tomorrow you avoided the forum." There can be no doubt that there's a plot afoot.

Late this afternoon, at the onset of twilight, I saw—I think—the werewolf's daughter. She's grown thinner, as if eaten away by disease. (Everyone, these days, looks to me eaten away by disease. My prostate's nearly plugged, and there's not a surgeon in Rome whom I'd trust to cut my fingernails.) She stood at the bottom step of the palace stairway, one shaky hand reaching out to the marble hem. She left herbs of some kind. Their use, whether for evil or good, is unknown to me. Then she fled. Later, it occurred to me that I hadn't really gotten a good look at her. Perhaps it was someone I don't know.

Strange news. You'll have heard it before you get this letter. Forgive the handwriting. My poor old nerves aren't all they might be. Would that I'd never lived to see this day. My stomach will be acid for a month.

Caesar was hardly seated, had hardly gotten out the call for prayer, before they rose like a wave from every side, 60 senators with daggers. He was stabbed a dozen times before he struggled to his feet—eyes rolling, every muscle in spasm, as if flown out of control, though it clearly wasn't that. You wouldn't have believed what strength he called up in his final moment! He dragged them from one end of the forum to the other, hurling off senators like an injured bear and shrieking, screaming his lungs out. It was as if all the power of the gods were for an instant contracted to one man. They tore his clothes from him, or possibly he did it himself for some reason. His blood came spurting from a hundred wounds, so that the whole marble floor was slippery and steaming. He fell down, stood up again, dragging his assassins; fell down, then rose to crawl on hands and knees toward the light of the high central door where, that moment, I was running for my life. His slaughtered-bull bellowings are still in my ears, strangely bright, like a flourish of trumpets or Jovian laughter.

General Plan
for *The Sunlight Dialogues*

*I*DISCOVERED THE GENERAL PLAN FOR THE
Sunlight Dialogues *uncatalogued among the papers of the Gardner Collection at the University of Rochester. The document from which it is taken is a photocopy of a typescript with only a few minor spelling corrections in ink. This is the only copy of the Plan unearthed so far; the original, I presume, no longer exists. John Gardner apparently wrote it either for his editor at Knopf, Robert Gottlieb, or his agent, Georges Borchardt. As a fan of the book and an aspiring novelist, I read his explication greedily. Possibly the last major unpublished Gardner document, the Plan is a map for the general reader and a treasure for scholars. Beginning writers who wished for more in-depth nuts-and-bolts examples in* The Art of Fiction *and* On Becoming a Novelist *will find answers here. On paper, Gardner makes sense of his huge, architectonic novel, explaining the intertwined mechanisms of character, action, and idea in specifics, hunting down connections, mapping out plots, and checking events against his timeline. Though he wrote the Plan for someone else, it's hard not to see Gardner urging himself on, telling himself that this monstrous project will come together in the end. It did and it does.* — S.O.'N.

A long, difficult metaphysical novel which explores the ideas of responsibility and freedom on many levels organized around two controlling metaphors, one a cops-and-robbers metaphor (developed in the main action), the other a philosophical contrast between the ancient Mesopotamian and Hebrew cultures (developed in the four dialogues themselves, sections VII, XI, XIV, and XIX). On a psychological level, responsibility means the struggle to resist withdrawal and alienation, on one hand, despotic self-assertion on the other; and freedom means either acceptance of suffering and limitation, and positive action despite one's suffering or limitation, or else freedom—a bad kind of freedom—means psychotic flight from reality. (As in *The Resurrection*, the controlling psychological theory is that of R. G. Collingwood and those who directly or indirectly follow him.) On a familial level, the ideas of freedom and responsibility characterize successful and unsuccessful relationships within an archetypal family pattern—father, mother, son, daughter. On a social level, the same ideas characterize relationships of ethnic groups, generations, and so forth. Further levels explored are the political and metaphysical or, loosely, religious. All levels of experience are interpreted, as in any good philosophical system, as parallel expressions of a single abstract set of relationships—in effect, the complex relationships of the archetypal cop and robber.

The two central characters in the novel establish the polar opposition: Chief of Police Fred Clumly, a just, moral, and responsible man who struggles to defend and support "law and order," and whose difficulty is that the ideal he seeks is an impossible one, finally—and the archetypal robber, known as "The Sunlight Man," who, confronted by the complexity of the modern world, has abnegated responsibility, social commitment, even sanity, and who has the experience and intelligence to make a convincing case for his position. The driving dramatic concern of the whole thick novel, and the central focus of its suspense, is the rising chaos which threatens both men. As head of a police force which is—as most small-town police forces now are—transitional, shifting from the once standard methods to the methods of modern technology, including the so-called "averaging strategy," whereby one calculates the relative importance of a given crime and fights crime with one eye on the time-product-factor—that is, the extent to which a given investigation pays off in terms of tax dollars (a nine-dollar theft is worth one policeman's effort for one hour, if the breakdown of police force time shows the operational cost per man to be nine dollars an hour)—as head of such a police force, Clumly endures pressures from the Mayor, the public, and the press which push him in divergent directions. The Mayor wants efficiency at low cost, in other words, a record of *apparent* success; the public wants both this and police success of the old-fashioned kind; the press wants yet another kind of success—interesting cases solved. And there are other difficulties as well: our laws, which Clumly would agree are just, are in fact outmoded. Present day criminal systems—the modus operandi of the new professionals—make detection under the present laws nearly impossible. And the courts, traditionally calculated to protect the innocent, increase the difficulty by adding to the odds for the criminal. Because Clumly is concerned with the old values of the cop—preventing or checking crime—he works as he sees fit, procrastinates with the Mayor, evades responsibilities he does not approve of (public talks, discussions of the civic parking problem, etc.) and hopes to save himself by a dramatic capture of the Sunlight Man before the police department roof falls in. Clumly is right that the capture of the Sunlight Man is important; and one approves of his defiance of the system being imposed on him, which limits his efficiency though it also has strong justifications. But as the novel progresses one fears that his chance of success according to his own individualistic and privately responsible code is very small. To make matters worse, Clumly is old (sixty-four), occasionally troubled by mental lapses, anility, and plagued by partly irrational fears. In short, Chief Clumly is a fictional embodiment of the problems facing the responsible man—personal, familial (his wife is unwell), social, political, and ultimately metaphysical as well. If we affirm him and all he represents, we cannot do so with any firm expectation that he will prevail. But time is running out for the Sunlight Man, too. He knows this, and he is resigned to his doom. His question, and the reason he persists in eluding capture, is that it is for him a psychological imperative that he know for certain whether or not he is right. He respects Clumly but sees clearly the impossibility of Clumly's ideal. As a result, the Sunlight Man holds a tentative position as a nihilist and anarchist, and to some extent as maniac, though he is not quite crazy in the usual sense. The necessity of remaining "free," eluding capture, forces him to repeated social contacts, repeated crimes, and increasingly desperate flight to unreality. Philosophically, he is as right about the world as Clumly—perhaps righter—and because he is, like Clumly, an absolutist, he stubbornly refuses to resolve his dilemma in merely pragmatic terms. True, his course must inevitably lead to his death, but he would rather die than submit to illusion or to what he thinks of as victimization by a confused and sick society. Insofar as the Sunlight Man is a character who wins the reader's sympathy—and for any thinking reader he must surely be worth respect—his queer race against time must be as suspenseful as Clumly's.

The ideas implicit in the relationship of these two characters are further explored in the lives of a broad cast of minor characters: an old country lawyer who for complicated reasons pursues Clumly just as Clumly pursues the Sunlight Man (that is, hunts down the areas of Clumly's neglected responsibility, searches out the evidence of Clumly's incompetence, and so forth); a younger lawyer, the older lawyer's son, who is a hunter of professional skips—people who set up paper businesses, milk a town, then vanish; a thief who has two identities, one as thief (Walter Boyle), the other as respectable suburbanite (Walter Benson), and who cannot resolve the conflict of the two; an Indian boy; a woman hell-bent on destroying the son she loves; and others. In every case, specific parallels of action and imagery subtly suggest the parallels between these people and the archetypes, cop and robber. The most explicitly philosophical analysis of the central conflict comes in the four dialogues of Clumly and the Sunlight Man—conversations which come at intervals in the novel, in which Clumly is forced to debate the Sunlight Man's position: an extremely one-sided debate, since Clumly is no logician and the Sunlight Man is. (He is also, and more important for the drama of the novel, an expert amateur magician.)

One of the central questions in the novel is the identity of the Sunlight Man. (See "The Identity of the Sunlight Man," below.) On the level of drama, the question is part of the controlling cops-and-robbers vehicle of ideas. But the question also involves the larger question of human identity itself. Because one's identity is, finally, a matter of one's choice between lawless freedom and responsibility. Ironically—and symbolically—at the very moment the Sunlight Man learns what his real identity is, that is, what his final values are, he is robbed of his identity: he is shot.

PLOTS

The main plot is that which concerns Clumly and the Sunlight Man, but threaded through this plot are a number of subplots, each developing, as I have said, implicit ideas in the main plot.

One problem every writer faces when he puts together an architectonic novel of this sort—an old-fashioned Victorian novel, in a way—is that of probability. What leaves one restless about Dickens, say, is that sooner or later every character comes into contact with every other—a thing which strains the reader's belief. In this novel the interwoven plots have moments of connection but no final connection. What must hold the book together is the thematic parallels, imagistic parallels, and similarities of action in the subplots. Further cohesive elements are the novel's concentration on, mainly, one important family, the Hodges (the lawyer and his son, the lawyer's ex-wife, the lawyer's younger son, and the lawyer's brother, and, finally—as one learns for certain only near the end—the Sunlight Man himself, a brother to the lawyer, who has been absent from the novel's locale for sixteen years but has returned to it, incognito, in hopes of setting right an old mistake). Another cohesive element is the figure of the old lawyer's father, a fine and brilliant man—once a Congressman—who established the ideal for his sons and grandsons, an ideal no longer meaningful because the world has changed, politics has changed, and family life has changed. The old ghost's values are at the heart of the lawyer's wife's hostility, the Sunlight Man's nihilism, and so on. Hopefully, the novel will also be held together by its use of a single, rich locale—western New York. And of course the novel's primary emphasis on the Clumly–Sunlight Man story will help to keep the rest in proper perspective.

The plots are as follows.

THE IDENTITY OF THE SUNLIGHT MAN
(A MYSTERY UNTIL THE END)

Taggert Faeley Hodge, who would now be forty, left Batavia sixteen years ago, in 1950, having been disbarred as a result of his having defrauded clients and robbed the government. He was the youngest

of the Congressman's sons, the darling of his family, the most brilliant
of the lot. In the army he was a minor hero. During his stint in the
service he married Kathleen Paxton, daughter of one of Batavia's relatively new rich. She was a little crazy, demanded more than Taggert
could afford. In time, he began to rob clients to meet his bills. (He had
expensive tastes of his own to support. Queer hobbies, gadgets, and,
above all, books and relics from the Near East.) Abandoning his wife
and two children, he fled New York State. Kept in touch with Will
Hodge's wife, his sole ally, and in six months returned for a secret
visit to his children, at Hodge's office. Betraying Hodge, he vanished
with the children, taking his car, which he abandoned in Cleveland,
mailing back the keys. Old Clive Paxton hunted Taggert but never
located him, remained a bitter man. Blamed Taggert Hodge for driving
Kathleen Paxton mad. She now occupies a room in Clifton. After about
five years, Taggert and the Hodges reestablish communication. All is
more or less forgiven. Taggert works as a used car salesman, shoeclerk,
custodian for the public school system of Phoenix. Marries, becomes
an imitation of his father. Begins to write articles on Assyriology. Also
begins to send Hodge feelers about a reconciliation with old Paxton.
Along with one such feeler he sends a clipping of himself in a magician's cape. A trifling detail, but one which recalls others, for Hodge.
In college, in the service, and occasionally even before, Taggert used
to do impersonations, card tricks, and so on, to entertain people. And
he's psychic.

On the night of August 22, Clive Paxton died in his study. His
heart had been bad for a long time, and no one was surprised. The
study window was opened, but no one noticed. His wife closed it
almost without thinking—as Clumly makes her remember later. What
happened, of course, is that Taggert Hodge paid him a visit, and the
man died of either shock or rage.

At Luke Hodge's house, where Millie and Luke are held prisoners, in
effect, by the Sunlight Man, the Sunlight Man for some reason makes
a point of never allowing anyone to see him. Millie would recognize
him, though she cannot—quite—recognize his altered voice. Luke theoretically could *not* know him. Luke was six when Taggert left Batavia.
And yet somehow—who knows how?—Luke does recognize him. "I
know you," he says just before the trip in which Luke dies.

What makes Clumly seek the identity of the Sunlight Man is Clumly's sense of order. Why should a man from California (Clumly's guess) appear precisely here in Batavia? Why should he release Nick Slater? Clumly isn't after a neat mystery-plot connection but something much grander—connections in the very substance of reality. Running out of time himself—Mayor Mullen breathing down his neck—and having no rational idea of where to turn, he begins, simply, to fumble, that is, follow his hunches. He questions everybody. People off the street. Fellow policemen. He hits a queer kind of paydirt when he visits the Woodworth sisters. He shows them a picture, and they say they recognize it. It's Taggert Villiers Hodge, father of the Congressman. T. V. Hodge died in 1908. Clumly sends a wire to Phoenix, Arizona. And visits Kathleen Paxton. Shown the picture, Kathleen screams—a high, mechanical, repetitive screech—then goes catatonic. (Kozlowski is with Clumly for this. He says, "It looks like you've got it, Chief." Clumly looks disgusted, bored. "You think he's *dangerous?*" Kozlowski asks. Clumly looks out the car window. "The *world* is dangerous, Kozlowski.")

A further identity complication: Walter Benson, shadowing his boarder at a revolutionary meeting, sees Will Hodge Jr and believes him to be the Sunlight Man. Same voice, same eyes. Will is fatter, appears younger, but even so the impression is so powerful that Benson is convinced. This too he must decide whether or not to tell the police. When Will Jr greets Benson, casually, Benson is terrified, feels the Sunlight Man knows all about him, has gotten inside his skin, so to speak. On an impulse, Benson shadows Will Jr that night, instead of shadowing his boarder. Sees Will Jr go home, greet his nice family. Outside Will Jr's house a car is parked. He's being watched. By whom? The next night Benson finds he himself is being shadowed.

CLUMLY'S STORY

Chief of Police Fred Clumly, a man who seeks honestly to control the area of his proper authority, be fully responsible. He recognizes the measure of waste of himself—the kinds of experience closed to him by virtue of his private and public commitments—and recognizes, though dimly, his human urge for fuller self-discovery, freedom from all social restrictions, even for evil, but suppresses the urge. Finds his responsible puritanism increasingly pointless in the populous and mechanized modern world. Sees on every side dehumanization and the decline toward bestiality. Strives to overcome both through personal force, assertion, but, like any man, lacks the power. Suffers paranoid delusions which increase as the novel progresses—the delusions of a bitter old man who has outlived his time. At the same time that he acts for justice in the old sense, he begins to spy nervously on his men, on the Mayor, and, confusedly, on himself, his own motivation, his capabilities.

His blind wife Esther, slightly self-pitying, thinks herself worthless, a burden on the world; plans to kill herself if she can ever "balance the score" with Clumly, who has sacrificed much for her, she rightly perceives. Thinks he has another woman, perhaps several (but only half thinks this)—he's been apparently impotent for years—and she has a habit of studying her face and the faces of all younger women she can get to with her fingers. When Clumly begins to stay out late (in connection with the Sunlight case, mainly), she begins to follow him. Learns he spies outside the Mayor's house (part of Clumly's paranoia).

Meanwhile Clumly has been having "dialogues" with the Sunlight Man. At first Clumly pretends to himself that his whole object is to crack the case, but eventually even he cannot hide from himself the fact that it is partly soul-searching, pointless and dangerous but psychologically necessary for him. He keeps tapes of the dialogues, takes them home with him and hides them. Esther discovers them. The lawyer, Will Hodge Sr, comes, asks questions about Clumly. Esther says very little. But gradually she becomes convinced that this is her chance to balance their score. Not knowing what is on the tapes, she imagines they reveal some plot in which the Mayor is involved. Knowing that Clumly is under fire from the Mayor and others, she takes them to Clumly's right hand man, Miller; tells him of Clumly's spying and asks to hear the tapes. Miller doesn't want to hear them, but gives in. Without understanding what the tapes mean, she knows she has ruined her husband. Goes home, bent on suicide. (Miller refuses to keep the tapes—from loyalty to Clumly.) But Esther cannot act. (*Continued below.*)

BOYLE'S STORY

Boyle is two men, Walter Boyle and Walter Benson, thief and middle-class "salesman," amateur poet and poetry lover (E. A. Guest). His life is one of studied irresponsibility: when the world requires him to be responsible he goes peculiarly blank (withdraws) as if by an act of will and thinks—as it seems to him—nothing. A prisoner in the Batavia jail at the time of the jailbreak in which the Sunlight Man releases the Indian boy, he sees the break and the murder of the young guard, Mickey Salvador, but says nothing, to avoid being implicated and thus exposed. Still, he is deeply disturbed by the incident. It connects, for him, with the plague of brutal and amateurish burglaries Batavia is enduring—a plague which increasingly forces Boyle-Benson to take stock of himself, his occupation, the changed times ("Mere anarchy is loosed upon the world" in effect).

Because of his wife Marguerite's nervousness, Boyle has advertised for and gotten a boarder, a radical, in fact revolutionary young man who paints signs, has a quietly disagreeable past, and is very proficient at hating the haters of Negroes, Jews, Communists, etc. He becomes a grotesque lover to Boyle's wife in Boyle's absence, and continues after Boyle's return. A connection forms in Boyle's mind between this man and the Sunlight Man as, little by little, he becomes aware of the love affair. He begins shadowing the man—Ollie Nuper—and slides toward the idea of killing him. What prevents it is, first, his poetry (here the novel burlesques the Kreutzer Sonata) and, second, his grudging love of the man's easy bestiality. Like Clumly, he begins to doubt, but with this crucial difference: whereas Clumly has behind him a clear and distinct morality, Boyle has behind him nothing but a moral suspension of disbelief. As his ambiguous hatred for Nuper increases, so his own sense of defilement increases. He should have told the police what he knew about the escape. His wife's dilletantish occultism (horoscopes, witchcraft, crackpot psychology) becomes real for Boyle. He begins to see Boyle as one man, Benson as another—Devil's man and God's man respectively, or Sunlight vs. Clumly. The full horror of his dilemma erupts when he throws open his bedroom door to catch Nuper in bed with his wife. (Cf. Kreutzer.) Rather than killing Nuper—his plan—he retires in anguish. He "knows" he cannot face Nuper's bestial evil until he has purified himself. He must go to the Batavia police. But he can't. After the news of the truck wreck in which Luke Hodge is killed (below) he becomes, simply, Boyle.

WILL HODGE SR'S STORY

He has settled for a small, unhappy life because he knows himself a limited man, a pale ghost of his vital and brilliant father the Congressman. To his wife he was coarse, stupid, gross; to his elder son he is a small-time shyster; to his younger son he is a weakling and a fool. He can tolerate self-accusation, but when accused of indirect responsibility for the murder of Mickey Salvador (by Salvador's mother)—as though not simply his professional protection of the accused but his very character were at the heart of it—he feels a fierce need to justify himself, atone. Like Clumly, he takes on the responsibilities of the world—more than a man can take. (In fact, he must atone for letting down both his sons, for robbing his wife of happiness, and above all for his blind selfishness, exactly like that of the Sunlight Man, as it seems to Hodge: he chose the small responsible life to avoid pain, and that is a crime as great, Hodge thinks, as choosing sensualism and unthinking self-fulfillment at any cost. (Here the argument gets very tricky: Hodge has spent a lifetime being responsible—satisfying or bending to or patching up after others, yet his object has been self-defense, the avoidance of pain—not Clumly's situation. Like his wise brother Ben, Will Hodge Sr is capable of love, but incapable of escaping cupidity—self-regarding joy.)

Goes to the Indian reservation, hunting Nick. Talks to Sun-on-the-water to no purpose. (Learns about a witch's irresponsibility.) Drives to Clumly's late that night. Finds car gone. Puzzling. Sees Esther in window watching. Begins to dog Clumly's tracks, learns of Clumly's possible incompetence, and becomes, like Clumly, a "watchdog" but also, like Sunlight, a destroyer. Learns all about Clumly but lacks the conviction and will to act, partly from cupidinous delight in the hunt itself.

MILLIE'S STORY

A sensualist; self-condemned bitch. Her one virtue seems to be that she sticks with her son Luke (as Clumly sticks to Esther, despite pain), not because she loves him or because she feels maternal instincts but, as she says, just because. She would willingly die for him, as she thinks. But she would more willingly see him dead. Like Boyle, she is socially irresponsible; like the Sunlight Man she is uncommitted and in some ways selfish, a destroyer. Truth is, Luke is her image of herself—but male, therefore more free, more powerful than she is. Her desire to reform him—make him go to college, put him in a position for power—is a desire to make him what she can't be herself; the desire to see him dead is hatred of his betrayal—his failure to live his life for her. When the Indian (Nick Slater) and Sunlight come and make her son and herself prisoners in her son's house, she gradually comes to see Sunlight as Luke's potential savior. As a truck driver, Luke can truck Nick and the Sunlight Man to freedom. If he will, renouncing his childish and puritanical rigidity (as Millie rightly thinks), he too will be free—a man at last (according to Millie's foolish definition of a man). Luke does as his mother wishes, or at any rate sets off with the two criminals in his truck. But instead of freeing them, he grandiosely kills himself in order to kill them.

Millie learns of the truck wreck from Clumly, by a fluke, and learns that there was only one body found. She takes a stiff drink, descends into herself, becoming pure selfishness, pure bestiality. Has a mad sense that she will never die.

WILL JR'S STORY

He has moved from a small-town, two man practice with his father to a junior-partnership in a firm of 39 lawyers in Buffalo. He chases skips, learns the mechanical heartlessness necessary for a bill collector; also, by appointment, again with professional indifference to right and wrong, defends felons he knows to be guilty and dangerous. All his life he has been responsible, but though he is capable of great anguish over justice, he is not quite capable of love. He needs physical contact (fierce handshakes, etc.), the only expression possible for him of this partially loving anguish. He is supremely controlled for a man of his sort, and extremely disciplined. But he never has time to see his children, never gets to talk with interesting people, feels himself losing all instinct for compassion, having been too often duped. Becomes feebly religious—a desperate attempt at return to innocence—takes piano lessons, studies languages, suffers, dreams of teaching school. He worships work, not people, and knows that that's no decent life. Or is it that he runs on ego? he wonders. Did he leave his father through idealism (because a country lawyer is not specialized enough to defend his clients, given the complexity of modern law) or through fear of self-knowledge? Cynical at heart, tortured by constant self-examination comparable to that in the Clumly–Sunlight dialogues. Wears no wedding ring.

The longer he chases skips, the more uncertain he becomes of why he is chasing them. If mere ego, why is he not a skip himself—they satisfy ego, he knows. If he doesn't become a skip merely from cowardice, what room for ego? So why chase skips?

In the California Zephyr, late at night, just outside Provo, Utah, he accidentally comes upon the man he has been after, R. V. Kleppmann. Stupidly, he can't decide to issue the subpoena he has with him. (Plenty of lawyers would, he knows.) He gives in to his bestial side, goes corrupt, gets nothing for it.

LUKE'S STORY

A total cynic, or so he thinks, except when driving his Road Ranger for the Paxton Trucking Company—a truck he thinks of in strictly sexual terms. He's a passionate boy, full of mingled love and hate, damnation and redemption. In the end, he destroys himself and the truck, thinking he's killing the escaped criminals, Nick Slater and Sunlight—but in fact they got off miles back, on another of the Sunlight Man's "hunches." For Luke it's self-crucifixion, an unspeakable joy.

CONCLUSION

Shaken by his son's death, Will Hodge Sr goes to Mayor Mullen with what he knows about Clumly. Tells Mullen the tapes are at Clumly's house—evidence that Clumly has been speaking with the Sunlight Man and making no attempt to capture him by means of his knowledge of where Sunlight will be at particular moments—the moments of the dialogues. Mullen et al pick up Miller and Kozlowski, cops, then

Millie, who of course knew where Sunlight was and can verify the meetings, at least in part. On the police radio they hear that Nick Slater has surrendered and that Sunlight is gone.

At Clumly's, Esther is waiting for them. When she hears the car drive up (Clumly's at the station) she pulls the master switch and waits in the dark, armed. Being blind, she has an advantage in the dark. She understands, now that she thinks she's going to die, that her long-standing wish to even the score was mere self-pity. They're equals, she and Clumly, and she is doing this as an equal. They will not get the tapes without killing her. (She has no idea whether the tapes will be worth it to them.) Duty is the intellectualization of love; without love, duty is meaningless and perverse. She also knows they'll get the tapes if they want them. One does not act to achieve something but simply because one must.

Meanwhile, the Sunlight Man gives up—not to Clumly but to Figlow, because Figlow happens to be at the desk. In panic, Figlow shoots him, though Sunlight makes no threatening gesture. The Sunlight Man's reason for surrendering (developed in the dialogues, here merely a matter of action) is that "the gods" have spoken to him: he must. (Cf. Esther.)

Ends with the image of the universe as metaphor: physical chaos for a moral rise to beauty. A final image of sunbeams. Final line: Figlow shot him through the heart.

Epilogue of dry, meaningless fact. (The reductio ad absurdum of the strictly ethical and intellectual side of the Hebrew-based Western culture and also, incidentally, a device for making a few details of the main action's mystery clear for any reader who didn't understand—e.g., the identity of the Sunlight Man.)

FUNCTIONS OF SOME VERY MINOR CHARACTERS

Miller (Capt. Dominic Sangirgonio), a normative cop—a good man, fond of kids, compassionate but also professional, not driven, not intense, pleasant. He is intelligent, loyal, capable of understanding Clumly's behavior though he himself would never get himself into such an extremity.

Ben Hodge, a normative citizen, not at all a hunter and not inclined to defy society either. His lay sermons at country churches contrast in their gentleness and willingness to suspend disbelief with the "sermons" of Sunlight.

Vanessa Hodge, sentimental and a little foolish, but good, a normative wife, mother, and schoolteacher, representative of society's values as they stand. Whereas the Sunlight Man finally capitulates to these values because though they are absurd they are the values of all the people to whom one is committed, Vanessa does not know there is anything wrong with the values that are in.

The ancient Woodworth sisters, straight representatives of the values of America in former times, before the population explosion became noticeable, before mechanization became a necessary evil, etc.

The novel's ministers, priests, and rabbis, representatives of alternative versions of religious experience, all decent and justifiable but also imperfect and potentially destructive. All of these essentially contrast with the Sunlight Man's true religious sense of the world as holy, at least as ideally conceived. (A true sense of life's holiness precludes mere theology, sectarianism, and the compromise of abstract ideal and concrete congregation.)

Mayor Mullen, representative of socially acceptable compromise resulting from insensitivity and a blunted sense of justice.

Marguerite Boyle, embodiment of the potential evil in brainless sentimentality.

Nick Slater and Kathleen Paxton (wife of the Sunlight Man in his former identity as Taggert Hodge)—stages of psychosis through withdrawal.

CONNECTIONS AND MEANING

My object in this novel is to present an image of the way we live now which is as complete as Melville's image of his time in *Moby-Dick*, in a narrative as dramatic and poetic as Melville's. What organizes the book on the level of mere intellect is its general concern with the conflict of principles summed up in the opposition of the two main characters, Clumly and the Sunlight Man. Clumly serves order, loves it, believes in it: he is one of those who seeks to shape his own destiny and he is heroic, however comic, because he hopes to serve all civilization as he would serve himself. The Sunlight Man, a Mesopotamian priest-like figure, submits to destiny, chaos, mystery. He is significant—no mere Emerson—because his submission is incomplete and in part grudging. He thinks too much and experiences too much for complete, comfortable scudding with the wind.

Like all important questions, the implicit question in the conflict of these two men is religious—works vs. faith. What torments the question is the old set of unanswerables: Is the universe ordered? Can man control even himself? Along the lines of these unanswerables lie the lives of the minor characters as well as the major. Millie, or Mama (Mesopotamian earth-sex-goddess), seeks to control; she differs from Clumly in that her control is thoroughly, though not quite ignobly, selfish. Against the ordered structure of Hodge family values and history she raises her own poor-girl assertion of personal value and virtue. (This defiance of the old values is at the heart of her lifelong attempt to destroy the Hodge name.) Her value is not moral (merely self-centered) and not articulate (intuition and instinct over intellect). Thus she combines the *processes* of the Sunlight Man—his surrender to larger forces (but in Millie's case, the forces of personal desire, not the mumbling of the gods)—and the goal of Clumly, control. Seeking freedom for her son (whether he wants it or not), antisocial and amoral freedom like her own, she effectually murders him.

In contrast to Millie, Esther Clumly seeks what is best for others. Like Clumly, she is selfless; but her object—her mode, really—is not to impose her order for the sake of others, but instead to withdraw her own identity from the scene—make peace by getting out of the way (in effect, by suicide). Like the Sunlight Man, she wishes to submit, to be a passive instrument; unlike the Sunlight Man, she has no faith whatever in gods, only in Clumly, and even here she is uncertain. But of course her wish to give Clumly freedom is parallel to Millie's wish to give her son freedom—at base, a selfish wish. Her effect is to murder (but in this case not literally) her loved one. If her final

defiance of Law, when she waits to fight with the police, is a step upward (since now she understands the selfishness in her earlier position),
it's a step upward only for its consciousness. In fact, both Millie and
Esther are recapitulating the gratuitous act of the Sunlight Man when
he "freed" Nick Slater from jail and thus made accidentally possible
the murder of the guard. His act was higher than theirs because it
is a universal act, not based on love or self-love but on a moral impulse
unshackled (but also, un-ordered) by ethical constraint or concern for
the larger good.

Will Hodge Jr, ultimately "freeing" Kleppmann, provides another
comment. He specifically and consciously frees Kleppmann from moral
order and responsibility because Will Jr cannot find, himself, reasons
for moral behavior. His recapitulation of the central mythical act (of
"freeing") is darkest of all, because most cynical, most corrupt.

In contrast to those who dismiss or renounce order, asserting the
flight into freedom—Millie, Esther, and Will Hodge Jr in the end, all
perversions of the Sunlight Man—are those who, like Clumly, are
mainly concerned with enforcing law and order. The figure mediate
between these two types is Walter Boyle-Benson, the thief. Boyle feels
impulses toward imposing order, but he constantly postpones it: rather
than deal with the split in his life, disastrous for his wife, he gets a
roomer. Rather than answer the roomer's radical political philosophy,
he says he must "do some reading," which he never gets to. Rather than
report what he knows about the jailbreak, he stews and procrastinates.

Chief of those who impose order—after Clumly—is Will Hodge
Sr. He is a faulty avenger not because, like Clumly, he is caught up in
the complexities of justice, but because he takes pleasure in pursuing,
judging, and condemning. From selfishness he hunts Clumly and cannot simply turn him in. And it is another selfishness, his reaction to
his son's death, which leads to his change of mind and his accusation.
Will Jr is of course another of the imposers of order, until his final
corruption turns him into one of the escapists.

The model cop, Miller, has an unthinking faith in life, a sense of
humor, dedication to work and decency. He does not get lost in abstruse
difficulties, like Clumly, yet does not simply pounce, either. He fights
crime (e.g., the teen-age burglars) with conviction but also with restraint
and compassion. He both catches men and lets men go in moderation
grounded on a firm sense of what it is to be human.

Pvt. Kozlowksi, Miller's disciple, functions mainly as Miller's straight man. He differs from Miller in that he is more self-conscious in his role as cop. And this self-consciousness (which reveals itself in his dealing with teen-age burglars) is potentially dangerous—as Will Hodge Sr, an extreme case, shows. The hunt becomes its own reward, and righteousness replaces holiness.

Nuper, Boyle's revolutionist roomer, a fierce critic of "society," a radical whose answer to the world's problems is BBB—"burn, baby, burn"—the complex of Protest and Power—P & P—an organizer of mobs for "punishment" of the sick social order, shows another aspect of the mythic cop or order-maker. Here the crime (society's) is vague, the enemy generalized. Nuper, like Mario Savio of Berkeley, does not want to be a dictator. But his selflessness is deluded. All his charitable impulses (e.g., toward Boyle's fat, ugly wife) are really perverse. The more he understands himself by analysis, the less he really understands. Through psychoanalytic jargon, Nuper manages to make *self* a concept as dehumanized and abstract as his concept of society.

THE ORDER OF SECTIONS AND EVENTS

I. *The Watchdog.* Clumly arrests the Sunlight Man, a magician who seems slightly mad but who vaguely frightens Clumly: it seems to Clumly that he is up to something, is dangerous; but Clumly cannot rationally support his hunch. His conflicts with the Mayor, with his men, etc., make his concern with the potential danger of the Sunlight Man dangerous: he should concern himself with other problems— unless his hunch is right. Section also shows Clumly's temptation to throw it all up, abandon his wife who's a burden, etc.—a temptation he admirably resists. He is something of a bungler, too late for the times, but worth respect, at least up to a point.

II. *When the Exorcist Shall Go to the House of the Patient . . .* Introduces the stories of the Indian, Nick Slater (arrested for a crime more serious than he could understand when he committed it, hence a victim of law), Walter Boyle, professional thief, and further develops Clumly's conflict with modern police methodology. Further signs of Clumly's paranoia. The Sunlight Man makes an escape, then, worse, returns to free the Indian—with the accidental result that a guard is killed. (The chapter title comes from a cuneiform tablet from ancient Mesopotamia. The Sunlight Man exorcises evil in Babylonian terms, commits evil in Hebrew and modern terms.)

III. *Lion Emerging from Cage.*   Story of Will Hodge Sr, who is made to feel partly responsible for the escape and murder, and who, after a life of ducking his head, is driven to action: he will help to recapture the Indian; later sees that Clumly's seeming incompetence stands in the way of the recapture. Becomes Clumly's hunter. Section also includes comment on Hodge's life with his wife and sons and on the influence of his father the Congressman's image on the lives of his family and himself.

IV. *Mama.*   Will Hodge Sr's wife. Her conflict with her younger son, her selfishness, her conscious and efficient destruction of the old Hodge family and its values. At the end of the section, Millie (the wife) and her son Luke are at Luke's house in the country, and are imprisoned there by the escaped Sunlight Man and the Indian boy.

V. *Hunting Wild Asses.*   (Like the title of section three, the title comes from a famous Mesopotamian tablet drawing.) Deals with Clumly's pursuit of the Sunlight Man, and the tightening net around Clumly himself—Mayor and Will Hodge Sr, as well as Clumly's own weaknesses.

VI. *Esther.*   (Based on the Biblical Esther.) Presents Clumly's wife's character and difficulty—her feeling of unworthiness, her religiosity, self-sacrifice, that is, her wish to balance the score with her husband.

VII. *The Dialogue on Wood and Stone.*   The first Clumly–Sunlight dialogue. Trapped, so that he is forced to listen to the Sunlight Man, Clumly hears the criminal's arguments for nihilism. (See "The Four Dialogues," below.)

VIII. *The Kleppmann File.*   Introduces Will Jr's pursuit of the professional skip, Kleppmann, and Will Jr's ambivalent feeling about Kleppmann, about his own life and family, about Law itself. Also explores Will Jr's feelings about law in the old days (as practiced by his country-lawyer father) and law now (highly specialized, expensive, and inhumane), as well as his feelings about his Congressman grandfather and the changing ideals of America.

IX. *"Like a Robber, I Shall Proceed According to My Will."* (From an old cuneiform manuscript about a king who renounced the will of the gods.) Deals with Clumly's continuing pursuit of the Sunlight Man, and others' continuing pursuit of Clumly. Hodge Sr, the Mayor, Clumly's wife.

X. *Poetry and Life.* Benson-Boyle's domestic troubles, his jealousy and shadowing of his boarder. His impulse to tell the police all he knows about the jailbreak, and his conflicting impulse toward self-preservation.

XI. *The Dialogue of Houses.* Second intellectual confrontation of Clumly and the Sunlight Man.

XII. *A Mother's Love.* Millie, the Sunlight Man, the Indian boy, and Millie's son, Luke. Millie's feeling that the nihilism of the Sunlight Man may be the key to her son's escape from his Congressman-inspired puritanism—may, in short, free him to be what she wants him to be.

XIII. *Nah ist—und schwer zu fassen der Gott.* A return to Will Hodge Sr's pursuit of Clumly, with emphasis on his increasing delight in the pursuit itself, the despotic power it gives one. He feels free of the old restrictions of his formerly timid, responsible life. He becomes increasingly destructive, though so far only in potential.

XIV. *The Dialogue of the Dead.* Clumly and Sunlight, third confrontation.

XV. *Love and Duty.* Esther takes the Sunlight dialogue tapes to Miller.

XVI. *Voyage to the Underworld.* Will Jr, pursuing Kleppmann, catches up with him but corruptly accepts a trifling bribe to free the skip. His anguish as he does this.

XVII. *Benson vs. Boyle.* Further development of the Benson story. Reaches the point of knowing he must go to the police. Can't do it.

XVIII. *Winged Figure Carrying Sacrificial Animal.* (Based on yet another famous tablet illustration.) Millie's decision to make Luke help Sunlight and the Indian escape, by driving them to safety in his Paxton truck.

XIX. *The Dialogue of Towers.* Clumly and Sunlight, fourth confrontation—conclusion of argument.

XX. *Luke.* Luke, driving the Sunlight Man and the Indian boy to freedom, chooses to wreck his truck and kill himself in order to kill his two riders. A joyful self-crucifixion—but Sunlight and the Indian have jumped off, and the self-crucifixion is pure waste.

XXI. *E silentio.* Prodded by his younger son's death, Will Sr acts, closing in on Clumly. The Indian surrenders.

XXII. *Law and Order.* Esther Clumly, knowing she is partly responsible for her husband's destruction, takes the responsibility for defending him, though only in an absurd gesture—she will not let the police get the Sunlight tapes. She prepares to fight the police in her house, with Clumly's pistol. Meanwhile, the Sunlight Man surrenders and is shot by a panicky policeman.

Epilogue: Documents. A death report on the Sunlight Man, now identified as Taggert F. Hodge, disbarred Batavia lawyer who has been living in Phoenix. Also other documents, cold, drab, and inadequate. The facts of a human life are merely facts, devoid of meaning.

THE FOUR DIALOGUES (SECTIONS VII, XI, XIV, AND XIX)

The four dialogues of Clumly and the Sunlight Man—in imitation of the Platonic technique—extend the central exploration of cops vs. robbers to its highest levels of abstraction and set contemporary questions against age-old questions summed up in the conflict of ancient Babylon vs. ancient Israel.

1. THE DIALOGUE ON WOOD AND STONE, OR THE PUPPETS OF BABYLON

The dialogue develops ideas implicit (for the Sunlight Man) in the Babylonian concept of the gods and of the human soul. The Babylonian gods are separate from the senses. (Whereas Greek and Hebrew holy sacrifices assume value to the gods of the offering's scent, the Babylonian priest purifies the air of all smell.) Babylonian civilization as a whole—brilliantly commercial and materialistic, on one hand, mystical and Eastern on the other—asserts a fundamental duality of life, a co-existence without necessary conflict of body and spirit, both of which are valued. The connection between body and spirit is in its very essence mysterious, and the health of each depends on the health of the other.

Whereas Judaism would solve the middle-aged man's sexual problems morally, by affirmation of duty and commitment, the Babylonian would grant the subtle workings of the unconscious (even psychic), would make the marriage vow *practical* (a unification of estates) and would leave satisfaction to mysterious instinct, any lawlessness whatever being allowable and culturally approved.

In politics, the Babylonian would assert a close connection between rulers and the mumbling gods (cf. the parallel structure of palace and temple), would make governing, contracts, etc., practical, but would finally leave the welfare of the state to the ruler's intuition, aided by the reading of omens by diviners. That this didn't work in ancient Mesopotamia is obvious (cf. Israel's failure). However, the principle that a ruler's great freedom and great responsibility makes possible great wisdom, an ability to act flexibly and impersonally, moment by moment, not on a basis of hard and fast principle but on a basis of action and reaction, is worth consideration. Cf. Goldwater's demand for a "policy," Johnson's evasion of fixed policy which may not fit tomorrow's situation.

In the sphere of social progress, the Babylonian disinterest in individual life (cf. Israel's assertion of the supreme importance of the individual and his stock) would suggest that civil rights cannot be made to come but must inevitably develop, at the usual gross natural cost in lives: a sickness cures itself. (Contrast physical medicine—a Judeo-Christian product.)

What is the Sunlight Man's answer to modern America's political and social problems? He has none. He does not deny that we should go on struggling for improvement. But he doubts that our system is in tune with, or keyed to, the actual nature of reality. If it is not, we must fail. And he thinks we will fail. And because he believes this, he cannot himself act. Cf. the Hell's Angel, or the beatnik who says he is "beyond protest."

2. THE DIALOGUE OF HOUSES

The dialogue is grounded on omen-watching in the ancient Near East, specifically on the Egyptian-Babylonian art of astrology. The Sunlight Man distinguishes between divination and magic—the attempt to make the gods act for one. Divination asserts holy passivity, not for spiritual fulfillment, as in the Far East, but for practical and spiritual life. He speaks of acting *with* the gods, being bodily possessed as one fires a machine gun, writes a poem, makes love, or rules a State.

Personal responsibility, in such a view, consists in two things: stubbornly maintaining one's freedom to act (in the Sunlight Man's case, evasion of capture by the police), and jumping when the spirits say jump. One of course never knows for sure that the gods will speak— cf. the case of the Assyrian king who behaved "like a robber"—but one must preserve the possibility.

Tentatively granting all this, what are the implications of the first imperative, maintaining freedom?

In the sexual sphere, one must either never marry, or one must maintain complete sexual independence in marriage. Is this possible? Is the "sexual revolution" of the West Coast a step in the right or the wrong direction? It is possible, says the Sunlight Man, but in our post-Judaic culture, possible only for superior people. The woman's problem is greater than the man's in that she has the more-than-cultural shame of menstruation (every animal has some measure of distaste for mess; it tells lions where one has been, if nothing else). For the male the problem is that he can't always achieve an erection—his potency depends heavily on his feeling of at least equality with the partner, among other things. If intercourse is a job (strictly a familial function), or a pitying gift, or an embarrassment, or a thing of no mystery—sex is poisoned for the male. And both male and female must contend with the family instinct by which each seeks to entrap and control the other. What are the necessary rules, then? Male and female must be *practically* protected from their weaknesses by the total culture, insofar as possible. It is not enough that males and females understand each other's problems, for this rationality leads to duty and guilt and to non-intuitive sex. Instead, the place of intellect is to establish the cultural norms—build the highway down which lovers can then unthinkingly speed. The "superior people" mentioned above, then, are not superior intellectually but superior by cultural gift: they are the accidental products of the right homes. The sexual revolution is a step in the wrong direction—anti-puritanism which must result in a loss of mystery, heightened guilt of a new, strictly psychological kind. But the wrong step might be transformed (by accident of history) to a mediate step toward a right step. Leading away from ancient Israel, it does not lead to Babylon but makes Babylon once more a live option.

There still remain problems: menstrual shame, mismatched desire, familial instinct, the particular difficulties of the excessively insecure, dominant male or female, and so on. So it was in ancient Babylon (horror stories of Babylonian sex conflicts). But granting the essential imperfection of the species, some cultural premises are better than others. Sexual independence remains a high value from which our culture (and every modern culture) seems closed off.

As for social and political implications, the imperative that one must remain free raises even more difficult problems. Socially, one must at once maintain one's ethnic identity and spurn ethnic identification— white, black, Irish, Jewish. Here cf. Babylonian and Israelean assimilation of foreigners. The Babylonian asked acceptance of ruler and gods, Israel asked circumcision and total transformation. Neither worked, both having built into the system the same error—both made an intellectual assertion. The only way men can really "love one another" is by coming to know one another, in personal, intuitive terms. Now, with our population, that is impossible, and our cultural heritage makes it even more impossible. Armed truce, that is, democracy, becomes the only hope—and it is not a hope. Truce always means regrouping: ultimately social problems will be resolved by the emasculation of all minorities. One answer: kill them now—the Rightist answer. Another: intermarry at once, an answer which destroys the individual social unit just as state religion destroys the citizen (i.e., Nazi worship of the abstract State). The Sunlight Man's solution, tentative and temporary, is great emphasis on each culture's understanding of itself—an unsentimental understanding of both virtues and defects, and minimization of concern with the other culture as a foil. If individuals want to intermarry, let them. If minority groups want to borrow majority values, let them. But let everybody know who he is. Does knowing who you are entail hatred of the man different from you, whose identity requires a modification of your identity? It can. The Sunlight Man would make social intercourse a practical concern, social individuality a spiritual and mystical concern, and the man who crosses the line—the bigot—he would execute.

The same argument can be made for international affairs. Nations are equivalent to ethnic or social blocs.

3. THE DIALOGUE OF THE DEAD

The dialogue, which develops a theme left unexplored in the second dialogue, deals with the ancient Babylonian concept of death and personal immortality.

If man must maintain his freedom to act as the gods will—if he must maintain his spiritual and to a lesser extent physical individuality—what is it that he will do when he acts? To what extent is the action itself individual—a personal as well as universal expression?

The Sunlight Man presents, in answer, an interpretation of the *Gilgamesh*, an analysis of the Babylonian concept of personal immortality (a mad goal) and death (a reality). In Mesopotamia, the struggle for personal fulfillment is a wrong-headed struggle. We are walled in from the outset. The pursuit of Youth (cf. America) is mad; so too fame (cf. America); lineage (cf. America); a great palace (or novel or industry). As for pursuit of Heaven, the answer in the *Gilgamesh* is that if there is an afterlife it is sealed up, walled in. Thus one acts to maintain the freedom to act, but the ultimate Act is impersonal, a movement of the universe, a stroke by, for, and of sole interest to—the gods. (Explication of the metaphor.)

Why act, then? Because that is the nature of life. That is the importance of Gilg. Bk. XII, the "actions" of the dead king among the ineffectual dead. The question is not shall I act or shall I not, but how shall I act? (Not to act is to die: even indecision is an act). Once one has said this, one must ask, shall I act within the cosmic order I do believe in? Or, again, shall I act by standing indecisive between the two orders—not striking out for the cosmic order because of my human commitment, not striking out for the cultural order because of my divine commitment (or devotion to the Real)? Which shall I renounce, my body (of which ethical intellect is a function) or my soul? The Sunlight Man has thus far chosen to hover, undecided. (But the pressure for decision is mounting.)

4. THE DIALOGUE OF TOWERS

The basis of the dialogue is the beautiful Babylonian Towers (Babel, for instance). Thematically, the dialogue continues from the last.

The towers are curious. Their height suggests to the Sunlight Man (as to the Jews) a wish in man to become like to God. But the god has his place not on top of the towers but in the base. He is an inner mystery from which the towers ascend. Or: from man's own inner mystery, the destructive principle in his blood (born for death), his achievements ascend, his godly will, his desire to become at one with the universe, total reality, either by merging with it or by controlling it.

For the Sunlight Man it is a matter of fact that our culture is not at one with total reality and can never control it or even match its force: sexually, socially, and politically we are doomed, as all civilizations have been doomed. He refuses to join his own culture not because he minds doom but because he has a vision of what would be possible in a better culture—one he does not expect ever to arise in the world. On the other hand, he will not openly turn on our culture because he has personal ties to it and because, increasingly now, he knows the effects of anarchistic actions on the innocent, for instance on Nick Slater.

Clumly asks, What happens if you do make a choice for the universe and against the culture which produced you?

Who knows? You can't act until the call comes, and then it may be a trifling act, an absurdity, the minds of the gods being indifferent to our values.

And what if you opt for those you love?

The Sunlight Man's elaborate answer brings the novel to its rhetorical and philosophical climax: the Sunlight Man's terrible vision of the

GENERAL PLAN FOR *THE SUNLIGHT DIALOGUES* / 283

future. (A vision which, by the way, is brilliant but wrong.) He sees an age of sexual catastrophe—increased bondage, increased violence and guilt, increased disgust and ennui. In the social sphere, shame and hatred and boredom. And he foresees total chaos in the political sphere. The capitalistic basis of the great values of Western culture will preclude solution of the world's problems. China and Africa will destroy Western civilization utterly, but for lack of respect for individual life will fail to build a free and responsible civilization of their own. (The Babylonian Towers blur with an image of New York's towers.) This grim vision of what our cultural errors must lead to is what keeps the Sunlight Man from choosing the ethical side—commitment to his imperfect but beloved culture.

At the end of this dialogue, which consists mainly of the Sunlight Man's monstrous vision of the future, Clumly gets possession of the gun. He "frees" the Sunlight Man for the following almost explicit reason: Clumly is outside his jurisdiction. It is not that Clumly accepts lawlessness or bends to it, but that here in the cavern of metaphysical anguish, Clumly has no authority. The Sunlight Man's crime is against life itself.

[The Sunlight Man's smile was scornful now. "You think I'll be arrested, then, by 'higher' authorities?"

Clumly thought deeply. "I *believe* so," he said. He rubbed his jaw. "Yes. That is what I believe."]

Clumly's faith proves right. After the accident, the death of Luke Hodge, the surrender of Nick Slater, the Sunlight Man—Luke Hodge's uncle, in fact—feels driven, "called" as if by the mumbling gods, to give himself up, confess his name and lineage, and, in short, affirm his culture for better or worse. Sgt. Figlow, reacting in pure terror *before he can think*, shoots him.

KINDS OF INTEREST THE NOVEL OFFERS

A first-rate novel is of interest in a variety of ways. The most obvious kind of interest in this one is its suspense—not only the suspense already described, in the main plot, but also suspense in subplots. The Boyle-

Benson subplot (the story of the double-identity thief) is equally suspenseful: Boyle's conflict with his boarder, the potential danger of the
young radical and his political activities, the potential danger in Boyle's
jealousy, the further potential danger in his accidentally crossing the
path of Will Hodge Jr, who is hunting the dangerous skip, Kleppmann.
In effect, the suspense in the Boyle-Benson subplot comes to nothing
because of Boyle's inability to act. And the same is true in the Will
Hodge Jr subplot. Will Hodge Jr hunts Kleppmann, a man capable
of killing to preserve himself from capture, but in the end Will Jr
capitulates, taking a paltry bribe and abnegating his responsibility. (More
may come of this, however. I don't know yet.) In any case, the suspense
built up in the two cops-and-robbers subplots, being based on the same
dilemmas dealt with in the main plot, are calculated to spill over into
the main plot, where a catastrophe does come and the reader's expectation is fully and grimly fulfilled. Another form of suspense builds
up in the conflict of Millie's selfishness and her wish to impose a similar
selfishness on Luke, on one hand, and, on the other, Luke's martyr-
like reaction to his mother's will—his wish to assert an idealistic
selflessness against her selfishness. In this subplot, the catastrophe is
ironic: Luke makes his assertion and, in hopes of killing the two criminals, kills himself alone. Here the bitter absence of poetic justice is
calculated to feed the intensity of the catastrophe in the main plot,
where poetic justice is realized, and for all the right reasons.

Setting and character provide another kind of interest. The locale
of the main action, Batavia, N.Y., is real—as are the locales of the minor
actions—and the character of the locale is closely analyzed: one gets
a valid sense of western N.Y. life and people, of western N.Y. geography—its peculiar lights and shadows, its stony hills, old-fashioned
barns, its conflict of the old and the new (going back to the time of
Seneca rule). Western N.Y. architecture, western N.Y. names, and so
on, even western N.Y. folklore are preserved and at the same time used
for their symbolic implications, so that one gets, as in *The Resurrection*, a very rich sense of place. At the same time, locales treated in
the minor plots—San Francisco, Los Angeles, Denver, Phoenix, and
southern Illinois—clarify by contrast and introduce a larger image of
American life. In the process of this long novel one gets close analysis
of a rich variety of houses and landscapes—a Harvester Avenue whore-
house in Batavia, one of those fine old brick houses found nowhere

but in western New York, old Ross Street houses in Batavia, modernistic houses overlooking Los Angeles freeways, a town house in San Francisco, and so on. All of which is to say that I believe Fielding is right about the novel, it must present a wide variety of settings and must always be absolutely convincing.

As for characterization, I believe the novelist should walk the tightrope between verisimilitude and romance. Every character in the novel, even the most minor, is larger than life—like the characters of Chaucer, for instance—yet more or less convincing. Absolute verisimilitude leads to plodding actuality; on the other hand, extreme and obvious distortion leads to a kind of thinness like that in fair tales or yarns. My object in creating characters is to make people just convincing enough that the reader never remembers to say "I don't believe it," yet not so pedestrianly convincing that the reader forgets to be interested. Thus Clumly is a cartoon of a man—hairless as a grub from an old sickness, more intense than police chiefs usually are, yet involved with real problems, suffering real emotions. And thus the Sunlight Man is an incredible person—a magician, somewhat psychic, unusually intelligent and well-read, yet also partly confused, torn by ordinary human anguish, capable of making foolish mistakes. All the characters, by the way, are based—remotely—on real people. In the final version, their professional activities will be very carefully researched—as carefully as the activities of Tolstoy's people. (Cf. the professional concerns of the philosopher, Chandler, in *The Resurrection*.)

In a novel of this size it is possible to treat closely and sensitively the whole gamut of human emotions, from puppy-love to the love of old people, from adolescent hostility to mature hatred, from befuddlement to madness. And part of the interest in all this is that all of these emotions can be interpreted in terms of the same system—contrasting kinds of responsibility and withdrawal.

Another point worth mentioning is that, unlike many modern novels, in which all significant characters are cry-babies suffering enormous sentimental pangs, this novel presents mature and sensible people, as well as immature, sentimental, or mad. From start to finish, the norm of the novel is optimistic, common sensical: though the central characters are extremists, confronting the world with the intensity of Melvillean heroes, there are all around them normative characters, reminders that there is a ho-hum workaday world in which the novel's concerns are not disastrous.

And then this. For the politically inclined, the novel has an original (?) and carefully worked out political thesis. For the religious, a theory of holiness vs. mere ritual. For the psychologically oriented, an analysis of mind and moral conflict. And so forth.

As for the poetic quality of a good novel, this novel has a refined and complex style, admittedly not a style to please readers of the popular novel, but one which ought to satisfy anyone seriously concerned with the novel as an art form. The Clumly sections are straightforward, humorous in a Kafkaesque sort of way, and fairly simple. The Will Hodge Jr sections —since Will Jr is intensely intellectual, almost an escapist—involve interior monologue, phantasy, and a fairly heavy use of foreign languages—one of Will's ways of evading life—French, German, Latin; but one can follow the story without knowing the languages (as well as in Thomas Mann, for instance). The most intensely poetic sections, and the most difficult, are the Sunlight dialogues themselves. Whereas Walter Boyle, the thief, is a popular poet, school of Eddie Guest, Sunlight is a true poet, for whom metaphor and allusion are a means of releasing essential reality. As for the larger poetic rhythm of the novel, it resides in recurrent images, parallel events, and the interplay of plot against plot, character against character.

Finally, the novel has poetic effect in that it presents a universe, something approaching the whole spectrum of American life in 1966— the whole political and social spectrum, as well as the relationship of the present moment to the flow of history, from the medieval formulation of the idea of modern civilization to the fall of the West through the predicted rise of a new and radically different, equally futile civilization grounded on the premises of Africa and Asia. (The individualistic values of capitalism, according to the Sunlight Man, cannot save the modern world; but the answers for modern times, proposed by China and Africa, though valuable in that they correct the error of capitalism, carry the seeds of their own destruction in that they find no value in individual human life. And neither can the Eastern answers evolve into a valid answer, because the sheer force of overpopulation must perpetuate the kernel weakness.) In terms of the Sunlight Man's metaphor, both Babylon and ancient Hebrew civilization are doomed to destruction. There can therefore be no answer for the world. There can only be an answer for the individual: love and commitment in a doomed universe. But this is no gloomy affirmation. Just as individual human consciousness arises directly because of human mortality, so social, political, and moral consciousness is a valuable product of the idea of death. (Cf. the theme of *The Resurrection*.)

LENGTH OF THE NOVEL

I cannot predict how long the finished novel will be. The first four sections are finished in rough draft and come to 400 ms. pages. The whole book will probably run to at least 1150 ms. pages. (I've also finished a few of the later sections.)

I can't accurately predict, either, how long the book will take to finish. I hope to have a complete first draft by this September—but that is no more than saying I hope to have the canvas blocked out, figures drawn in in some detail. In any case, I'll need to sit and fret with the rough draft for several months at least.

INDEX

Aaron, Hank, 99
Abbot, Bud, 191
Abe, Kobo, 130
Absent-Minded Professor, The, 83
Accent, 176
Acts of King Arthur and His Noble Knights, The, 112–18
Ada, 71, 185, 195
Adams, Samuel, 95
Adventurer, The, 86–89
After Julius, 24
Aiken, Joan, 219
Albee, Edward, 173
Alice in Wonderland, 60–64
Alienation, 22
Allen, Ethan, 95
Allen, Woody, 91
Alley Jaggers, 42, 48
All the King's Men, 177
American Dream, An, 71, 167
Anna Karenina, 37, 196
Apollonius of Rhodes, 79, 181, 184, 231
Aristotle, 28, 103
Arkin, Alan, 224
Armies of the Night, 167
Art of Fiction, The, vii, xvii, xviii, 258
Art of Walt Disney, The, 79

As I Lay Dying, 221
Aspects of Alice, 60
Assassins, The, 199, 200, 201, 202
Auden, W. H., 60, 62
Austen, Jane, 41, 75, 232

Bach, Johann Sebastian, 108, 162
Bad Man, A, 74, 75, 167
Baldwin, James, x
Baron in the Trees, The, 130, 131, 205
Barth, John, xi, 71, 72, 118, 134,
    139, 164, 165, 170, 171, 173,
    179, 181, 182, 183, 184, 186,
    187, 189, 191, 192
Barthelme, Donald, 73–74, 75, 76,
    86, 164, 170, 173, 191
"Bartleby the Scrivener," 1–12
Baudelaire, Charles, 166
Bazzaris, 16
Beagle, Peter S., 165
Beardsley, Aubrey, 143
Beckett, Samuel, 33, 41, 48, 50, 56,
    73, 88, 91, 170, 176, 222
Bedknobs and Broomsticks, 81
Beethoven, Ludwig van, 111, 162,
    220, 231
Beetle-Leg, The, 169, 195

Behan, Brendan, 51
Being There, 72
Bellamy, Joe David, xiv, xvi, 111, 182
Bellefleur, 199–204
Bellow, Saul, xvii, 13, 18, 164, 165,
    167, 168, 170, 175, 176, 189, 194
Bennett, Arnold, 91
Benny, Jack, 190
Beowulf, xiv, xx, 87, 140, 174, 232,
    233
Bergson, Henri, 48
Beyond the Bedroom Wall, 90–94
Bhagavadgita, 72
Biely, Andrei, 185, 231
Big Rock Candy Mountain, The, 90, 155
Blake, Peter, 79
Blake, William, 171, 231
Blanshard, Brand, 123
Bleak House, 45
Bledsoe, Thomas, 41, 43
Blood Oranges, The, 169
Bloodshed, 185
Bloom, Allan, xxi
Boccaccio, Giovanni, 206, 220, 221
Boethius, Anicius Manlius Severinus,
    143
Boheme, La, 230
Borchardt, Georges, 258
Borges, Jorge Luis, 88, 130, 173, 194
Born Free, 83
Bourjaily, Vance, 176
Braithwaite, R. B., 63
Breakfast of Champions, 174
Breast, The, 65–69
Brockway, James, 22
Brooks, Cleanth, 176, 232
Brothers Karamazov, The, 123
Brower, Brock, 71
Browning, Robert, 125, 229
Buchanan, Pat, xxi
Bullet Park, 55–59, 128, 168
Burgess, Anthony, 18, 26, 27, 49–50
Burke, Kenneth, 61
Burroughs, William S., 71, 73, 171,
    178, 188, 195
Byron, George Gordon, Lord, 12

Calvin, John, 59
Calvino, Italo, 130–33, 176, 205–11

Camus, Albert, 177, 231
Cannibal, The, 169
Canterbury Tales, The, 233
Capote, Truman, 14
Capp, Al, 34
Carlyle, Thomas, 231
Carroll, Lewis, 60–64
Carter, Jimmy, xxi
Carver, Raymond, xviii
Casanova, Giovanni, 87, 88
Castaneda, Carlos, 196
Castle of Crossed Destinies, The, 130–33,
    205
Catch-22, xix
Cato, 86
Caulfield, Holden, 73
Caute, David, 41, 52–54
Caxton, William, 112, 113
Centaur, The, 184
Charlotte's Web, 219
Chaucer, Geoffrey, xiv, 37, 68, 74,
    85, 98, 131, 143, 174, 181, 220,
    221, 232, 285
Chayevsky, Paddy, 123
Cheever, John, xvii, 55–59, 71, 90,
    124–29, 145–48, 168, 169, 176
Chekhov, Anton, 13
Childwold, 199, 202
Chimera, 173, 179, 183
City Life, 74
Clegg, N. C., 22
Clinton, Hillary, xxi
Cloven Viscount, The, 130, 132, 205
Coenen, Frans, 22
Coleridge, Samuel Taylor, 168, 191, 231
Collector, The, xix, 134
Collingwood, R. G., ix, 259
Collins, Wilkie, 231
Comedians, The, 25
Compson, Quentin, 193
Confessions of Nat Turner, The, 156, 157
Confidence-Man, The, 9, 11, 106, 169
Conrad, Joseph, 185
Coover, Robert, 71, 164, 165, 169, 170,
    172, 173, 178, 190–91, 195, 196
Cosmicomics, 130, 132, 205
Couples, 76
Cozzens, James Gould, 176, 194
Crane, Stephen, 185

Crews, Harry, 169
Criers and Kibitzers, 75
Crime and Punishment, 156
Crouch, Stanley, xvii
Crumb, R., 85

Dahl, Roald, 219
Daniel Martin, 134–39
Dante Alighieri, 143, 174, 231
"Dead, The," 221, 224
"Death in Venice," 235
Decameron, The, 206, 221
Decline of the West, The, 41, 52–54
Defoe, Daniel, xix, 87
de la Mare, Walter, 60
Delaney, Samuel R., xv
Delbanco, Nicholas, 152
Deliverance, xix
de Sade, Marquis, 88, 171, 218
Dickens, Charles, ix, xvi, 19, 37, 43,
    82, 91, 105, 222, 229, 230, 234,
    235, 262
Dickey, James, viii, xix, 161
Dick Gibson Show, The, 74, 75, 191
Dink's Blues, 15
Disney, Walt, viii, 34, 78–85, 142, 143,
    156, 174, 229, 230, 231, 234, 235
Divine Comedy, The, 232
Doctorow, E. L., 134, 167, 168
Donne, John, 172
Don Quixote, 101
Dostoyevsky, Fyodor, 19, 53, 91, 156,
    220, 225, 231, 234
Double Image, The, 16
Douglas, Lloyd C., 196, 229
Dove of the East, A, 195
Doyle, Sir Arthur Conan, 231
Dreyfuss, Richard, 224
D'Souza, Dinesh, xxi
Dubin's Lives, 149–53
Dubliners, 224
Dumbo, 79
Dunlap, Lennis, 175

Eastlake, William, 176
Ebony Tower, The, 134
Einstein, Albert, 150
Eisenhower, Dwight D., 168, 177

Eliot, T.S., 49
Elkin, Stanley, 68, 74–75, 76, 85, 86,
    152, 167, 170, 191
Ellington, Duke, 156
Elliot, George P., 175
Ellison, Ralph, xix, 168, 194
Elsschot, William, 18, 19
Emerson, Ralph Waldo, 71, 74, 167, 272
Empedocles, 33
Encounter, The, 25, 26
End of the Road, The, 139, 165
Epstein, Edmund, 64
Erikson, Erik, 94
Euripides, 184

Faecke, Peter, 15, 27
Fair, Ronald L., 40
Faith and the Good Thing, ix, 169
Falconer, 124–29, 146, 168
Fantasia, 78, 79, 84, 142
Faulkner, William, 25, 31, 37, 54, 70,
    71, 82, 91, 159, 177, 178, 185,
    193, 213, 221, 224, 227
Faust, xix
Fellini, Federico, 91
Fiction and the Figures of Life, 71, 171,
    186, 187
Fiedler, Leslie, 182
Fielding, Henry, 217, 231
Finch, Christopher, 79, 80, 81, 83
Finnegans Wake, 27, 28, 33, 85, 101
Firebugs, The, 15
Fitzgerald, F. Scott, 71
Floating Opera, The, 165
Forms of Fiction, The, viii, 175
Fowles, John, xix, 68, 134–39
Frame, Janet, 43, 44
Franchiser, The, 167
Franklin, Benjamin, 95
Freddy's Book, xxi
French Lieutenant's Woman, The, 134,
    135
Freud, Sigmund, 28, 50, 54, 61, 62,
    63, 67, 174
Frye, Northrop, 193
Fulgentius, xiv
Fuller, R. Buckminster, x
Fullerton, Alexander, 16, 17

Gaddis, William, 101-11, 127, 164, 165, 169, 172, 197
Galsworthy, John, 91
García Marquez, Gabriel, 130
Gardner, John, vii–xxi, 173, 181, 258
Gass, William H., viii, xi, 21, 27, 30–34, 43, 68, 71, 72, 76, 85, 86, 111, 156, 164, 169, 170, 171, 172, 173, 175, 178, 185, 186, 187, 188, 189, 191, 192, 197, 218, 221
Gates of the Forest, The, 51–52
Gershwin, George, 156
Gide, Andre, 177, 183, 192
Giles Goat-Boy, 71, 173, 183
Gilgamesh, 87, 281
Goethe, Johann Wolfgang von, xix, 111
Gogol, Nikolai, 65, 69
Gold, Herbert, 175
Goldwater, Barry, 278
Goodbye, Columbus, 194
Gordimer, Nadine, 41, 42, 43, 45
Gordon, Caroline, 193
Gottlieb, Robert, 258
Graves, Robert, 61
Gravity's Rainbow, 169
Gray, Donald J., 63
Greene, Graham, 14, 25, 26
Green Light, The, 196
Gregory, Horace, 60
Grendel, viii, x, xx, 171, 174, 235
Guest, Edgar A., 228, 266, 286
Gupta, Roberta, 214

Haley, Alex, xix
Hansen, Ron, 214
Happy Days, 73
Hardy, William M., 40
Hassan, Ihab, 164, 166
Hawkes, John, 164, 169, 172, 173, 174, 175, 184, 189, 194
Hawthorne, Nathaniel, 76, 168, 218
Hecht, Anthony, 164, 192
Heidegger, Martin, 66
Heller, Joseph, xix, 176
Helprin, Mark, 164, 195
Hemingway, Ernest, 53, 82
Henderson the Rain King, 165, 167, 194
Herbert, George, 172
Hersey, John, 35

Herzog, 18, 189
Hess, Rudolph, 158
Higgins, Joanna, 214
Hobbit, The, 140, 141
Hoff, Marilyn, 15
Hoffman, Dustin, 224
Hog Butcher, The, 40
Holquist, Michael, 63, 64
Holy Land, The, xix, 45–48
Home Is Where You Start From, 15
Homer, 53, 88, 155, 166, 181, 188, 220, 231
Horowitz, Gene, 15, 16, 22
Horton, Chase, 112, 113
House on the Canal, The, 22
Howard, Elizabeth Jane, 24, 25
Howells, William Dean, 71
Huck Finn, 70, 72, 73, 74, 77
Humboldt's Gift, 189, 194
Humperdinck, Engelbert, 230
"Hunting of the Snark, The," 63, 64
Hurston, Zora Neal, xix

Iliad, The, 87, 89, 166, 220
Ingarten, Roman, 123
In Cold Blood, 14
Indian Summer, 37–40
In the Heart of the Heart of the Country, 72, 191, 221
"In the Region of Ice," 60, 75
Invisible Cities, 130, 205
Invisible Man, xix, 194
Iowa Review, 237
Irving, Washington, 200
Italian Folktales, 205–211
Itaya, Kikuo, xvii

Jack and the Beanstalk, 221
Jakes, John, 216, 217, 218
James, Henry, 71, 75, 76, 77, 90, 134, 232
James, William, 199, 235
Jason and Medeia, xii, xiii, 181-82, 184, 186
Jefferson, Thomas, 98
Johnson, Charles, 169
Johnson, Lyndon Baines, 278
Johnson, Samuel, 152
Jones, James, 176, 194

Jonson, Ben, 103, 106
Joyce, James, 27, 28, 33, 54, 64, 152, 166, 179, 224, 225, 227, 232, 234
JR, 101-11, 165, 169
Jubjub Bird, The, 40
"Julius Caesar and the Werewolf," 237-57
Jung, Karl, 63
Jungle Book, The, 82

Kafka, Franz, 65, 67, 131, 178, 192, 286
Karamazov, Ivan, 120
Kazin, Alfred, 177
Keats, John, 231
Kelly, Walt, 85
Kentfield, Calvin, 174
Kenyon Review, 176, 232
Kerr, Walter, 63
Kesey, Ken, 174
Kierkegaard, Soren, 15, 122, 123, 177, 225
Kimball, Roger, xxi
King's Indian, The, 181
Kirk, Russell, 193
Kissinger, Henry, 86
Knowles, John, 37-40, 43
Kosinski, Jerzy, 70, 72-73, 173
"Kreutzer Sonata, The," 266
Kumin, Maxine, 219

Lagerkvist, Pär, xix, 43, 45-48, 50, 52
Lancelot, 119-23
Lane, Margaret, 16
Last Gentleman, The, 119
Late Bourgeois World, The, 41
Late Great Creature, The, 71
Lawrence, D. H., viii, 150
Lawrence, T. E., 88
Lebowitz, Al, 175
Lee, Peggy, 94
Leg, The, 19
Let Noon Be Fair, 16
Levin, Harry, 61
Lie Down in Darkness, 156
Limbaugh, Rush, xxi
Lime Twig, The, 169
Lincoln, Abraham, 83-84, 96
Lionheart, 16

Lolita, 71
Longfellow, Henry Wadsworth, 229
Longinus, xiv, 17, 171
Long March, The, 156
Lord of the Rings, The, 140, 141
Love and Death, 91
Love and Death in the American Novel, 182
Love Bug, The, 83
Love in the Ruins, 119
Lytle, Andrew, 176, 194

MacInnes, Helen, 16
Magic Mountain, The, 101
Magus, The, 135
Mailer, Norman, 38, 71, 88, 164, 167, 176, 194
Malamud, Bernard, 149-53, 164, 167, 168, 170, 227
Malory, Sir Thomas, xix, 112-18, 122, 174
Malraux, André, 87, 88, 177
Manhunt, 232
Mann, Thomas, 232, 235, 286
Martin, Valerie, xv
Mary Poppins, 82
Mary Reilly, xv
Mather, Cotton, 59
Matthews, William, 113
Maupassant, Guy de, 66, 190
McCarthy, Joseph, 177
McCullers, Carson, 178, 193
McDonald, Ross, 218
McGalliard, John, 174, 176
Meanwhile Back at the Henhouse, 41
Melville, Herman, xvi, xix, 1-12, 15, 37, 54, 71, 73, 76, 81, 106, 149, 152, 164, 168, 169, 171, 192, 216, 217, 218, 219, 230, 271, 272, 285
Meyer, Nicholas, 134
Michaelson, Greg, 214
Michener, James, 218
Mickelsson's Ghosts, xxi
Miller, Arthur, 164
Miller, Heather Ross, 20
Milton, John, 10, 172, 230, 231
Mishima, Yukio, 20, 21
Miss MacIntosh, My Darling, 27-30
Moby-Dick, 45, 271

Month of Sundays, A, 171
Moravia, Alberto, 178
Morrison, Toni, viii
Morte d'Arthur, xiv, xix, 112–18
Mother in History, A, 17
Motley, Willard, 16
Moviegoer, The, 119
Mozart, Wolfgang Amadeus, 109, 110, 150, 230
Mrs. Stevens Hears the Mermaids Singing, 22, 23
MSS, viii, 212–15

Nabokov, Vladimir, xvii, 13, 27, 63, 70, 71, 91, 173, 185, 195
Nader, Ralph, 97
Naked and the Dead, The, 167, 176, 192
"Narrative of A. Gordon Pym, The," 88
Nathan, John, 20
Nemerov, Howard, 176
Network, 123
New Fiction, The, 111
Newman, Cardinal, 231
New Yorker, The, 101, 147, 176, 218
Nickel Mountain, viii, 181
Nietzche, Friedrich, 21, 54, 87, 88, 120, 123, 177, 208, 225, 231, 232
Night at Sea, A, 16
Nightside, 199, 200
98.6, 179
Nonexistent Knight, The, 130, 132, 205
Nova Express, 188
Nunez, Sigrid, 214

Oates, Joyce Carol, viii, 60, 74, 75–76, 77, 175, 199–204
O'Bowen, Robert, 174
O'Brien, Tim, 194
Ocean of Story, The, 183
O'Connor, Flannery, xi, 17, 174, 178, 193
October Light, xxi
Odyssey, The, 87, 88, 89, 166, 220
Of the Farm, 23, 24
Old Wives' Tale, The, 101
Oliver Twist, xx
Omensetter's Luck, 14, 27, 30–34, 72, 169, 170, 185, 186, 189

On Becoming a Novelist, 258
On Being Blue, 188
Once and Future King, The, 115
One Hundred and One Dalmatians, 82
On Moral Fiction, xx
Origin of the Brunists, The, 71, 169, 170
Otis, Elizabeth, 112, 115
Our Mutual Friend, 101
Out, 179
Ozick, Cynthia, 185, 194

Painted Bird, The, 72
Palmer, William, 169
Paradise Lost, 231
Patch of Blue, A, 229
Pearl, 140
"Pedersen Kid, The," 72, 185, 191
Percy, Walker, 119–23, 159
Perspective, 176
Peter Pan, 79
Phillips, Robert, 61–63
Picasso, Pablo, 82
Pictures of Fidelman, 150
Pierre, 9
Pilgrim's Progress, 169
Pinocchio, 78, 80, 174
Pitcher, George, 63
Plato, 53, 64, 231
Platonism, 28, 29, 202, 277
Playboy, 237
Plotinus, 33
Poe, Edgar Allan, 20, 81, 82, 87, 88, 111, 166, 168, 176, 177, 192, 229
Porter, Katherine Anne, 193
Portnoy's Complaint, 67
Portrait of the Artist as a Young Man, A, 224
Power, Crawford, 25, 26
Price, Reynolds, 163
Price, William, viii
Pricksongs and Descants, 169
Proust, Marcel, 93, 111, 166, 177, 192, 231
Purdy, James, 68
Pynchon, Thomas, 91, 164, 165, 169, 172, 173, 189, 197

Queneau, Raymond, 187

Rabbit Redux, 73, 76, 77
Racine, Jean, 166
Rackin, Donald, 63
Ragtime, 134, 167
Rand, Ayn, 123
Ransom, John Crowe, 176, 193
Recognitions, The, 103
Redford, Robert, 224
Reed, Ishmael, xv, 156
Remembrance of Things Past, 101
Resurrection, The, 168, 235, 259, 284, 285, 287
Revere, Paul, 100
Richler, Mordecai, 176
Rilke, Rainer Maria, 66
Robbe-Grillet, Alain, 63
Robe, The, 196
Robin Hood, 82
Robinson Crusoe, xix, 87
Roots, xix
Roth, Philip, 65–69, 125, 170, 172, 175, 176, 194, 195
Russ, Joanna, xv

Sailor Who Fell from Grace with the Sea, The, 20, 21
Salinger, J. D., 178, 213, 227
Sarton, May, 22, 23, 24
Sartre, Jean-Paul, ix, 24, 59, 66, 67, 87, 88, 177
Saturday Evening Post, The, 178, 213, 232
Scholes, Robert, 194
Scott, Walter, 229
Seal Island, 83
Searches and Seizures, 167, 191
Sedgwick, George, 123
Set This House on Fire, 156
Seven Pillars of Wisdom, The, 88
Sewanee Review, 176
Shadows, vii
Shakespeare, William, 37, 155, 218, 220, 228, 229, 231
Shreve, Susan, 219
Silmarillion, The, 140–44
Sinatra, Frank, 224
Singer, Isaac Bashevis, 194

Sir Gawain and the Green Knight, 87, 140
Sir Orfeo, 140
Smollett, Tobias, 231
Snopes, Flem, 177, 192
Snow White (Barthelme), 73
Snow White (Disney), 78, 82
Socrates, xviii, 68
Soft Soap, 18, 19
Son of the Morning, 199, 202
Sophie's Choice, 154–62
Sot-Weed Factor, The, 36, 71, 134, 171, 183, 186
Sound and the Fury, The, 185
Sound of Music, The, 222
Southern Review, The, 14
Stafford, Jean, 17, 177, 178
State of Siege, A, 43, 44
Stegner, Wallace, 90, 155
Steinbeck, John, 112–18
Steiner, George, 101
Steps, 72–73
Stevens, Wallace, 87
Stevick, Philip, 178
Stillness, vii
Stillness and Shadows, viii
Stoppard, Tom, 123, 173
Stories of John Cheever, The, 145–48
Strauss, Richard, 231
Styron, William, 154–62
Sukenick, Ronald, 179–80, 183, 186, 189
Sunlight Dialogues, The, xiii, 174, 258–87
Swift, Jonathan, 65, 68, 106, 165, 191
Sylvie and Bruno, 62

Tale of Two Cities, A, 230
Tales of Hoffmann, The, 230
Tate, Allen, 60, 193
Taylor, A. L., 61
Taylor, Larry, 76
Taylor, Peter, 15
Tenants of the House, 20
Tengu Child, xvii
Tenniel, Sir John, 61
Tennyson, Alfred, Lord, 229
Them, 76
Thesée, 183

Thomas, Lowell, 177
Thompson, Stith, 208
Thoreau, Henry David, 73, 150, 167
Thousand and One Nights, The, 183
Through the Looking-Glass, 62
Thurston, Jarvis, 176
Ticket That Exploded, The, 73, 171
Tolkien, J. R. R., 140–44
Tolstoy, Leo, ix, xvi, xviii, 15, 37, 52,
    53, 68, 90, 124, 128, 131, 134,
    152, 168, 177, 190, 196, 217,
    220, 222, 224, 225, 227, 285
Tracy, Don, 16
Transcendentalists, The, 70, 73, 167
Treasure Island, 82
Tremor of Intent, 49–50
Troilus and Criseyde, 221
Tsukui, Nobuko, xvii
Tunnel, The, 111
Twain, Mark, 71, 73, 74, 150, 168,
    172
20,000 Leagues Under the Sea, 82
Types of Fiction, The, 175
t zero, 130, 132, 205

Ulysses, 33, 166, 225
Universal Baseball Association, The, 169
Up, 179
Updike, John, xvii, 23, 24, 68, 71,
    73, 74, 76, 127, 171, 174, 176,
    184, 189, 195, 197

van Gogh, Vincent, 110
Van Oudshoorn, J., 22
Vergette, Nicholas, viii
Very, Jones, 167
Vidal, Gore, 176
Vinaver, Eugene, 113
Virgil, 18, 231
Vision of Battlements, A, 18
Vittorini, 192
Vonnegut, Kurt, 71, 174, 176, 178,
    213, 216

Wagner, Richard, 230

Walford, Naomi, 45
Wallant, Edward Lewis, 176
War and Peace, 101
Ward, Jay, 85
Warren, Austin, 176
Warren, Robert Penn, 159, 177, 232
Washington, George, 95, 96, 98
Watcher and Other Stories, The, 130,
    132, 205
Watt, 48
Weiss, Paul, 123
Wellek, René, 176
Welty, Eudora, 178, 193
West, Paul, 42, 43, 45, 48
West, Ray B., 176
Western Review, 176
"Wheel of Love, The," 75
When She Was Good, 67
White, T. H., 115
Whitehead, Alfred North, ix
Whitman, Walt, 70, 114, 167, 194
Why Are We in Vietnam?, 167
Wiesel, Elie, 51–52
Willard, Nancy, 219
Williams, Charles, 169
Williams, John A., x
Willie Masters' Lonesome Wife, 71, 171,
    173, 186
Winnie-the-Pooh, 78
Wittgenstein, Ludwig, 48, 63
Woiwode, Larry, xvii, 90–94
Wolfe, Thomas, 159
Wolitzer, Hilma, 219
Wonderland, 60, 199
Woolcott, Alexander, 60
Woolf, Virginia, 60, 62, 87
Wouk, Herman, 176, 194
Wreckage of Agathon, The, xiii
Wright, Richard, x
Wurlitzer, Rudolph, 189

Young, Marguerite, xvii, 27–30, 174
Yurick, Sol, 194

Zweig, Paul, 86–89

CREDITS

" 'Bartleby': Art and Social Commitment," *Philosophical Quarterly*, January 1964.

"An Invective Against Mere Fiction," *Southern Review*, Spring 1967.

"More Smog from the Dark Satanic Mills," *Southern Review*, Winter 1969.

"*Bullet Park*, by John Cheever," *New York Times Book Review*, October 24, 1971.

"*Alice in Wonderland*, by Lewis Carroll," *NYTBR*, January 30, 1972.

"*The Breast*, by Philip Roth," *NYTBR*, September 17, 1972.

"The Way We Write Now," *NYTBR*, July 9, 1972.

"Saint Walt," *New York*, November 12, 1973.

"*The Adventurer*, by Paul Zweig," *NYTBR*, December 22, 1974.

"*Beyond the Bedroom Wall*, by Larry Woiwode," *NYTBR*, September 28, 1975.

"Amber (Get) Waves (Your) of (Plastic) Grain (Uncle Sam)," *New York Times*, October 29, 1975.

"*JR*, by William Gaddis," *New York Review of Books*, June 10, 1976.

"*The Acts of King Arthur and His Noble Knights*, by John Steinbeck," *NYTBR*, October 24, 1976.

"*Lancelot*, by Walker Percy," *NYTBR*, February 20, 1977.

"*Falconer*, by John Cheever," *Saturday Review*, April 2, 1977.

"*The Castle of Crossed Destinies*, by Italo Calvino," *NYTBR*, April 10, 1977.

"*Daniel Martin*, by John Fowles," *Saturday Review*, October 1, 1977.

"*The Silmarillion*, by J. R. R. Tolkien," *NYTBR*, October 23, 1977.

"*The Stories of John Cheever*," *Chicago Tribune Book World*, October 22, 1978.

"*Dubin's Lives*, by Bernard Malamud," *Washington Post Book World*, February 25, 1979.

"*Sophie's Choice*, by William Styron," *NYTBR*, May 27, 1979.

"A Writer's View of Contemporary American Fiction," *Dismisura*, 1980.

"*Bellefleur*, by Joyce Carol Oates," *NYTBR*, July 20, 1980.

"*Italian Folktales*, edited by Italo Calvino," *NYTBR*, October 12, 1980.

"Fiction in *MSS*," *MSS*, Spring 1981.

"What Writers Do," *Antaeus*, Winter/Spring 1981.

"Cartoons," *NYTBR*, January 30, 1983.

"Julius Caesar and the Werewolf," *Playboy*, September 1984.

"General Plan for *The Sunlight Dialogues*," from the Gardner Archive, ca. 1971.